New Faces, New Voices

*

New Faces, New Voices

THE HISPANIC ELECTORATE
IN AMERICA

*

MARISA A. ABRAJANO
R. MICHAEL ALVAREZ

PRINCETON UNIVERSITY PRESS

PRINCETON AND OXFORD

Second printing, and first paperback printing, 2012
Paperback ISBN 978-0-691-15435-0

The Library of Congress has cataloged the cloth edition of this book as follows

Abrajano, Marisa A., 1977–

New faces, new voices : the hispanic electorate in america / Marisa A. Abrajano,
R. Michael Alvarez.

p.   cm.

Includes bibliographical references and index.

ISBN 978-0-691-14305-7 (cloth : alk. paper)

1. Hispanic Americans—Politics and government.   I. Alvarez,
R. Michael, 1964–   II. Title.

E184.S75A65 2010

323.1168′073—dc22   2009029524

British Library Cataloging-in-Publication Data is available

This book has been composed in Palatino
Printed on acid-free paper. ∞
Printed in the United States of America

3   5   7   9   10   8   6   4

WE DEDICATE THIS BOOK TO OUR FAMILIES.

*

* Contents *

* Preface *

THIS IS A BOOK about the political behavior of Hispanics in America, focusing mainly on elections since the late 1990s. Like most large-scale research projects, this book has a long and complex history, and its origins lie in our mutual teaching and research interests. We began working together on some of these issues in 2001, when Marisa was a graduate student at New York University and we were working on collaborative research with Jonathan Nagler. Over the next few years, the three of us worked on a variety of research projects together.

Along the way, as we presented our work at a number of professional conferences and began to submit our joint work for review, we began to realize that there was need for broader and more synthetic research on Hispanic political behavior than we could fit within the narrow confines of academic journal articles. Especially when we taught political behavior to undergraduate and graduate students, we saw that there was a need for a book that covered many of the important dimensions of Hispanic political behavior, and that could present these dimensions of Hispanic political behavior within some of the important theoretical models used to study political behavior.

That's the basic genesis of this book.

But before we get to the book itself, we both have a number of people and institutions to acknowledge. First, our joint acknowledgments. One we have already alluded to is our intellectual and professional debt to Jonathan Nagler. We have both worked closely with Jonathan, and without our other research with Jonathan this book would never have been possible. We also both thank the many scholars along the way who have given us comments and raised questions about our joint research before this book, especially those who discussed our research papers at academic conferences going back to 2002. Specifically, we wish to thank Lisa García Bedolla and Rene Rocha.

We both wish to jointly acknowledge those institutions that have produced data and analyses about the Hispanic population and electorate in the United States in the last decade. In our work reported in this book, we draw heavily upon data from the American National Election Survey, the National Annenberg

Election Survey, the U.S. Census Bureau, the media consortium who have provided exit poll data from recent federal elections, and the recent Latino National Survey. We appreciate their efforts and thank them for making their data available to researchers.

Finally, we thank the anonymous reviewers of our manuscript, as well as Chuck Myers and the rest of the editorial and production team at Princeton University Press. We hope that the reviewers will see that their work helped to improve our research.

MARISA'S ACKNOWLEDGMENTS

I would especially like to thank Jonathan Nagler for being such an incredibly dedicated and committed advisor. Without his guidance in graduate school, I would not have become the scholar that I am today. I would also like to thank my colleagues at the University of California, San Diego (UCSD)—Sebastian Saiegh, Megumi Naoi, Keith Poole, and Zoltan Hajnal—for their friendship, support, and encouragement. Special thanks go to Hans Hassell for his research assistance on this project. I owe a great deal of thanks to Lisa García Bedolla, who has provided me with endless advice and support both professionally and personally. I also could not have completed this project without the unconditional love and support of my family—my parents, Jess and Mary Abrajano, and my siblings, Joseph Abrajano and Marilou Abrajano.

Much of the impetus to write this book emerged from my courses on Latino politics and racial and ethnic politics in the United States, so I would also like to acknowledge the students enrolled in these courses over the past several years for their insightful comments and discussions. They were my sounding board for many of the topics and issues that we raised in this book, and I am grateful for their enthusiasm and interest in the subject matter. Finally, I would also like to acknowledge institutional support that I received from UCSD to work on this project—the Faculty Career Development Program and the University of California Latino Research Initiative.

MICHAEL'S ACKNOWLEDGMENTS

I'd like to begin by thanking the people I worked with at Greenberg, Quinlin, and Rosner Research (GQR), and GQR's Democracy Corps project, especially Stanley Greenberg. Others at GQR and Democracy Corps I'd like to thank are Jim Gerstein, Anna Greenberg, Matt Hogan, and Ana Iparraguirre. Working with this team was a fantastic experience, and it also provided me with access to a great deal of amazing data.

Along the same lines, I want to thank Mark Mellman, and the others of the Mellman Group, who provided a unique opportunity for Lisa García Bedolla, Jonathan Nagler, and I to assist with the development, design, implementation, and analysis of Hispanic focus groups and polling in 2004. This unique experience also provided access to great data, fantastic people, and the inner workings of a presidential campaign.

In the academic world, my previous work with Lisa García Bedolla has played an important role in shaping the focus of much of my work on this book. Lisa is a great friend and collaborator, and without both her friendship and knowledge, the work reported herein would have suffered. A number of graduate students, past and present, have also factored into my research on Hispanic and Latino political behavior, and those who have contributed directly to this book are Delia Bailey, Melanie Goodrich, Ines Levin Fiorelli, and Morgan Llewellyn. Ines collected the data used in our postscript, and we thank her for her work. Gloria Bain proofread our manuscript and provided indispensable administrative assistance along the way.

New Faces, New Voices

*

Introduction

Dear friends, the wife of senator John Kennedy, candidate for the U.S. presidency, is talking to you. In these very dangerous times, when the world peace is threatened by communism, it is necessary to have in the White House a leader able to guide our destinies with a firm hand. My husband has always cared for the interests of all the portions of our society who need the protection of a humanitarian government. For the future of our children and to reach a world where true peace shall exist, vote for the Democratic Party on the eighth of November. Long live Kennedy!

> —*Jacqueline Kennedy, in a speech from John Kennedy's 1960 presidential campaign*

We share a dream, that with hard work our family will succeed. If we are sick, we will have health insurance, and that our children will receive a good education, whether we are rich or poor. This is the American dream. I ask for your vote, not just for me and the Democrats, so that we can also keep the dream alive for you and your children.

> —*Barack Obama, in a speech from his 2008 general election campaign*[1]

WHILE MORE THAN forty-five years separate the broadcast of these two Spanish-language television advertisements, it is remarkable how both messages touch upon similar themes: the ideas of hope and the future, and the importance of having a candidate who understands the needs of the Spanish-speaking community. These advertisements provide a glimpse of how politicians have communicated with the Hispanic electorate, but they also raise a

---

[1]Kennedy's speech is available at http://www.livingroomcandidate.org/commercials/1960/mrs-jfk (translated by the authors). The second quotation is from Barack Obama's Spanish-language ad, "Un Mensaje de Barack Obama" (A Message from Barack Obama). The ad may be viewed at http://pcl.stanford.edu/campaigns/2008/index.html.

number of interesting questions.[2] Why have candidates' appeals to Hispanics remained so similar over such a long period of time? And on what basis do politicians believe that such messages are the ones Hispanic voters will respond to?

It remains an open question why, despite the technological advances in political campaigns from 1960 to 2008—including the introduction of focus groups, demographic targeting, and polling (Shea and Burton 2006)—candidates still appeal to Hispanics using messages nearly identical to that of Jacqueline Kennedy in 1960. This could mean that the Hispanic population has remained relatively unchanged over the past forty-eight years; it could also indicate that politicians have not really made an effort to understand the Hispanic community, which has led them to rely on general themes in their advertisements. We know that the first proposition is untrue, as Hispanics have now surpassed African Americans as the largest racial minority group in the United States (as of 2004, Hispanics made up 14.2 percent of the U.S. population) and the Hispanic population has diversified dramatically in recent decades. And by 2025, 20.1 percent of the U.S. population will be made up of Americans of Hispanic descent. Moreover, Hispanics are the largest racial or ethnic minority group in nineteen states.[3] The rapid growth of the U.S. Hispanic population can be attributed to Hispanics' steady rates of immigration as well as their higher fertility rates when compared to the total U.S. population. Not only is the Hispanic population much larger today than it was in 1960, but also its composition has changed, shifting toward an increasingly large proportion of foreign-born Hispanics (approximately 40 percent).

[2]Throughout this book, we use the term "Hispanic," though we could just as easily have used the term "Latino" to describe individuals who identify themselves as Hispanic or Latino. We use the term "Anglo" to describe non-Hispanic Whites, "Asian" to describe non-Hispanic Asian Americans, and "Black" to describe non-Hispanic African Americans.

[3]U.S. Census Bureau, "U.S. Interim Projections by Age, Sex, Race and Hispanic Origin," http://www.census.gov/ipc.www/usinterimproj/natprojtab01a.pdf (accessed July 2, 2008).

What We Know about Hispanic Political Behavior

Candidates' messages to Hispanics may have remained relatively similar because of the difficulty they have in understanding the political preferences and attitudes of this rapidly growing and heterogeneous community. The "American voter" that Angus Campbell, Philip Converse, Warren Miller, and Donald Stokes wrote of forty years ago may not be the same as the American voter of today, as it is likely that this new voter is of Hispanic origin. But, it does not follow that either scholars or politicians have a clear understanding of what the new American voter believes. Moreover, the compositional shifts within the Hispanic electorate indicate that the Hispanics Kennedy campaigned to in 1960 and those Obama targeted in 2008 are likely to be quite different. As such, understanding Hispanic political behavior is a complex and constantly changing endeavor, so that the commonly held beliefs used to characterize the average Hispanic voter of the 1960s may no longer be applicable to today's Hispanic voter.

The primary goals of this book are twofold. First, we will demonstrate why the Hispanic electorate is such a diverse and complex group, particularly when compared to other ethnic and racial minority groups in the United States. Thus, some of the most well-understood theories on racial politics and political behavior may not always adequately explain Hispanic political behavior in American politics. For instance, despite the presumption that ethnic and racial minorities will naturally lend their support to racial/ethnic minorities running for office (Browning, Marshall, and Tabb 1984), in the 2008 Democratic presidential primaries, Hispanics overwhelmingly supported then U.S. senator Hillary Rodham Clinton. While we explore this phenomenon later in the book, this example highlights why we cannot assume that Hispanic political behavior will follow the same trajectory as that of other racial/ethnic groups (e.g., Blacks) in the United States. The second aim of this book is to dispel some of the pieces of conventional wisdom about the Hispanic electorate, many of which have affected the way in which campaigns, elected officials, the media, and even the average American voter, perceive this group. Perhaps the most contentious assertion that emerged from this past presidential campaign is that Hispanics are unwilling to support an African American candidate.[4] To the extent that this observation is true has been the subject of much debate by both academics and the popular press. We therefore explore, in our chapter on intergroup relations, whether evidence exists to support this claim.

Most of the conventional wisdom on the Hispanic electorate can be traced to the popular press, political pundits, academics, and elected officials. The following section explores what we believe to be the most commonly regarded "facts" regarding Hispanic political behavior.

> Conventional Wisdom #1: Hispanics are an ethnically, racially, and geographically diverse population, and their concentration in politically important states makes them attractive to politicians.

Indeed, great diversity exists in the Hispanic population, with salient differences between numerous subgroups based on ethnicity, culture, language use, national origin, religion, and historical experiences. In fact, there is no such thing as a "Hispanic," in the sense that this is a pan-ethnic label created by the U.S. Census in 1970 (Garcia 2003).

Hispanics are concentrated in the key battleground states of Florida, Colorado, Nevada, and New Mexico; many also reside in states with a large number of Electoral College votes. According to 2004 U.S. Census estimates, approximately 80 percent of the Hispanic population resides in California (34.9 percent of the state population), Texas (34.9 percent), New York (16.1 percent), Florida (19.1 percent), Illinois (14 percent), Arizona (28.1 percent), New Jersey (15 percent), and Colorado (19.2 percent). The state with the largest Hispanic population is New Mexico, where Hispanics make up 43.4 percent of the population (U.S. Census 2007). In addition, states in which Hispanics have not traditionally settled, such as Georgia, North Carolina, Iowa, Arkansas, and Nebraska, have also witnessed an unprecedented increase in their Hispanic populations in recent years. Thus, the political landscape of these states may likely change in the next several decades.[5]

[4]This statement was made by longtime Hispanic pollster, Sergio Bendixen. See the postscript for a more in-depth discussion, as well as chapter 5 for the possible reasons behind this assertion.

[5]The Hispanic population's concentration at the county and city levels is also staggering: 4.2 million reside in Los Angeles County, California; 1.3 million in

The Hispanic population's rapid growth can be explained by several factors. High levels of migration from Latin America have contributed to the growth of the Hispanic population; as of 2000, 51 percent of the foreign-born population in the United States hails from Latin America (Lollock 2001). The Hispanic population is also younger, on average, than the rest of the U.S. population. The median age of the Hispanic population in 2005 was 26.9, while it was 40.1 for the non-Hispanic Anglo population (U.S. Census 2007). Hispanics in the United States also have higher fertility rates than do non-Hispanics. While the U.S. Hispanic population increased by 57.9 percent in the 1990s, from 22.4 million in 1990 to 35.3 million in 2000, the rest of the U.S. population increased by only 13.2 percent over the same period (Guzman and McConnell 2002). The Mexican American subgroup grew most rapidly in this decade, outpacing the population growth among Cubans and Puerto Ricans. According to del Pinal and Singer (1997), the high fertility rate among Hispanics has contributed most to their population growth. Hispanics' large numbers have translated into economic power: U.S. Hispanic purchasing power is estimated at $700 billion, with estimates reaching $1 trillion by 2010.[6] This rate of increase is approximately three times that of the estimated overall national rate for the past ten years. There are an estimated 2 million Hispanic-owned businesses in the United States, with annual revenues of approximately $300 million.[7]

Conventional Wisdom #2: Hispanics are assimilating into American political life in the same manner as previous immigrants to the United States.

Miami-Dade County, Florida; 1.1 million in Harris County, Texas; and 1.1 million in Cook County, Illinois. Hispanics make up almost half the residents of Los Angeles (46.5 percent), more than half the residents of San Antonio (58.7 percent), and more than two-thirds of the population of El Paso (76.6 percent). These numbers indicate that Hispanics can be, and increasingly are becoming, important political players at all levels of government.

[6]Estimates based on analysis from HispanTelligence, which uses data from the U.S. Bureau of Economic Analysis, http://www.hispanicbusiness.com/news/2004/5/5/hispanic_purchasing_power_surges_to_700.htm.

[7]Jessica Seid, "Hispanic-Owned Businesses Thrive," http://money.cnn.cm/2006/0913/smbusiness/hispanic_biz/index_htm.

Casual scrutiny of contemporary American politics and culture might lead some to think that the only thing that distinguishes Hispanics from the rest of the population is their ethnicity. Why should that have any impact on their political behavior? And given the immigrant foundations of the United States, it seems reasonable to suppose that Hispanics will assimilate and integrate themselves into the American political system in the same manner as the Irish, Italian, and German immigrants of the early twentieth century.

However, the pattern of Hispanic immigration to the United States is markedly different from those of earlier immigrations. Hispanic political behavior is distinct from that of the rest of the American electorate because of the constant and steady rates of immigration, which make the classic political assimilation model used to understand the behavior of previous European immigrants insufficient to explain the political behavior of Hispanics. Many Hispanics now in the United States retain close connections to their countries of origin, remaining culturally, politically, and even economically linked to friends, families, and colleagues there. At home, many Hispanics strive to maintain their ethnic identities by, among other things, speaking Spanish with friends and family members. The retention of ethnic identity, the maintenance of connections to countries of origin, and the continued influx of new immigrants into existing Hispanic communities all imply that Hispanics today might not be assimilating in the same ways or to the same degree as previous waves of immigrants to the United States.

While Hispanic population growth is remarkable, the issue of Hispanic political preferences and ideologies would be of little interest to politicians if Hispanics were solidly aligned with one political party. This leads us to the next piece of conventional wisdom regarding Hispanic political behavior:

Conventional Wisdom #3: Hispanics are a monolithic voting bloc and overwhelmingly support the Democratic Party.

Hispanics are not a monolithic voting bloc, a theme that we constantly emphasize in this book. The reason why Hispanics have received such a great deal of attention from politicians and candidates is because their political alliances are still up for grabs. Hispanic support for George W. Bush in 2004 marked the first time that a Republican presidential candidate received at least 40 percent of the Hispanic vote (Abrajano, Alvarez, and Nagler 2008). This outcome signaled to Republicans that they had a real opportunity to win over Hispanic voters to the Republican Party. Moreover, larger numbers of Hispanics report being independent in their partisan affiliations than do non-Hispanics (Hajnal and Lee 2008). Our analysis in chapter 2 provides further evidence revealing how many Hispanics do not think of themselves as Democrats or Republicans. As a result, we have seen presidential, congressional, and gubernatorial candidates from both parties investing an increasingly larger share of their advertising budget in Spanish-language advertising (Segal 2002, 2006). Securing the Hispanic vote has clearly become a priority for both political parties, and this makes the study of Hispanic political preferences increasingly important.

Yet some of the most well-understood theories of political behavior may not be applicable to a group of individuals who do not undergo the same type of political socialization process as does the rest of the American population, who are socioeconomically worse off than the rest of the population, who have only recently been actively courted by political elites in meaningful and substantive ways, and whose population is being rapidly replenished with new immigrants. All of these factors suggest that the salience of a political identity based on Hispanic ethnicity may remain strong for years to come—and that analyzing the shape of that political identity is a matter of some practical urgency.

At the same time, however, significant socioeconomic discrepancies continue to separate Hispanics from the rest of the American population. This observation leads many pundits and others to our next nugget of conventional wisdom:

Conventional Wisdom #4: Hispanics participate in politics at lower rates than other racial and ethnic groups, and therefore continue to be the "Sleeping Giant" of American politics.

Despite the large concentration of Hispanics in many politically important (and electoral-vote-rich) states, socioeconomic discrepancies create numerous challenges for Hispanics' becoming as politically involved and active as they might be. Estimates from the U.S. Census indicate that while just over half of Hispanics graduate from high school by age twenty-five, at least 80 percent or more of the Anglo, Black, and Asian U.S. population of the same age have completed high school. Thus, an educational achievement gap of 23 percent exists between Blacks and Hispanics and an even larger gap of 28 percent between Hispanics and Anglos. Hispanics also have a lower median household income ($35,929) than do non-Hispanic Anglos ($48,784), and a greater percentage of Hispanics live below the poverty line (22 percent) relative to non-Hispanic Anglos (9 percent) (U.S. Census 2007).

Research on political participation over the past thirty years has consistently confirmed that political participation is strongly influenced by voters' resources (Verba, Schlozman, and Brady 1995; Rosenstone and Hansen 1993; Wolfinger and Rosenstone 1978; Leighley and Nagler 1992). To participate in politics, an individual must have the proper resources (e.g., time or interest) to do so. Furthermore, recent work has focused on other ways of increasing turnout and participation, such as through personal contact: people are more likely to participate in politics if someone asks them to participate (Verba, Schlozman, and Brady 1995). This is particularly true of ethnic and racial minorities, as shown by recent work by Leighley (2001), Michelson (2003), and de la Garza, Abrajano, and Cortina (2008). These two strands of research, when paired together, point out why studying Hispanic political participation is so important: according to the resource model, many Hispanics are unlikely to have the necessary resources to participate fully in politics, while according to the contact model, it may be the case that candidates and parties are not asking Hispanics to participate—or perhaps not asking them in ways that are consistent with their ethnic identity and culture.

Despite the current size of the Hispanic population in the United States and impressive gains in Hispanic population growth in recent decades, many skeptics might argue that there is no such thing as "Hispanic" or "Latino" politics, and that we can expect Hispanic political behavior to mirror that of other Americans. However, the following sentiment is more often expressed, which we phrase as yet another piece of conventional wisdom (see Ramos 2004):

Conventional Wisdom #5: Hispanics are primarily concerned with issues that are "Hispanic specific," e.g., immigration, bilingual education, and, to a somewhat lesser extent, affirmative action.

Given the diversity of the Hispanic population, the presumption that all Hispanics are concerned with the same issues is somewhat problematic. For example, given that Puerto Ricans are U.S. citizens, their views on immigration differ from those of Cubans and Mexicans (Abrajano and Singh 2009).

In order for Hispanics to care about the same issues, a distinct Hispanic political identity would have to exist. According to Garcia (2003), Hispanics and other minority groups can draw on the notion of cultural politics as a source of pride and identity. Unfortunately, cultural politics have not been powerful enough to provide a clear political agenda for Hispanics, precisely because of their diversity. But, in light of the fact that the central component to cultural politics is language, it has become one of the central components, if not the central component, that defines the Hispanic population. The question of how language plays a role in Hispanic political behavior is one of the main themes of our book.

The notion of a Hispanic political identity is not only an individual construct but also an identity that has been shaped and will continue to be shaped by perceptions of shared histories and by political, social, and economic events. For example, California governor Pete Wilson used the issue of immigration in his 1994 reelection campaign to mobilize Anglo voters and to polarize the state's electorate along racial and ethnic lines. Some observers of California politics have argued that such a tactic led to a surge in Hispanic participation in California elections after 1994 (Scott 2000); in particular, some research has found that Hispanics who naturalized during the early 1990s in California are much more likely to participate in politics than those who naturalized in other eras (Pantoja, Ramirez, and Segura 2001). Similarly, we might expect the resurgent interest in the immigration issue across the nation over the past several years, which crested in the spring of 2006 in demonstrations in many American cities, to further galvanize the evolution of a unique Hispanic identity. Though as our postscript discussing the 2008 presidential campaign reveals, when other pressing issues take center stage, which in this case was the economy, the issue of immigration can fall to the wayside.

A similar logic leads us to the final commonly held belief regarding Latino political behavior:

> Conventional Wisdom #6: Having elected officials who are co-ethnic (that is, Hispanic) are important to Hispanic voters. It is also important for representative democracy.

The scholarly research on this subject provides a number of insights. One study examining self-reported survey responses finds that the majority of Hispanic survey respondents stated a candidate's race made little difference in their vote decision (Abrajano 2005). However, in an analysis of the Los Angeles mayoral election in 2005, Abrajano, Alvarez, and Nagler (2005) find that Hispanic voters in Los Angeles overwhelmingly supported the Hispanic candidate, Antonio Villaraigosa, even among those Hispanics whose political ideology differed from that of the candidate. While shared ethnicity was not the deciding factor for all Hispanic voters, in some instances, ethnicity did trump political ideology. Accounts by Vaca (2004) reveal a similar dynamic in the mayoral elections of Houston, Texas. Related research by Barreto (2007) and Barreto, Segura, and Wood (2004) finds that Hispanics living in areas represented by Hispanic officials are more likely to vote than those who live in areas with no Hispanic representatives. Thus, Hispanics may not openly admit that race matters in their vote decision, though in their voting patterns, this appears to be the case.

The study of political representation in academic political science has a deep normative and philosophical tradition, but more recently a quantitative study of political representation has emerged. There are many ways of trying to quantify the degree to which any group in society is represented, including, for example, descriptively (Are there many Hispanics who are able to capture and hold political office?) and substantively (Are there representatives in office who share and seek to implement the same concerns that are held by Hispanics?).

Studying the political representation of Hispanics in America is beyond the scope of this book, but we do provide some data herein on the descriptive representation of Hispanics to help motivate later research. Owing to our comparative focus, we first looked at the best available data on the number of African Americans and Hispanics who hold political office at the local, state, and federal levels.[8] At the state and local level in 2001, there were 9,430 African Americans in office, as compared to 4,303 Hispanics. (We use 2001 data, since that is the most recent year that the U.S. Census Bureau has provided comparable statistics for the Hispanic and African American populations.) In the 109th Congress (2005), there were 42 African Americans in the House of Representatives and 1 African American senator. In the same Congress, there were 23 Hispanics in the House and 2 in the Senate. Keeping in mind that the African American and Hispanic populations are of roughly comparable size, by this particular metric of descriptive representation it can be argued that Hispanic representation lags behind that of African Americans.[9]

Another way to think about political representation is to examine how it changes over time in response to demographic changes. In the case of Hispanics in the United States, we know that in recent decades their population has increased dramatically—a fact we will continue to stress throughout this book. Thus, another question we can pose about Hispanic political representation is, to what extent is it responsive to the dramatic rise in the Hispanic population in the United States? To offer a preliminary answer to this question, we turn again to data provided by the U.S. Census. On the population side, we have Hispanic population estimates from the 1980 and 1990 census enumerations; we also have annual estimates of the Hispanic population from 1994 through 2006.[10] For information on political representation at the

[8]These data come from the U.S. Census Bureau, "The 2008 Statistical Abstract," http://www.census.gov/compendia/statab/cats/elections/elected_public_officialscharacteristics.html. We use data from tables 394, 402, and 403. Table 394 provides data on members of Congress (House and Senate representatives). Table 402 gives data on the number of African Americans holding state and local office as of January 2001, while table 403 gives data on the number of Hispanics holding state and local office through 2005.

[9]Table 6 of the 2008 *Statistical Abstract* provides a variety of estimates of the African American and Hispanic populations. In 2006, for example, there were nearly 36 million African Americans and nearly 44 million Hispanics or Latinos. See http://www.census.gov/compendia/statab/tables/08s0006.pdf.

[10]For the former, we obtained Hispanic population data from the U.S. Census Bureau's population estimates, http://www.census.gov/population/documentation/twps0056/tab01.pdf. For the data from 1994 through 2006, we

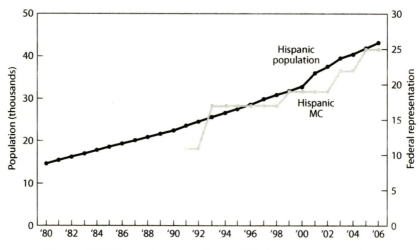

FIGURE I.2: Hispanic population and federal representation

While the latter has typically examined the political experiences of racial and ethnic minorities in isolation from those of nonminorities, the former has focused mostly on the attitudes and opinions of Anglo Americans. Our aim is to combine these two research areas and draw on theoretical and empirical contributions from both of these subfields of the American politics literature. Thus, we study Hispanics from a comparative standpoint and analyze their behavior in light of well-understood theories about political participation, turnout, voting, and partisanship.

Recent research that we have conducted, new work being done by other scholars, and the research we present in this book all point out that the established theories of American political behavior, such as those pertaining to political participation, mobilization, political socialization, and information processing, as well as partisanship acquisition, need to be revisited when we think about the new politics of Hispanic political behavior. Because of the distinct characteristics of the Hispanic electorate, some of which we have discussed in the introduction (e.g., ethnic diversity, large foreign-born population, constant influx of new immigrants), many of these theories need to be reassessed to better explain Hispanic political behavior. For instance, how one learns about politics, especially with respect to party identification, has largely been attributed to parental socialization (Valentino and Sears 1998; Vaillancourt 1973). That is, children learn about politics from their parents and typically adopt the same partisan preferences as their parents. Among foreign-born Hispanics, this socialization process is likely to differ, given that their parents were socialized into a political system outside of the United States. This raises a host of questions and implications for the future of American politics: From where and through what channels do these Hispanics learn about politics? Do the standard terms of liberal, conservative, Democrat, and Republican mean the same thing to foreign-born and recently naturalized Hispanics as they do for the rest of the American electorate? Implications such as these highlight the importance of studying current American politics from this perspective.

A Road Map of Our Book

We organize our study into six chapters, a conclusion, and a short postscript on the 2008 presidential election. In an appendix we provide a discussion of the data sources we use in our research. In chapter 1, we discuss the concept of Hispanic political identity. Because ethnic identity has been found to influence the political behavior of racial and ethnic minority groups, it is important to know what constitutes Hispanic political identity. We review the work in this area from the political science, sociology, and Hispanic studies literatures. This discussion would be incomplete without discussing the major cleavages within the Hispanic population (including ethnic, generational, and language differences) and their impact on the formation of Hispanic political identity, so we also tackle that subject in the first chapter.

Chapter 2 examines Hispanic public opinion and partisanship. How do Hispanics' opinions on social and economic issues compare to those of non-Hispanics? We focus on major issues like the economy, health care, foreign policy, and education. We also look at policies that are directly linked to the Hispanic community (e.g., immigration and bilingual education), and we explore whether Hispanics' attitudes are homogeneous or whether variations emerge as a result of generational status and ethnicity. On a related matter, we study the acquisition of partisanship among Hispanics. Do traditional predictors of partisanship, such as ideology and demographics, influence their decision to identify with a party, or do other characteristics unique to Hispanics, such as ethnicity and generational status, play a role in this decision?

Chapter 3 focuses on the cornerstone of mass political behavior: turnout and participation. At the most basic level, we ask whether Hispanics turn out to vote at the same rate as non-Hispanics and whether Hispanics are registered to vote at the same rates as non-Hispanics. We also ask who in the eligible Hispanic electorate participates in presidential elections, why more Hispanics are not registering to vote, why Hispanics are not turning out to vote, and what reforms might increase Hispanic participation in presidential elections.

Chapter 4 examines the factors contributing to Hispanics' levels of political knowledge. Since little is known about how Hispanics acquire political knowledge and information, particularly because many are immigrants whose political socialization occurs largely outside the United States, it is unclear what resources Hispanics turn to in order to learn about politics. Moreover, some of the socioeconomic barriers that Hispanics face may also lead to variations in their knowledge about and interest in politics.

In chapter 5, we turn to the politically important issue of determining whom Hispanics vote for in federal elections. Of course, voting for a presidential or congressional candidate is only one of the choices that Hispanic voters are asked to make when they go to voting booths every two or four years. Hispanics also vote in statewide races and local contests. We choose here to focus on federal election voting because the offices of the president, U.S. House, and U.S. Senate are one of the most important positions Hispanics can vote for, because presidential and congressional election voting has long been a mainstay of academic research on voting behavior, and because they are subjects for which we have detailed and extensive polling data that includes relatively large samples of Hispanic voters. We use exit poll data from recent presidential and midterm elections to look at which candidates Hispanic voters support and to study in more detail the variety that exists in the Hispanic electorate when its voters cast ballots.

It does not make sense to study Hispanic politics today in isolation from the politics of the other major racial and ethnic groups in the United States. As such, chapter 6 examines the prospects for intergroup relations not only among racial and ethnic minorities but also between Anglos and Hispanics. We explore those issues on which Hispanics, Anglos, and Blacks could potentially coalesce, as well as perceptions of a linked fate or shared interests among these various groups. Moreover, we discuss whether the benefits derived from these coalitions might outweigh the costs associated with them, especially considering that the size of the Hispanic population is considerably larger than that of the other two racial/ethnic minority groups.

We summarize and review our findings in the conclusion. We also discuss how our research contributes to the race and politics literature, as well as the political behavior literature. This conclusion returns to the themes that we discussed in this introduction. In light of the growing diversity of the American electorate, the manner in which we think about American political life needs to be reassessed. While some of the well-understood theories of political behavior do an adequate job of explaining Hispanic and non-Hispanic behaviors and attitudes, others need to be reassessed to take account of the new voices of Hispanic voters in America.

Finally, we close our study with a short postscript that presents some early analysis of the 2008 presidential election, and ties that analysis into some of the larger themes of our work. There is no doubt that the landmark 2008 presidential election will generate substantial quantities of research, and in our postscript we discuss the significant role that Hispanics played in the 2008 election.

Hispanic Political Identity

DESPITE MORE THAN three decades of scholarship on Hispanic politics, there is little consensus on the meaning of "Hispanic political identity." Scholars such as Lisa García Bedolla (2005) and Rodney Hero (1992) have examined the development of Hispanic political identity in the United States, but, as both authors point out, much work still needs to be done. Hispanic political identity is important to understand because ethnic or racial group identity is a key factor in the political behavior of racial and ethnic minorities in the United States (Dawson 1994; Barreto, Segura, and Woods 2004; Hero 1992; García Bedolla 2003; Meier et al. 2005; Sanchez 2006; Stokes-Brown 2006; Abrajano, Alvarez, and Nagler 2004) as well as in other countries (see Horowitz 1985; Fearon 2006; Chandra 2004; Posner 2005). García Bedolla (2005) defines identity as "an individual's self-conceptualization that places the individual either within or in opposition to a social grouping." This definition looks at identity formation from both an individual and a contextual perspective. Accounting for both of these factors is particularly salient for immigrants, since their identity can change based on where they immigrate to and what identity or identities they assume.

DEFINING A POLITICAL IDENTITY FOR ETHNIC AND RACIAL MINORITIES IN THE UNITED STATES

Research on African American politics demonstrates the importance of racial group identity to African American political behavior. Dawson (1994) provides an in-depth explanation of this. The cornerstone of his argument is known as the African American utility heuristic, which he defines in the following way: "Blacks' evaluations of candidates, parties and public policies will be influenced by the extent to which they believe that it will impact the interests of the Black community, as a whole" (61). Dawson's reasoning is based on the historical experiences of African Americans with racism in America. Until the late 1960s, the life chances and opportunities of African Americans were largely determined by their race. The structural barriers and discrimination faced by African Americans forced them to turn to their own leaders and organizations for clues about what would be best for them both socially and politically. Race therefore functions as a useful and meaningful heuristic so long as one identifies with one's racial identity. Based on survey responses from the National Black Election Studies, the notion of a linked fate still continues to exist among African Americans; the percentage of African Americans who perceive that they share a common or "linked fate" with other African Americans has ranged from 73.5 percent in 1984 to 77.4 percent in 1988 to a high of 83 percent in 1996 (Jost 2004).

But any attempt to apply Dawson's theory of linked fate to Hispanics requires some careful consideration. The biggest challenge is that Hispanics, overall, do not share a linked fate based on a common history—primarily because "Hispanic," or "Latino," is a socially constructed pan-ethnic label developed by the U.S. Census (Espiritu 1992; Skerry 1997). No shared history exists that is easily comparable to the experiences of Blacks for all the individuals who are placed in the category of Hispanic or Latino. The predominant commonality that helps bring Hispanics together is cultural affinity, especially one associated with their shared common language of Spanish. The historical experiences of the three major Hispanic subgroups—Cubans, Puerto Ricans, and Mexicans—have been dramatically different, and their reasons for immigrating to the United States also vary. For instance, most Cubans immigrated to the United States at the height of the cold war as refugees seeking political asylum from Castro's Communist regime (Garcia 1996). Mexicans, in contrast, have had a long presence in the United States, since much of the U.S. Southwest was once part of Mexico. The United States and Mexico also share a common land border, and in some parts of the nation, such as New Mexico, many families that now identify as Hispanic have lived in what is now the United States since well before the nation's East Coast founding. The more recent experiences of many Hispanics of Mexican descent began with the systematic importation of Mexican labor through the Bracero program, which was established in the 1940s (Hero 1992); though in recent decades the flow of new immigrants from Mexico has continued in the Southwest. Finally, individuals from Puerto Rico are unique because the country is a U.S. protectorate, making all Puerto Ricans American citizens. Thus, the possibility of having a historically linked fate akin to Blacks' shared experiences of slavery and legal segregation simply does not exist for the Hispanic population. The constant and steady rates of Hispanic immigration make it even more difficult for a conception of linked fate to develop between those Hispanics who are already in the United States and those who have recently arrived. According to political scientist Michael Jones-Correa, "With Blacks, there is this sense of linked fate, that what happens to any one of us could happen to me.... Hispanics don't have that same feeling, the same group identity, because they don't have same group history that Blacks do" (quoted in Jost 2004, 236).

Hispanic political identity as it exists today must be understood as having formed in a manner that is distinct from the formation of Black political identity. García Bedolla (2005) develops an insightful explanation of the factors that contribute to a Hispanic individual's political identity. She argues that Hispanic political identity comprises three factors: power, collective identity, and place. The first factor, power, is closely related to stigma, which is "imposed on individuals who possess or are believed to possess some attribute, or characteristic, that conveys a social identity that is devalued in a particular social context" (5). Experiences of stigma could serve to mobilize Hispanics into political action, as demonstrated by the protests organized by Hispanic high school students in the wake of the passage of Proposition 187 (García Bedolla 2005). On the other hand, being stigmatized as a racial minority could also lead individuals to become politically disengaged and distrustful.

Collective identity refers to an individual's personal ideology, combined with his or her beliefs about the ability to make an impact on the world. In deciding to become involved in politics, Hispanics have to feel like they are part of a community or group. Thus, social capital plays a large role in determining the extent to which Hispanics perceive that they are part of the larger Hispanic community, and their attitudes and feelings toward the community are critical in determining whether they get involved in politics.

Place, or where Hispanics live, is also a significant factor in shaping their political identity. Contextual capital is important, especially for immigrants, because it determines what social networks they can develop and what types of institutions they will have access to. For example, if a recent Mexican immigrant settles into a neighborhood where a large number of Mexican American–based organizations and groups already exist, then not only will that person have a ready-built social network, but also his or her ethnic identity may become more politicized as a result of the shared histories and experiences in this neighborhood. Structural features such as these may contribute to a positive conception of racial or ethnic identity, while the absence of these institutions is likely to have the opposite effect on the formation of a racial or ethnic political identity.

Thus, the construction of Hispanic political identity depends on a host of factors, many of which are not in the hands of Hispanics themselves but are largely determined by where they live, the institutional structures that exist in their neighborhoods, and how society responds to and interacts with them. Hispanic political identity is also shaped by explicitly political factors (hence our use of the term "political" identity). Political candidates, parties, and organized groups have used, and will continue to use, the idea of a shared Hispanic identity to mobilize Hispanics for their own political goals. And it is also the case that Hispanics and symbols associated with Hispanics have been used to mobilize non-Hispanics: we have mentioned the example of the 1994 gubernatorial election in California, in which negative imagery and campaign rhetoric were used by Pete Wilson to mobilize Anglo voters mainly around the issue of illegal immigration (the slogan used for his television advertisement was "They keep coming," in reference to Mexican immigrants).[1] Hispanic political identity is therefore contingent on both individual and contextual factors—contextual factors that are social, economic, and political. Accounting for these variables is particularly salient for immigrants, since their identity can change based on the place where they emigrate.

[1]Wilson's support for Proposition 187, which aimed to restrict noncitizens from receiving public social services, further added to the perception that he was anti-immigrant and anti-Hispanic.

This overview suggests that the assumption that Hispanics possess a strong, collective group identity is not necessarily correct and is contingent on a number of different factors. Indeed, the survey evidence on Hispanics provides little support for the notion that most Hispanics perceive a linked fate with other Hispanics. In the 1989 Latino National Political Survey (de la Garza and Hero 1992), which was the first nationally representative survey of Hispanics in the United States, only about one-fifth of the members of the three major subgroups believed that they had any cultural similarities with other Hispanics: 19.7 percent of Mexicans, 20 percent of Puerto Ricans, and 18 percent of Cubans felt this way. When probed about political similarities, the differences were even greater. Fifty-five percent of Mexicans and 54 percent of Puerto Ricans felt that they were not very politically similar to Cubans. Moreover, 46.7 percent of Mexicans and 62.6 percent of Cubans perceived that they had very little in common politically with Puerto Ricans. A plurality of Mexicans (46.7 percent) and Puerto Ricans (49.8 percent) believed that very few political similarities existed between them and Cubans. More than a decade later, in the Pew Hispanic Survey in 2002, only 24 percent of Hispanics identified themselves as "Latino" or "Hispanic," while the majority of respondents (54 percent) chose to identify with their country of origin. Such evidence provides little support for the notion of a linked fate among Hispanics, and this lack of commonality suggests the difficulty Hispanics might encounter in sustaining a pan-ethnic collective identity.

More recent findings from the 2006 Latino National Survey (LNS) suggest that many Hispanics are choosing to identify themselves in various ways, whether with their country of origin or as "American" or "Hispanic." Cubans and Spaniards are the least likely to identify with a pan-ethnic label, while Central Americans, Dominicans, and Puerto Ricans are the most likely to do so. In comparing these survey results to the 1989 Latino National Political Survey (LNPS), a greater percentage of Hispanics are identifying as pan-ethnics: about 50 percent of the respondents perceived a great deal of commonality between their own ethnic group and other Hispanics. This growth in pan-ethnic identity from 1989 to 2006 may be correlated to the increase in Spanish-language media outlets (e.g., newspapers, television stations, radio) during this time.[2] Typically, these media outlets, especially television stations, target Hispanics as a pan-ethnic group, and they may serve to prime and socialize Hispanics to think of themselves as having a pan-ethnic identity. Also, anti-Hispanic policies and ballot initiatives introduced over the past fifteen years may have motivated more Hispanics to think of themselves in a pan-ethnic manner. Despite these changes, however, the Hispanic community's subscription to the idea of a linked Hispanic fate is still far weaker than is the allegiance of Black Americans to their own collective racial identity.

HISPANIC POLITICAL IDENTITY TODAY

Data from a survey by the Pew Hispanic Center in 2004 allow us to build upon the existing research on Hispanic political identity. We specifically look at survey questions that asked Hispanics to reveal their opinions on the role of ethnic identity in their political attitudes and behaviors. Overall, we see a consistent pattern in Hispanics' attitudes toward their racial/ethnic identity, one that is primarily driven by their generational status. For first- and second-generation Hispanics, ethnic identity is more salient in political attitudes and decisions than it is for third-generation Hispanics. Moreover, on measures of political assimilation and acculturation, we see that clear differences exist between earlier and later generations of Hispanics.

In table 1.1, we present the responses to several questions pertaining to Hispanics' views on assimilation and the concept of the melting pot, as well as their views on acculturation. Table 1.2 presents information on Hispanics' attitudes toward the opportunities and values in the United States versus their countries of origin. With regard to Hispanics' views on assimilation, a strong majority believes that it is either very important or somewhat important to change in order to blend in with larger society (69.1 and 72.2 percent, respectively). Hispanics possess a similar view when this question is directed toward them specifically as when

[2]"The State of the News Media 2004: An Annual Report on American Journalism," http://www.stateofthenewsmedia.com/narrative_ethnicalternative_spanish press.asp?media=9.

23

TABLE 1.1
Hispanic Opinions on Political Identity

Variable	Very important	Somewhat important	Not too important	Not important at all
Importance of racial/ethnic minorities changing to blend into larger society	35.8	33.3	12.5	10.8
Importance of Hispanics changing to blend into larger society	38.5	33.7	11.2	10.0
Racial/ethnic cultures maintaining distinct cultures	57.7	27.7	7.1	5.0

Source: 2004 Pew/Kaiser Hispanic Survey.
$N = 1,144$; cell entries are row percentages.

it is directed at racial and ethnic minorities in general. Respondents from the 2006 LNS were also asked a very similar question, and 56.9 percent feel that it is very important to change in order to blend into larger society. These responses suggest that Hispanics do believe in the importance of assimilation. At the same time, though, 85.4 percent of Hispanics from the Pew Survey feel that retaining one's racial/ethnic culture is either very important or somewhat important. And as a point of comparison, 77.4 percent of the respondents from the LNS also believe that maintaining a distinct culture is very important. Thus, a disconnect seems to be at play here: while a solid majority of Hispanics place importance on the need to change in order to blend into larger society, an even greater number of Hispanics also believe in the importance of preserving their racial/ethnic culture. Respondents may not perceive that changing to blend into the larger American so-

TABLE 1.2
Hispanic Opinions on Political Assimilation and Acculturation

Variable	Better in the U.S.	Better in parents'/ home country	Same
U.S. or country of origin better in the treatment of the poor	67.0	9.7	19.9
U.S. or country of origin better in the moral values of society	26.1	39.4	30.4
U.S. or country of origin better in the opportunity to get ahead	89.7	2.6	6.9

Source: 2002 Pew/Kaiser Hispanic Survey.
Note: N = 2,919; cell entries are row percentages.

ciety excludes the possibility of retaining and preserving their own racial/ethnic culture, but this is what the question, and the concept of assimilation, implies. As Park (1928) outlines, the classic assimilation model expects that after several generations, immigrants will abandon their cultural ties and backgrounds as they advance at the socioeconomic, residential, and occupational levels. An alternative theory of immigrant assimilation known as acculturation (Gordon 1964) suggests that immigrants are able to retain their own culture while adopting the ways of dominant society. In this view, immigrants do not need to completely relinquish all ties with their racial/ethnic culture in order to become part of the dominant society.

Moving on, the data presented in table 1.2 focus on questions that asked Hispanics to consider whether treatment of the poor, moral values, and the opportunity to get ahead are better in the United States or their country of origin/their parents' country of origin, or whether they are the same in both countries. These questions are useful in explaining Hispanics' attitudes toward the United States and gauging areas in which assimilation would be easy, since Hispanics may perceive more advantages in the United States relative to their homelands or their parents' homelands. Two-thirds (67 percent) of respondents believe that the United States is better than their country of origin in its treatment of the poor, 9.7 percent believe that it is better in their country of origin, and about one-fifth (19.9 percent) feel that the treatment of the poor is the same in both countries. In the same vein, an overwhelming majority of Hispanics perceive that opportunities to get ahead are better in the United States than in their country of origin (89.7 percent). In fact, only 2.6 percent of Hispanics feel that opportunities are better in their home country, and 6.9 percent feel that the opportunities are equal in both countries. Of course, we would expect Hispanics to respond in this manner, as they immigrate to the United States primarily for economic reasons and as a way to improve their life circumstances (Portes and Rumbuat 1992).

When asked about the moral values of a society, however—a term that can encapsulate abortion, gay marriage, and prayer in schools, among many other cultural touch points—Hispanics are less inclined to favor the United States: 39.4 percent feel that the moral values are better in their own country, 30.4 percent perceive that they are the same for both countries, and 26.1 percent believe that the moral values in the United States are better. Given that most Hispanics are from Catholic countries and therefore possess socially conservative views and attitudes (Pew Hispanic Center 2007), it is understandable why they would assess their country of origin or their parents' country of origin as having better moral values than the United States. So while Hispanics' evaluations of economic and life opportunities in the United States are highly positive, their evaluations of U.S. moral values are less so. This finding is particularly notable, since Republicans have long used "values" appeals to attract Hispanics to the Republican Party. In fact, Bush's success with Hispanics in the 2004 presidential election can partially be attributed to his position on and discussion of moral values during that campaign (Abrajano, Alvarez, and Nagler 2008).

In table 1.3, we provide several unique measures of group identity based on questions posed to respondents about the role of ethnic identity in their voting behavior. In situations in which a Hispanic is on the ballot, a majority of Hispanics either strongly or somewhat agree that this will improve the probability of Hispanic turnout. A moderate gap exists between earlier- and later-generation Hispanics on this question, however: while 40 percent of third-generation Hispanics strongly agree that Hispanic turnout

TABLE 1.3
Hispanic Attitudes toward Group Identity, by Generational Status

Measure of group identity	First and second generation	Third generation
Hispanics are more likely to vote if Hispanics are on the ballot		
Strongly agree	52.0	40.0
Somewhat agree	26.9	25.5
Somewhat disagree	8.8	19.1
Strongly disagree	7.6	10.9
Don't know	4.3	5.0
Hispanics are more likely to vote for a Hispanic instead of a non-Hispanic candidate running for the same office if they are equally qualified		
Strongly agree	42.8	40.0
Somewhat agree	30.4	27.7
Somewhat disagree	12.1	13.6
Strongly disagree	8.7	14.1
Don't know	5.4	4.1
[Respondent] is more likely to vote for a Hispanic instead of a non-Hispanic candidate running for the same office if they are equally qualified		
Strongly agree	30.4	19.4
Somewhat agree	15.1	13.3
Somewhat disagree	20.0	20.9
Strongly disagree	30.2	44.1
Don't know	3.6	1.8
[Respondent] is more likely to vote for a Hispanic instead of a non-Hispanic candidate running for the same office even if the non-Hispanic is more qualified		
Strongly agree	19.7	10.8
Somewhat agree	9.0	7.1
Somewhat disagree	16.9	17.0
Strongly disagree	48.1	63.5
Don't know	4.4	1.3
*Hispanics from different countries. . .**		
Share one Hispanic culture	22.5	17.8
All have separate and distinct cultures	74.8	80.1
Don't know	2.1	1.2

(continued)

TABLE 1.3 (*cont.*)

Measure of group identity	First and second generation	Third generation
Hispanics from different countries are. . .*		
Working together to achieve common political goals	56.7	52.1
Not working together politically	33.9	40.4
Don't know	8.4	6.9

Source: 2004 Pew Hispanic Center National Survey of Hispanics: Politics and Civic Participation.

Note: N = 1120 in 2004; cell entries are column percentages.

*From the 2006 Pew Hispanic Immigration Survey (N = 1,873).

will increase when a Hispanic is on the ballot, 52 percent of first- and second-generation Hispanics strongly agree with this sentiment. At the other end of the spectrum, a far greater percentage of third-generation Hispanics disagree with this statement relative to first- and second-generation Hispanics (30 percent versus 16.4 percent). This result suggests that, consistent with previous research, for later-generation Hispanics, the role of shared ethnic identity and descriptive representation is less salient than it is for more recent Hispanic immigrants.

Another scenario asks Hispanics whether Hispanic voters are more likely to support a Hispanic candidate if both the Hispanic and the non-Hispanic candidate are equally qualified. In this case, generational differences are once again apparent. A larger percentage of third-generation Hispanics strongly disagree with the statement than do first- and second-generation Hispanics (14.1 percent versus 8.7 percent), while a greater percentage of earlier-generation Hispanics agree with this sentiment than do third-generation Hispanics (72.3 percent agree or strongly agree, versus 67.7 percent).

The Pew Survey then asked whether a respondent would himself or herself be more likely to support a Hispanic candidate when: (1) both the Hispanic and the non-Hispanic candidate possess the same qualities or (2) the non-Hispanic candidate is more qualified than the Hispanic candidate. Here, we notice a significant decline in the percentage of Hispanic respondents who agree with these two statements relative to when the question was asked of Hispanics in general. It is still the case, however, that a greater percentage of first- and second-generation Hispanics agree with these statements than do third-generation Hispanics. In the first scenario, where both candidates are equally qualified, 30.4 percent of first- and second-generation Hispanics strongly agreed with this statement, but a smaller percentage of third-generation Hispanics (19.4 percent) responded in this manner. In fact, nearly half of the third-generation Hispanics (44.1 percent) strongly disagreed with this statement, while only 30.2 percent of the first- and second-generation Hispanics responded in this manner. Thus, we see how generational status affects Hispanics' perceptions of the importance of ethnic identity and descriptive representation in their political decisions: descriptive representation appears to be more important and salient to the earlier-generation Hispanics, whereas for third-generation Hispanics, shared ethnic identity between themselves and a candidate is somewhat less likely to lead them to lend their support to the candidate.

In the second scenario, where the respondents were asked whether they were more likely to vote for a Hispanic than a non-Hispanic candidate even if the non-Hispanic candidate is more qualified, a smaller percentage of Hispanics strongly agreed with this statement when compared to the scenario in which both candidates possessed equal qualifications. It is still the case, however, that a larger percentage of first- and second-generation Hispanics strongly agreed with this statement (19.7 percent) than did third-generation Hispanics (10.8 percent). In fact, more than a majority (63.7 percent) of third-generation Hispanics strongly disagreed with this statement, as did a near majority of first- and second-generation Hispanics (48.1 percent). These responses suggest that Hispanics, particularly those who have been here the longest, are more concerned about a candidate's qualities and skills than his or her ethnic background. Thus, while the notion of descriptive representation is important to first- and second-generation Hispanics when both Hispanic and non-Hispanic candidates are on equal footing in terms of their background and qualifications, descriptive representation becomes less salient when the candidates' qualities are unequal.

Another set of noteworthy patterns are the variations in the responses that Hispanics provided based on the way the questions were worded. When respondents were directly asked their opinions on these scenarios, as opposed to what they thought were the opinions of Hispanics in general, fewer strongly agreed in the salience of descriptive representation. For instance, while 42.8 percent of first- and second-generation Hispanics strongly agreed with the notion that Hispanics are in general more likely to vote for a Hispanic than for a non-Hispanic candidate when both of the candidates are qualified, only 30.4 percent of these respondents strongly agreed with this statement when they were asked about their own personal opinions on this matter. And for third-generation Hispanics, the difference is even greater: while 40 percent strongly agreed with this statement when the question was framed as being about Hispanics generally, this number dropped by half to 19.4 percent when the question asked the respondent for his or her own personal opinion. Indeed, more than a majority (65 percent) of third-generation Hispanics either somewhat disagreed or strongly disagreed with this statement when they were asked directly for their position, as did 50.2 percent of first- and second-generation Hispanics. These variations may have emerged due to respondents' unwillingness to admit that ethnicity trumps candidate quality or due to their perception that Hispanics overall care more about ethnicity than a candidate's background and qualifications. These bivariate distributions cannot tell us which is the case, but they are important to think about and consider.

The last two questions presented in table 1.3 directly speak to Hispanics' views on the existence of a pan-ethnic identity. Regardless of generational status, approximately 75 percent of Hispanics believe that Hispanics possess separate and distinct cultures. This indicates that the notion of a linked fate is not something that a majority of Hispanics believe in; instead, as previous research and our own work have shown, the diversity of the Hispanic community makes it difficult for Hispanics to think of themselves in these pan-ethnic terms. Interestingly, a greater percentage of first- and second-generation Hispanics believe that Hispanics share one culture than do third-generation Hispanics (22.5 percent versus 17.8 percent). A longer presence in the United States seems to make Hispanics *less* likely to believe in a pan-ethnic identity and instead *more* likely to think of themselves in terms of their ethnic identity. On a more positive note, a majority of Hispanics believed that they are working together to achieve common political goals, although, consistent with the previous patterns, third-generation Hispanics are more pessimistic than are first- and second-generation Hispanics. While only one-third (33.9 percent) of earlier-generation respondents perceive that Hispanics are not working together politically, 40.4 percent of the third-generation respondents view the Hispanic community in this manner. Given third-generation Hispanics' views on pan-ethnicity, these survey results do not bode well for the prospects of forging a politically strong and united Hispanic community, since longer residence in the United States does not appear to be uniting Hispanics as a single and cohesive political entity.

Table 1.4 presents Hispanics' attitudes toward assimilation and acculturation in the United States. Respondents in the Pew Survey were asked, "To be part of American society, Hispanics should a) speak English; b) believe in the U.S. Constitution; c) be a U.S. citizen; d) vote in U.S. elections." Respondents could answer "yes, they have to" or "no, they do not have to" for each question. Again, we examine the data based on respondents' generational status, since previous research indicates that immigrants' attitudes on assimilation and acculturation differ according to the length of time they have spent in the United States. The general pattern that emerges is that a smaller percentage of third-generation Hispanics feels that Hispanics need to engage in these four activities than do earlier generations of Hispanics. While the ability to speak in the host country's primary language has long been the main benchmark of assimilation (Dahl 1961; Portes and Rumbaut 1992), for example, only 53 percent of third-generation Hispanics believe that Hispanics need to become proficient in English to be part of American society.

For earlier-generation Hispanics, however, a slightly greater percentage (59.3 percent) believes that language acquisition is a key to assimilation. And furthermore, while 70 percent of first- and second-generation Hispanics believe that voting is an important aspect of assimilation, only 55.3 percent of third-generation respondents feel this way. These patterns in Hispanics' opinions may be understood in the context of the segmented assimilation theory (Zhou 1999; Portes and Rumbaut 1992), which focuses

TABLE 1.4
Hispanic Attitudes toward Assimilation and Acculturation,
by Generational Status

Political assimilation	First and second generation		Third generation	
	Yes, they have to	No, they do not have to	Yes, they have to	No, they do not have to
To be part of American society, Hispanics should. . .				
Speak English	59.3	38.4	53.0	45.2
Believe in the U.S. Constitution	83.6	11.5	80.4	17.1
Be a U.S. citizen	52.4	44.1	57.9	39.8
Vote in U.S. elections	70.0	27.6	55.3	42.0
Importance of future generations of Hispanics living in the U.S. to speak Spanish				
Very important	73.4		54.9	
Somewhat important	19.4		28.6	
Not important	4.5		9.2	
Not important at all	1.9		6.9	

Source: 2004 Pew Survey.
Note: N = 2,288.

specifically on the experiences of second-generation immigrants. It recognizes that society is composed of segregated and unequal segments. In particular, experiences with discrimination may reverse the assimilation process, so that these later-generation Hispanics become more aware and cognizant of their ethnic identity and the structural inequalities that result from it. Thus, instead of believing in the need to speak English, to believe in the U.S. Constitution, and to vote, third-generation Hispanics may see little benefit in either thinking or behaving in these ways, since their experiences with discrimination may lead them to believe that they will always be outsiders in American society, no matter how well they speak English or how often they vote in elections.

The only activity that a larger percentage of third-generation respondents, as opposed to the first- and second-generation respondents, feel that Hispanics need to engage in is acquiring U.S. citizenship: 57.9 percent of third-generation Hispanics perceive that Hispanics need to become U.S. citizens in order to be part of U.S. society, whereas 52.4 percent of first- and second-generation Hispanics responded in this manner. Perhaps the reason for this can once again be traced to segmented assimilation theory: As a result of their encounters with discrimination, third-generation Hispanics may feel that U.S. citizenship is one of the most definitive ways to assert their presence in and belonging to American society, as well as to garner rights and protections that are associated with citizenship. On the other hand, this finding could also be understood in the context of classic assimilation theory, since citizenship is the ultimate indicator of political incorporation (Bloemraad 2006).

Given all the discussion, not only in the popular media but also in academic research, of the importance of language acquisition as an indicator of assimilation (Park 1928), table 1.4 presents the results from a survey question probing Hispanics' attitudes toward the importance of "having future generations of Hispanics living in the U.S. speak Spanish." Again, the responses vary by generational status. Consistent with the previous findings, sustaining the Spanish language for future generations of Hispanics is much more important to first- and second-generation Hispanics than to third-generation Hispanics: 73.4 percent of the first- and second-generation Hispanics believe that it is very important, compared to only 54.9 percent of third-generation Hispanics.

Moreover, 16.1 percent of third-generation Hispanics believe that the retention of Spanish by future generations is "not important" or "not important at all"; in contrast, a significantly smaller percentage (6.4 percent) of first- and second-generation Hispanics responded in this manner. These patterns suggest that Hispanics are, at least culturally and linguistically, assimilating in the manner that traditional immigration scholars predict: the importance of preserving one's mother tongue diminishes from one generation to the next. Given that language is the primary indicator that numerous scholars, particularly Huntington (2004), use to measure assimilation, the responses to this survey question can alleviate his and others' fears that Hispanics are unwilling to linguistically assimilate into the United States.

Conclusion

This chapter demonstrates the many layers and facets that contribute to Hispanics' attitudes toward assimilation, acculturation, and the future of Hispanic political identity. While the large influx of immigrants from Latin America continues to alter and shape what Hispanic political identity currently is and what it will be in the future, it seems to be the case that as Hispanics' time in the United States increases, unless other changes in the political environment occur or rates of immigration continue to increase, their ties to their culture and ethnic identity are likely to wane. For skeptics and critics of Hispanics and their ability to assimilate into U.S. society, the survey evidence we present here should alleviate their fears that Hispanics may be culturally "inassimilable." Certainly, by the third generation, the role of shared ethnic identity and the importance of maintaining the mother tongue become less important to Hispanics.

Given these findings, identifying a single Hispanic political identity may be a challenge. As García Bedolla (2005) and others have pointed out, the vast diversity of the Hispanic population, coupled with varying experiences pertaining to stigma, discrimination, and place of residence, all imply that Hispanic political identity is constantly changing and fluid. Thus, making predictions about Hispanics' political attitudes, opinions, and behavior may not be easy or as straightforward as many politicians expect. Unlike African Americans, whose racial/ethnic identity can be used as a readily available shortcut to predict their political behavior, Hispanics' racial/ethnic identity may not explain their political behavior to the same extent, for reasons discussed in this chapter. For Hispanics to become fully involved in the U.S. political system and for candidates to reach out to them in the most effective and appropriate manner, candidates and politicians need to pay attention to the distinctions within the Hispanic community and understand that Hispanic political identity will continue to evolve.

Hispanic Public Opinion and Partisanship

RECENT RESEARCH on American public opinion has explored the origins of political attitudes and opinions and has looked at their stability (Zaller 1992; Alvarez and Brehm 2002). Instead of seeing public opinion as completely fickle and capricious, contemporary research views American public information as influenced by current information flows, as well as by the predispositions and values held by the public. Americans are not completely informed about political affairs, nor are they completely ignorant about political issues; instead, most Americans have opinions about some issues that are of importance to them, and when asked about other issues they have deeply held values and predispositions they draw upon to formulate an attitude or opinion if necessary.

Detailed research that applies contemporary theories of public opinion to Hispanics has yet to be done, we suspect mainly because available data on Hispanic public opinion are still too sparse to allow for the sorts of detailed studies undertaken by Zaller (1992) or Alvarez and Brehm (2002). Thus, at this point, we can only use contemporary theories of public opinion to speculate about the political attitudes, particularly those pertaining to the partisan preferences, of Hispanics in the United States and especially to argue that there is considerable reason to believe that the nature and origins of Hispanic public opinion and partisanship likely differ in important ways from those of their Anglo counterparts, who have received the bulk of the research attention.

First, from work that one of us has undertaken, we know that in some ways the flow of information to Hispanics in the United States differs from the flow to non-Hispanics; Abrajano's studies of presidential campaign communications targeted at Hispanics show that Hispanic voters are provided with political information that is more symbolic in nature than that provided to non-Hispanics (Abrajano 2010). Second, because of a variety of factors, we expect that Hispanics in America have different predispositions and values than do Anglos; we hypothesize that

Hispanic attitudes as well as their partisanship preferences are shaped by, for example, their affinities with the Catholic Church; social, cultural, and economic backgrounds in Central and South American and other Hispanic-influenced nations; the use of Spanish-language media; and the immigration experience itself. Because of these differences in information, predispositions, and values, we anticipate that Hispanic public opinion will differ in important ways from Anglo public opinion, though we await the sorts of data and future analyses that will test these expectations in more detail.

The data we have at the present time allow us to ask more proximate questions: How do Hispanics' opinions on both domestic and international issues compare to the opinions of other Americans? Does Hispanic public opinion on issues that are directly relevant to the Hispanic community, such as immigration and bilingual education, vary based on their generational status? Do these issues, along with other factors, explain Hispanic partisanship as well? These are the questions that we address in this chapter, using public opinion data from three sources: the Pew Hispanic Center, the National Annenberg Election Survey (NAES), and the 2006 Latino National Survey. Both the Pew and the LNS data allow us to examine Hispanic public opinion on specific issues that directly affect the Hispanic community, including responses to a detailed set of questions on immigration policy, unauthorized immigrants, and the recent reforms proposed by Congress to overhaul the immigration system in the United States. We also use the LNS data to explore the factors that explain Hispanic partisanship. And finally, with the Annenberg data, we can compare Hispanics' attitudes toward domestic and foreign policies with those of Anglos and African Americans.

Little systematic research and understanding of Hispanics' views and attitudes, particularly as they compare to those of the rest of the population, has taken place. On the other hand, a commonly held belief regarding Hispanic political behavior, as we discussed in the introduction, is that Hispanics' opinions on issues such as moral values and immigration differ considerably from those of Anglos and African Americans. The reason for these conjectures is rather straightforward: immigration is viewed to be an issue that directly affects the Hispanic community, while moral values issues (which include abortion, school prayer, and gay marriage) are presumed to be important to Hispanics because many are Catholic and therefore tend be socially conservative. We examine Hispanic public opinion on these issues as well as those pertaining to foreign policy, the economy, and education. Along with examining Hispanics' issue opinions relative to those of the rest of the American electorate, we also look at preferences within the Hispanic community, particularly based on generational status. As previous research (e.g., Hood, Morris, and Shirkley 1997; Branton 2007) indicates, Hispanics' opinions on an issue like immigration vary according to their generational status.

ISSUE SALIENCE

Table 2.1 provides a snapshot of Hispanic public opinion in 2006. Respondents in the Hispanic Immigration Study conducted by the Pew Hispanic Center were asked, in an open-ended manner, what they believed was the most important problem in 2006. As the results reveal, Hispanics considered two issues to be most important that do not normally top the list as the most important concerns facing the country: the issue of immigration (21.8 percent) and the war in Iraq (21.6 percent). Much of the reason why these two issues ranked the highest can be attributed to the context in which this survey was conducted: foreign policy concerns, and in particular the war in Iraq, have been at the top of the American policy agenda in recent years, and this survey was conducted in the wake of the major immigration reforms being discussed by Congress and the mass marches and rallies that ensued in the spring of 2006. Thus, Hispanics may have ranked these issues as the two most important problems facing the country due in part to timing and the political context.

When asked more specifically about what they perceived to be the most important problem for themselves and their families, survey respondents still ranked immigration high on the list (16.9 percent), but the domestic issues of jobs/economy and education emerged as more important to individual Hispanic families (at 22.2 percent and 18.6 percent, respectively). The fourth most important problem for Hispanic respondents and their families was the issue of health care, with 9.1 percent considering it to be their

TABLE 2.1

Hispanic Opinions on the Most Important Problem (MIP) in 2006

Issue	MIP facing the country*	MIP to R and R's family**
Crime/violence/drugs	3.2	1.2
Education	1.9	18.6
Health care	0.8	9.1
Homeland security	7.1	1.8
Immigration/immigrants	21.8	16.9
Jobs/economy	10.5	22.2
Moral/religious values	0.8	0.5
None	3.1	0.1
War/war in Iraq	21.6	1.8
N	939	936

Source: 2006 Pew Hispanic Center Hispanic Immigration Study.
*This question was asked in an open-ended format.
**This question was asked in a closed-ended format.

most important concern. The results from these two questions paint an interesting picture of Hispanic public opinion in 2006: while Hispanics, along with the rest of the American electorate, recognized that the war in Iraq was the most pressing problem facing the country, domestic issues trumped foreign policy concerns when it came to their own personal lives. In line with previous research (Abrajano, Alvarez, and Nagler 2008), Hispanics consistently rank the economy/jobs as the most important issue, typically followed by education and health care.

Table 2.2 provides a different perspective on issue salience, using comparative data from the 2004 NAES, wherein we can examine the issues that Anglos saw as important in comparison to the issues that Hispanics saw as important in 2004. For Anglos, the top three issue concerns in 2004 were the economy (17.3 percent), the Iraq War (14.9 percent), and terrorism (10.7 percent). The same three issues were seen by Hispanics as important in 2004, but their respective rank ordering differed: Hispanics saw the Iraq War as the most important issue (19.3 percent), followed by the economy (16.7 percent) and terrorism (10.1 percent). Among the other issues, Hispanics were more likely than Anglos to see health care and moral values as of concern, and, surpris-

TABLE 2.2
Hispanic and Anglo Opinions on the Most
Important Problem (MIP) in 2004

Issue	Anglos	Hispanics
Crime/violence/drugs	2.7	1.0
Economy	17.3	16.7
Education	5.0	3.5
Health care	3.8	6.5
Immigration/immigrants	2.5	0.9
Moral/religious values	2.9	6.0
Terrorism	10.7	10.1
Unemployment/jobs	8.9	7.8
War/war in Iraq	14.9	19.3
N	48,358	4,644

Source: 2004 National Annenberg Election Survey.

ingly, both Anglos and Hispanics viewed immigration as relatively unimportant. (Among Anglos, 2.5 percent viewed immigration as an important issue in 2004, and less than 1 percent of Hispanics saw it as an important issue.)

IMMIGRATION

The issue of immigration is particularly important to look at, since it not only is an issue that directly affects a large portion of the Hispanic community, but also is a policy area that is inextricably linked to the Hispanic population (Jimenez 2007). We should note that the time span examined (2004–2006) for this study may have been unique, in that millions of individuals participated in marches and other events nationwide to protest the immigration reforms proposed by Congress just before the 2006 survey went into the field. The immigration opinions that Hispanics provided in the 2006 survey may have been affected by this momentous series of events.

Previous research has found that Hispanics' immigration attitudes vary based on generational status (Binder, Polinard, and Wrinkle 1997; Hood, Morris, and Shirkley 1997, de la Garza and DeSipio, 1992, 1996; Newton 2000; Branton 2007; Abrajano and Singh

2009). One explanation can be found in the structural integration hypothesis, which predicts that immigrants who are more structurally integrated into U.S. society will possess a more restrictionist view of immigration than will their less structurally integrated counterparts. Since structural integration by way of socioeconomic status is often correlated with generational status, the expectation is that later-generation Hispanics will favor a more restrictive stand on immigration policy than will earlier-generation Hispanics. Moreover, recent work by Jimenez (2007) finds that Mexican Americans' opinions on immigration are influenced by a cost-benefit assessment of immigration's impact on their own economic, social, and cultural well-being.

Table 2.3 presents the answers to several detailed questions related to Hispanics' views on the rate of immigration to the United States, proposed immigration reforms, and the role of undocumented immigrants in the United States. Here, we present Pew Survey data from interviews taken in 2004 and 2006 and examine Hispanic public opinion toward immigration based on respondents' generational status. When asked to evaluate the current rate of legal immigration by Latin American immigrants in the United States, the modal response in 2004 was that the status quo ought to be maintained. Generational differences did emerge in this response, with later-generation Hispanics exhibiting a more restrictionist attitude than earlier-generation Hispanics; this result is consistent with the existing literature on Hispanic attitudes on immigration. In 2004, a larger percentage of third-generation Hispanics (19.5 percent) favored a reduction in the number of legal immigrants coming to the United States than did first- and second-generation Hispanics (7.9 percent). Similarly, a smaller percentage of third-generation Hispanics, 26.8 percent, supported an increase in the number of legal immigrants than did first- and second-generation Hispanics, at 36.4 percent. But by 2006, an entirely different perspective on the existing rates of Latin American immigration had emerged. In the 2006 survey, almost a majority of Hispanics, irrespective of their generational status, favored an increase in the number of legal immigrants from Latin America being admitted to the United States, and the percentage of Hispanics who supported a decrease in the rates of immigration also dropped significantly from 2004: only 9.3 percent of first- and second-generation Hispanics versus 13.9 percent of third-

TABLE 2.3
Hispanic Public Opinion on Immigration

Immigration	2004		2006	
	First and second generation	Third generation	First and second generation	Third generation
Number of legal Latin American immigrants to the U.S....				
Increase	36.4	26.8	55.0	48.4
Reduce	7.9	19.5	9.3	13.9
Allow the same number	44.2	46.4	26.5	32.5
Don't know	10.7	6.8	8.0	4.3
Illegal immigration...				
Helps the economy by providing low-cost labor	72.8	54.6	74.9	63.3
Hurts the economy by driving wages down	17.2	36.0	17.3	26.7
Don't know	9.2	8.4	6.8	7.8
President Bush's guest worker program				
Favor	56.2	50.5	66.1	54.4
Oppose	37.1	42.0	27.6	38.0
Don't know	6.1	6.8	5.7	6.7
Guest worker program with a pathway to citizenship				
Favor	93.0	80.1	—	—
Oppose	4.2	15.6	—	—
Don't know	2.6	4.2	—	—
View on immigrants				
All immigrants should have a chance to become U.S. citizens	73.1	72.6	56.8	42.7
Some immigrants should come to the U.S., but return home	20.5	22.3	37.3	46.8
Don't know	5.6	4.4	2.9	1.9

Source: 2004 Pew Hispanic Survey, 2006 Pew Hispanic Center Hispanic Immigration Study.

Note: N = 2,061; cell entries are column percentages.

generation Hispanics were in favor of reducing the number of legal immigrants coming to the United States. Whether it was due to the mass protests and rallies or to the national attention that immigration had attracted two years later, a definite shift in Hispanics' attitudes toward immigration had occurred. Not only did generational distinctions in Hispanics' views toward immigration dissipate by 2006, but also a majority of Hispanics supported increasing the immigration rates of Latin Americans as opposed to maintaining the status quo, as they had just two years earlier.

The Pew Survey also provided Hispanics with an opportunity to express their attitudes toward undocumented immigrants. In both 2004 and 2006, a majority of Hispanics took the position that undocumented immigrants were an asset to the U.S. economy because they provide low-cost labor. However, a greater percentage of first- and second-generation Hispanics adopted this view than did third-generation Hispanics. In 2004, 72.8 percent of first- and second-generation Hispanics held this belief, whereas 54.6 percent of third-generation Hispanics felt this way. A similar gap existed between earlier- and later-generation Hispanics in 2006, though the gap was slightly smaller than in it was in 2004 (74.9 percent versus 63.3 percent). Moreover, third-generation Hispanic respondents in 2004 were twice as likely to believe that undocumented immigrants hurt the economy by driving wages down when compared to first- and second-generation Hispanics.

Hispanics' opinions toward the proposed immigration reforms being debated by Congress from 2004 through 2006 were also captured in this survey. Overall, a majority of Hispanics in both years favored Bush's guest worker program, a plan that would allow immigrants to work in the United States legally and for a temporary period of time without a pathway to U.S. citizenship. Consistent with the structural integration hypothesis, third-generation Hispanics were less supportive of this program than were first- and second-generation Hispanics. Moreover, when asked about the alternative proposal that would include a pathway to citizenship (2004), a much larger percentage of third-generation Hispanics were opposed to it, 15.6 percent, than were first- and second-generation Hispanics, 4.2 percent. This once again confirms the significant variations in the opinions that earlier- and later-generation Hispanics possess on the issue of immigration. And when Hispanics were asked about their opinions toward the opportunity to attain citizenship, more than 70 percent of all respondents in 2004 felt that all immigrants should be given this chance. By 2006, these attitudes had shifted, with 56.8 percent of first- and second-generation Hispanics believing that all immigrants should have the opportunity to gain citizenship and 42.7 percent of third-generation Hispanics adopting this view.

The structural integration argument suggests that these generational distinctions may also exist due to later-generation Hispanics' unwillingness to associate themselves with earlier immigrants (Jimenez 2007)—that they may favor more restrictive immigration policies and reforms as a way of setting themselves apart. According to classic assimilation theory, third-generation Hispanics should be more assimilated into U.S. society than first- and second-generation Hispanics and may therefore adopt the policy views of the dominant society. Later-generation immigrants may also be engaging in "selective dissociation," wherein they maintain their identity but try to exclude those within the group that they believe are perpetuating a negative image (García Bedolla 2005). In this case, the negative image from which third-generation Hispanics may wish to distance themselves from is the idea that all new immigrants are in the United States illegally or that immigrants take jobs away from native-born workers. First-generation Hispanics have also been found to be more politically active than later-generation Hispanics on policies that directly impact their communities (García Bedolla 2005).

The Latino National Survey also included several questions pertaining to immigration and bilingual education. We present the responses to these questions, again based on one's generational status, in table 2.4. In particular, respondents were asked to provide their opinions on a recently proposed piece of federal legislation known as the Development, Relief and Education for Alien Minors (DREAM) Act. This bill would have granted academically successful, unauthorized high school students who wished to attend college or enter the military with legal status in the United States. The LNS queried Hispanics on a specific aspect of the DREAM Act—whether or not undocumented immigrants should pay a higher tuition rate at public colleges and universities, even if they have lived for a long period of time and attended high school in the United States. Respondents were also

TABLE 2.4
Hispanic Public Opinion on Hispanic-Related Issues

	First and second generation	Third generation
DREAM Act: Undocumented immigrants should pay a higher college tuition, even if they went to high school in the U.S.		
Strongly oppose	59.6	47.3
Oppose	24.8	28.2
Support	7.8	11.5
Strongly support	7.9	13.1
N	7,976	948
Replace multiyear bilingual education with English only after one year		
Strongly oppose	24.3	26.1
Oppose	25.1	32.7
Support	28.3	21.0
Strongly support	22.3	20.2
N	3,724	495
Use matricula consular (ID issued by foreign countries) as an acceptable form of identification for immigrants in the U.S.		
Strongly oppose	11.6	22.8
Oppose	11.9	22.5
Support	32.4	29.7
Strongly support	44.1	25.0
N	3,586	404

Source: Latino National Survey of 2006.
Note: Cell entries are column percentages.

asked to provide their position on bilingual education programs and the use of a *matricula consular*, which is an identification card issued by Mexican consulates, as a suitable form of identification in the United States.[1]

Hispanic opinions on the DREAM Act are relatively similar across generations, with an overwhelming majority either opposed or strongly opposed to requiring unauthorized students to

[1]This proposal has become the topic of discussion in recent years, since numerous U.S. states now require individuals to show proof of legal residency in order to receive a driver's license.

pay a higher tuition rate. Considering that some first-generation Hispanics would be affected by this proposal, a somewhat larger percentage of first- and second-generation Hispanics were against this provision, 84.4 percent, relative to third-generation Hispanics, 75.5 percent.

Turning to Hispanic attitudes on bilingual education, among third-generation Hispanics, 58.8 percent oppose replacing multiyear bilingual education with English after just one year, while 41.2 percent support this initiative. For earlier-generation Hispanics, their views on bilingual education appear to be more evenly divided; 49.4 percent oppose replacing multiyear bilingual education with English after just one year, and 50.6 percent support this type of program. Perhaps because of their own experiences, third-generation Hispanics may be less inclined to support bilingual education programs in which the English immersion process occurs so quickly.

Finally, Hispanics' responses to the use of the *matricula consular* as a form of identification are also shaped by their generational status. Among first- and second-generation Hispanics, 76.5 percent support this proposal, whereas only 59.7 percent of third-generation Hispanics responded in this manner. Thus, while the majority of third-generation Hispanics support the use of a *matricula consular* as a form of identification, their degree of support is not as great as it is among first- and second-generation Hispanics. Of course, the high level of support among first- and second-generation Hispanics could be attributed to the fact that many might benefit from such a policy.

Hispanic public opinion on immigration goes beyond their policy views and positions. As we discussed previously, the period of time that we study also gives us the opportunity to examine the impact of proposed immigration reforms on Hispanic political participation. Table 2.5 presents Hispanic public opinion on the nationwide immigration marches and rallies that took place in May 2006. Recall that the Republican efforts at immigration reform were especially infuriating to the Hispanic community, as the Republican bill would have deemed those entering the country illegally and those assisting undocumented individuals as felons. Thus, these public outcries were directly in response to congressional efforts to reform the current immigration system. Hispanic organizations and advocacy groups, along with the

media and political pundits, all contemplated the political consequences following these highly publicized events. Would Hispanics punish Republicans by lending most of their support to
the Democrats in the 2006 elections? Would these marches motivate Hispanic citizens to register to vote? The 2006 Pew Survey on Hispanics offers us some insight into this matter, since it
asked Hispanics for their opinions about the ramifications of
these political demonstrations for the future of Hispanic political
participation.

As table 2.5 indicates, regardless of a Hispanic's generational
status, more than a majority of Hispanics (64.1 percent and 64.2
percent) viewed the marches as the "beginning of a new social
movement that will go on for a long time" rather than as "a one-
time event which will not necessarily be repeated." Overall, it
appears that Hispanics were generally optimistic and viewed the
marches as a positive response from the Hispanic community.
This view is also echoed in the responses to the survey question
asking Hispanics whether they believe that the "debate over immigration policy in Washington will result in many more Hispanics voting in November." The response to this question was overwhelmingly positive: more than three-quarters, 77.0 percent, of
first- and second-generation Hispanics responded in the affirmative, while 75.1 percent of third-generation Hispanics agreed. Although a slightly larger percentage of third-generation Hispanics,
20.4 percent, felt that the protests would do little to affect Hispanic
political participation than did first- and second-generation Hispanics, at 16.5 percent, a sense of optimism was shared by most of
the Hispanic respondents in this survey.

But when Hispanics were asked about the impact of the marches
on the attitudes of the American population, their overall optimism was not as great, particularly among third-generation Hispanics. While 59.4 percent of first- and second-generation Hispanics felt that the marches had a "positive effect on the way the
American public thinks about undocumented immigrants," only
44.5 percent of third-generation Hispanics offered this response.
In fact, a significantly larger proportion of third-generation Hispanics perceived the marches as having had a negative effect on
Americans' attitudes toward undocumented immigrants than
did first- and second-generation Hispanics (28.2 percent versus
18.6 percent). Moreover, 19.3 percent of third-generation Hispan-

TABLE 2.5

Hispanic Public Opinion on 2006 Immigration Marches and Protests

	First and second generation	Third generation
Immigration marches are. . .		
Beginning of a new social movement that will go on for a long time	64.1	64.2
A one time event which will not necessarily be repeated	23.3	25.4
Don't know	11.8	8.7
Immigration marches had a. . .		
Positive effect on the way the American public thinks about undocumented immigrants	59.4	44.5
Negative effect on the way the American public thinks about undocumented immigrants	18.6	28.2
No effect	13.4	19.3
Don't know	8.3	7.2
The debate over immigration policy in Washington will result in. . .		
Many more Hispanics voting in November	77.0	75.1
Not much of an effect on political participation	16.5	20.4
Don't know	6.0	4.3
If another march was going to be in [R's] hometown. . .		
[R] Would participate	57.4	42.1
[R] Would not participate	37.2	53.4
Don't know	5.1	4.3

Source: 2006 Pew Hispanic Center Hispanic Immigration Study.
Note: N = 1,998; cell entries are column percentages.

ics perceived the marches to have had no impact on the immigration attitudes of Americans, whereas 13.4 percent of first- and second-generation Hispanics held this point of view. Overall, Hispanics viewed the protests as having a positive effect within the Hispanic community, but generational differences emerged when Hispanics were asked about the impact of these protests on the immigration attitudes outside of the Hispanic community:

Hispanics with the longest presence in the United States appear to have been more negative and pessimistic than recent Hispanic arrivals.

Finally, Hispanics were asked whether they would participate in another march if it were to be held in their hometown. Consistent with the selective disassociation theory and the segmented assimilation model, a larger percentage of first- and second-generation Hispanics responded that they would participate than did third-generation Hispanics, 57.4 percent versus 42.1 percent. Interestingly, while a solid majority of Hispanics viewed the marches to have had a positive impact on their community, 10–15 percent fewer Hispanics planned to participate in future marches than those who expressed this opinion.

As public opinion polls of the American population reveal, the issue of immigration is a highly sensitive topic, one that generates divisions not only within communities, such as generational differences among Hispanics, but also between communities. Oftentimes, we also see how the public's immigration views can contradict one another. These recent public opinion polls quell popular notions that all Hispanics view the issue of immigration in the same manner. As the survey results from the Pew Hispanic Center demonstrate, Hispanics' views on immigration policy, the proposed reforms, and undocumented immigration differed considerably, with generational status playing some role in these distinctions. In light of these differences, the use of immigration as a "wedge" issue by candidates and politicians ought to be carefully considered, since all Hispanics do not share the same view on this policy.

MORAL VALUES

One issue area that gained prominence in the 2004 presidential and congressional elections is collectively referred to as "moral values." This term encompasses issues such as abortion, gay marriage, and prayer in schools. Moral and cultural values have long played a role in presidential election voting (Abramowitz 1995; Layman 2001; Layman and Carmines 1997; Layman and Green 2005; Leege et al. 2002). As Leege et al. (2002) demonstrate, cultural politics has been an important component of American campaigns and elections in the post–New Deal era. For instance, Republicans' presidential campaigns throughout the 1980s and 1990s capitalized on cultural themes (e.g., moral order) as a means to mobilize and turnout their base. Leege et al. (2002) define cultural or moral values issues as one's beliefs about how individuals should live, and those that evoke one's fundamental social values. These issues should therefore resonate well with voters, since they can be characterized as "easy issues"—symbolic and normative in nature and easy to communicate to voters (Carmines and Stimson 1980). Again, because Hispanics are socially conservative, Republicans have used these issues to appeal to them. In the 2004 presidential election, Bush and the Republicans were successful in capturing a greater percentage of the Hispanic vote by emphasizing moral values, along with foreign policy, in their campaigns (Abrajano, Alvarez, and Nagler 2008).

The politics of abortion have deeply shaped partisan and ideological debates in American politics, and abortion is one of the most important issues that separate the policy stances of the Democratic and Republican parties. Abramson, Aldrich, and Rohde argue, "Indeed, abortion is one of the most contentious issues in government at all levels, between the two parties, and within the public" (2002, 144; see also Adams 1999). Given the importance of abortion as a divisive and salient issue in American politics, it has been well studied by many scholars. One component of the research literature has focused on the determinants of public opinion about abortion; that research has found that certain "core beliefs" structure abortion opinions (Luker 1984; Ginsburg 1989) but that the conflict between these core beliefs is profound (Alvarez and Brehm 1995). A second component of the literature has examined the abortion issue from a racial perspective, looking specifically at differences between Anglos and Blacks on the issue (Combs and Welch 1982; Hall and Ferree 1986; Wilcox 1990).

In recent election cycles, Republicans have hoped to attract Hispanic votes away from the Democrats by emphasizing the party's antiabortion stance. This is because a large majority of Hispanics not only identify themselves with organized religion but also attend church on a regular basis: 68 percent of Hispanics report being Catholic, and 15 percent are born-again or evangelical Protestants (Pew Hispanic Center 2007). Moreover, the same survey revealed that two-thirds of Hispanics believe that their

TABLE 2.6
Hispanic Public Opinion on Moral Values

	2004		2006	
	First and second generation	*Third generation*	*First and second generation*	*Third generation*
Abortion should be. . .				
Legal in all cases	13.9	20.6	12.3	22.6
Legal in most cases	26.1	30.9	19.5	25.6
Illegal in most cases	21.3	23.6	19.8	17.6
Illegal in all cases	31.0	19.6	39.8	24.9
Don't know	6.9	4.1	7.3	7.6
Favor/oppose a constitutional amendment defining marriage as a union between one man and one woman				
Favor	43.0	43.4	—	—
Oppose	44.2	48.4	—	—
Don't know	9.5	7.4	—	—

Source: 2004 and 2006 Pew Hispanic Center Surveys.
Note: N = 2,061; cell entries are column percentages.

religious beliefs influence their political attitudes, ideology, and partisan identification. Thus, religiosity is likely to play a role in Hispanics' attitudes toward abortion. Respondents' opinions on the moral values issue of abortion are presented in table 2.6.

Most of the first- and second-generation Hispanics' interviewed in 2004 and 2006 believe that abortion "should be illegal in all cases." In 2004, 31 percent of first- and second-generation Hispanics responded in this manner, and an even larger percentage of first- and second-generation Hispanics, 39.8 percent, felt this way in 2006. But the modal view for third-generation Hispanics was that "abortion should be legal in most cases" (30.9 percent in 2004 and 25.6 percent in 2006). Thus, we see a generational difference in Hispanics' attitudes toward abortion that suggests that Hispanics may become more secular the longer they reside in the United States, though the recent rise in the number of Hispanics identifying as born-again or evangelical Protestants (Pew Hispanic Center 2007) raises the possibility that this trend may not continue.

Hispanics' opinions on a "constitutional amendment defining marriage as a union between one man and one woman" do not reveal as distinct a pattern based on nativity as did their attitudes toward abortion. Hispanics overall tend to oppose this type of constitutional amendment, with 44.2 percent of first- and second-generation Hispanics and 48.4 percent of third-generation Hispanics in opposition to it. Despite Hispanics' religiosity and conservative tendencies, then, most do not see the need to establish a constitutional amendment that defines marriage as heterosexual in nature. Overall, we see that depending on what moral values one is referring to, Hispanics' length of time and degree of integration in the United States helps to explain some of their views on these matters, as we saw in the case of abortion, and less so on others.

FOREIGN POLICY

In recent years, American foreign policy has weighed heavily on the minds of the American public, particularly the specific issues of terrorism, homeland security, and the ongoing war in Iraq. While public support for the war was initially high, it has steadily declined in recent years (Jacobson 2006). Table 2.7 provides Hispanics' responses to questions about their attitudes toward the war in general and to more specific questions pertaining to President Bush's handling of the war. Overall, a majority of Hispanics in 2004 did not hold a positive view of the Iraq War. Sixty percent of first- and second-generation Hispanics either disapproved somewhat or strongly disapproved of Bush's handling of the war, and almost equal percentage of third-generation Hispanics, 61.1 percent, felt the same. These opinions differ from the views held by Anglos, the majority of whom either somewhat approved or strongly approved of Bush's handling of the war. But Hispanics did share similar attitudes with Blacks, as 77.5 percent of Black survey respondents disapproved of Bush's handling of the war (Abrajano, Alvarez, and Nagler 2008).

We also find slight variations in Hispanic public opinion on the war based on generational status. While the bulk of first- and second-generation Hispanics believed that it was the wrong decision to use military force (44.5 percent), most third-generation

TABLE 2.7
Hispanic Public Opinion on Foreign Policy

Foreign policy	First and second generation	Third generation
Views on Iraq		
Bush had a clear plan for Iraq	32.2	27.4
Bush had no clear plan for Iraq	52.2	64.6
Approve of Bush's handling of the war		
Strongly approve	23.2	22.7
Somewhat approve	16.1	16.2
Somewhat disapprove	20.5	16.0
Strongly disapprove	40.2	45.1
Use of military force by the U.S. in Iraq		
Right decision	39.9	48.0
Wrong decision	44.5	43.5
Don't know	15.1	7.3
Bush administration deliberately misled Americans about how big a threat Iraq was to the U.S. before war		
Yes, administration misled	42.6	53.5
No, administration did not mislead	40.9	38.0
Don't know	15.5	7.8
N	2075	211

Source: 2004 Pew Hispanic Survey.
Note: Cell entries are column percentages.

Hispanics felt that the United States made the correct decision in employing force (48 percent). However, these opinions do not appear to be driven strongly by one's generational status. In addition, a larger proportion of third-generation Hispanics, 64.6 percent, believed that "Bush had no clear plan for Iraq" than did first- and second-generation Hispanics (52.2 percent). Finally, when they were asked whether they felt misled by the Bush administration "about how big a threat Iraq was to the U.S. before the war," most Hispanics responded that they did feel that they were being misled by the Bush administration. A larger proportion of third-generation Hispanics felt misled than did first- and second-generation Hispanics, at 53.5 percent versus 42.6 percent. Later-generation Hispanics appear to be more pessimistic and perhaps less trustful of the government than earlier-generation Hispanics.

This generational difference may once again be explained partially by the selective disassociation theory and the segmented assimilation model. The more negative and cynical views exhibited by third-generation Hispanics are also consistent with Hispanics' levels of government trust. Recall that first-generation Hispanics are much more trusting of the federal government than are second- and third-generation Hispanics (Abrajano and Alvarez, forthcoming; Michelson 2001). Likewise, we would expect first-generation Hispanics to exhibit a greater amount of confidence in the foreign policy decisions of the federal government (and its current administration) than we would of second- and later-generation Hispanics.

DOMESTIC ISSUES: EDUCATION

Education is one policy domain that is particularly salient to Hispanics in the United States. In most public opinion surveys conducted on Hispanics in the past decade, Hispanics have consistently ranked education as one of the most important issues to them. Given the substandard educational opportunities available to Hispanics in this country (see Orfield and Lee 2004; Pew Hispanic Center 2007; and Kozol 2005), as well as their lagging performance on many education indicators, it is understandable that Hispanics would view education as a highly salient concern.

To better understand Hispanics' views on the different facets of education reform and how they compare to the views held by Anglos and Blacks, we once again turn to data gathered by the Pew Hispanic Center. In 2004, Pew conducted a national survey of Hispanics and non-Hispanics regarding their attitudes toward education policies and proposed reforms in the United States. This highly detailed survey included a series of questions pertaining to the current state of education; it also asked respondents to evaluate the performance of elected officials on education. In this survey, 1,193 Anglos, 1,508 Hispanics, and 610 Blacks were interviewed. Table 2.8 presents the various survey questions pertaining

TABLE 2.8
Public Opinion on Education Policies and Reforms

	Anglos	Blacks	Hispanics
Education policies			
Importance of teaching English in public schools to children of immigrants			
Very important	87.9	84.1	91.6
Somewhat important	10.1	12.9	7.1
Not too important	0.9	1.3	0.6
Not important at all	0.8	1.3	0.5
Support for government vouchers to send children to private schools			
Favor	37.4	41.0	40.9
Oppose	29.4	23.6	13.8
Don't know/haven't heard enough	33.1	35.4	45.0
Support for charter schools programs			
Favor	34.3	33.8	25.7
Oppose	13.0	12.6	8.4
Don't know/haven't heard enough	52.3	53.2	65.6
Federal government should require states to set strict performance standards for public schools			
Agree	70.2	70.3	66.0
Disagree	27.0	24.4	23.3
Don't know	2.7	4.9	10.4
Standardized tests are. . .			
An unbiased measure of a student's abilities	56.7	41.8	58.4
Biased against nonwhite students	30.8	46.7	25.5
Don't know	11.1	10.7	14.9
Racially integrated schools. . .			
Better for kids	62.9	58.5	47.7
Worse for kids	6.0	8.2	6.6
Doesn't make much of a difference	29.3	30.5	44.2
Affirmative action for university admissions			
Favor	27.1	68.2	67.2
Oppose	69.0	28.9	28.3
Don't know	3.4	2.8	4.2

TABLE 2.8 (*cont.*)

	Anglos	Blacks	Hispanics
Political evaluations			
Rate President Bush's handling of education and schools			
Excellent	7.5	2.0	9.6
Good	26.2	13.4	27.9
Fair	35.0	35.3	38.7
Poor	24.9	44.4	18.1
Don't know	5.8	4.6	5.5
Rate state governor's handling of education and schools			
Excellent	4.4	4.8	8.7
Good	26.6	23.4	30.2
Fair	36.0	38.9	36.7
Poor	25.7	28.2	19.4
Don't know	7.2	4.3	5.0
Political party that does a better job at improving education and the schools			
Democrats	38.2	62.3	41.5
Republicans	32.9	10.5	19.0
Both	3.8	3.9	7.4
Neither	17.6	16.6	13.1
Don't know	6.0	6.2	17.6
Since Bush became president, public schools in this country have become. . .			
Better	10.1	6.7	20.7
Worse	14.6	29.3	13.5
Stayed about the same	70.2	61.2	60.7
Don't know	4.7	2.8	4.8
N	1,193	1,508	610

Source: 2004 Pew National Survey of Hispanics: Education.

to education. The first question, which asked respondents for their opinions on the importance of teaching English to the children of immigrants, drew a similar response across the board: 84.1 percent of Blacks, 87.9 percent of Anglos, and 91.6 percent of Hispanics believe that it is "very important" to teach English in public schools to immigrant children.

The survey also asked respondents about their opinions on alternatives to the public education system. More specifically, respondents were asked to provide their views on two of the most popular alternatives to public schools: voucher programs and charter schools. A plurality of Anglo and Black respondents support government vouchers that would allow children to attend private schools. But a plurality of Hispanics, 45 percent, were sufficiently unfamiliar with the voucher program to respond that they "did not know" whether they favored or opposed it. Note that approximately one-third of Anglos and Blacks also responded in this fashion. Thus, one of the most popular proposals for education reform discussed in recent years may require more explanation from policymakers, since many Americans are unaware of its details.

Another alternative to public schools are charter schools; these schools are not under the jurisdiction of the school district, which allows them to be more lax and flexible in their guidelines, rules, and policies. Across all three racial and ethnic groups, a majority of respondents did not have enough information about charter schools to offer an opinion: 52.3 percent of Anglos, 53.2 percent of Blacks, and 65.6 percent of Hispanics. For those who provided a response, a larger proportion of individuals supported rather than opposed charter schools; this was true for all ethnic and racial groups.

Individuals were also asked for their opinions about standardized tests, which serve as the centerpiece of Bush's major education initiative, the No Child Left Behind Act of 2002 (NCLB). According to the Department of Education, this legislation set out to achieve "accountability for results, more choices for parents, greater local control and flexibility, and an emphasis on doing what works based on scientific research."[2] A strong majority of Anglos, Blacks, and Hispanics are in favor of the federal government establishing performance standards for public schools. Only about one-quarter of Anglo, Black, and Hispanic respondents are opposed to these efforts. When asked about the purpose of standardized tests, the majority of Anglos and Hispanics viewed them as an unbiased measure of a student's abilities (56.7 percent and 58.4 percent, respectively), while most Blacks perceived these tests as being biased against non-Anglos (46.7 percent). The existence of this bias in America's public schools certainly exists (see Orfield and Kornhaber 2001), particularly in the post-NCLB

[2]U.S. Department of Education, Answers, "What Is No Child Left Behind?" http://answers.ed.gov/cgi-bin/education.cfg/php/enduser/std_adp.php?p_faqid=4.

era. Such attitudes are also consistent with Blacks' exhibiting a lower level of trust in government (Abrajano and Alvarez forthcoming), as well as their more pessimistic outlooks on the economy and the future (Baldassare 2004).

One area of education policy that directly relates to racial minorities is the increasing rates of racial segregation in U.S. public schools, as well as the issue of affirmative action. Both school desegregation policies and affirmative action generate strong differences of opinion among Anglos, Blacks, and Hispanics. While a solid majority of Blacks and Hispanics support affirmative action in university admissions (68.2 and 67.2, percent respectively), the majority of Anglos are opposed to such policies (69 percent). Because the use of affirmative action in the university admissions process would primarily benefit minorities, we expect that Anglo support for such programs would be minimal, especially because affirmative action is one policy that requires many to sacrifice for the benefit of a small, concentrated group of individuals. As Hetherington (2005) finds, the American public also does not have enough trust and faith in government to believe that it can carry out affirmative action policies competently.

Another pressing problem in the current public education system pertains to the growing rates of racial segregation and racial isolation (Kozol 2005; Orfield and Lee 2004). In numerous public schools across the United States, minority children are increasingly attending primary and secondary schools where 80 to 90 percent of their classmates are made up of racial and ethnic minorities (Orfield and Lee 2004). While this shift is largely driven by patterns of residential segregation, the growing number of schools that are racially segregated has raised serious concerns among policymakers advocating diversity in public education. Turning to the public's opinions on this matter, we see that of the three racial and ethnic groups, a larger percentage of Anglos, 62.9 percent, believe that racially integrated schools are better for students than do Blacks, at 58.5 percent, or Hispanics, at 47.7 percent. That ethnic and racial minorities, particularly Hispanics, are less likely to see the value in racially integrated schools than Anglos is somewhat surprising, though it is worth noting that such questions are not being asked of the students themselves. Thus, the value individuals place on racial diversity in public education may also be influenced by where they were raised, e.g., whether or not it was in the

United States, since its meaning may not be the same in other contexts outside of the United States.[3] Moreover, a large percentage of Hispanic respondents, 44.2 percent, do not believe that racial diversity in public schools makes much of a difference. We also see that more Hispanics adopt this view when compared to Anglos (29.3 percent) and Blacks (30.5 percent).

The Pew Survey on Education also asked respondents to evaluate the performance of elected officials on education policies. A plurality of Anglos (35 percent) and Hispanics (38.7 percent) gave President Bush a "fair" evaluation for his efforts in education policy. But 44.4 percent of Blacks gave the president a "poor" assessment for his handling of schools and education. As a point of comparison, only 24.9 percent of Anglos and 18.1 percent of Hispanics rated President Bush "poor" for his education policies. These trends are consistent with our previous results demonstrating Blacks' tendency to have more pessimistic views of the government when compared to Anglos and Hispanics. And when asked about the state of U.S. public schools since Bush took office, a majority of Anglos, Blacks, and Hispanics responded that the public schools have "stayed about the same." However, a somewhat greater percentage of Anglos feel this way (70.2 percent) than Blacks (61.2 percent) or Hispanics (60.7 percent). Consistent with Blacks' views on the president's overall performance on education, about one-third (29.3 percent) feel that public schools have become worse since Bush's presidency began. Hispanics, on the other hand, appear to be more optimistic, with 20.7 percent believing that schools have actually become better since Bush became president.

Respondents also had the opportunity to evaluate their governor's performance on education. Here, a plurality of Anglos, Blacks, and Hispanics gave their respective governor a "fair" evaluation. A larger percentage of respondents from all three racial and ethnic groups rated their governor's performance as "poor" as opposed to "excellent." At both the state and the federal level, then, it seems that the American public was not overwhelmingly impressed with the performance of President Bush and state governors on education reforms and policies.

[3]This is especially true if we consider that the U.S. concept of racial diversity is distinct from that of Canada or Western Europe. See Bloemraad (2005) for an extensive discussion of this topic.

On a related point, respondents were also asked to evaluate the efforts made by political parties to improve education and schools. Across all three racial and ethnic groups, the largest number of respondents felt that the Democrats were better at improving education than Republicans. While an overwhelming majority of Blacks favor Democrats to Republicans on education by a margin of 6 to 1, the Democratic edge among Hispanics is not as great (41.5 percent versus 19 percent). With regard to Anglo respondents, the Democrats' advantage on education is even smaller, at 38.2 percent versus 32.9 percent for Republicans. Nonetheless, it is clear that the American public still views education as an issue "owned" by the Democrats, since this is one policy domain that has traditionally been aligned with the Democratic Party (Petrocik 1996).

DOMESTIC ISSUES

The 2004 National Annenberg Election Survey included numerous questions pertaining to the public's views on the state of the economy, Bush's economic performance, and issues pertaining to taxes, jobs/unemployment, and the budget deficit. We present the answers to these questions in table 2.9. Here, we compare the opinions of Hispanic and Anglo respondents. One of the most basic and general attitudinal questions available in the survey asked respondents to evaluate the current economy. Overall, we see that Anglos were more optimistic about the current state of the economy than were Hispanics. While the largest number of Anglos and Hispanics evaluated the economy as "fair" (43.9 percent and 47.8 percent, respectively), a greater percentage of Anglos rated the economy as "good" than did Hispanics, at 27.7 percent versus 19.8 percent. When asked to evaluate their expectations for the economy in the following year, both Anglo and Hispanic respondents conveyed optimism: 43.6 percent of Anglos and 44.6 percent of Hispanics expected the economy to be "somewhat better" in 2005, and a slightly larger percentage of Hispanics, 11.2 percent, expected the economy to be "much better" in 2005 than did Anglos, at 8.7 percent. While Hispanics appear to have been more pessimistic about current economic conditions, they were somewhat more positive about future economic conditions

TABLE 2.9
Anglo and Hispanic Opinions on Economic Issues

	Anglos	Hispanics
Economic evaluations		
Rate economic conditions today		
Excellent	2.3	2.7
Good	27.7	19.8
Fair	43.9	47.8
Poor	26.2	29.7
N	6,058	62,763
Rate economic conditions next year		
Much better	8.7	11.2
Somewhat better	43.6	44.6
Same	28.6	24.0
Somewhat worse	9.9	10.4
Much worse	2.4	3.9
N	63,124	6,108
Rate personal economic situation today		
Excellent	9.1	5.0
Good	44.7	27.3
Fair	33.6	47.2
Poor	12.6	20.5
N	62,821	6,083
Bush's handling of the economy. . .		
Approve	49.0	41.4
Disapprove	47.6	53.0
N	63,668	6,155
Bush's economic policies are making the economy. . .		
Better	34.4	24.8
Worse	35.6	39.6
No effect	25.5	28.7
N	62,861	6,099
Taxes		
Federal government reducing federal taxes		
Strongly favor	47.9	54.2
Somewhat favor	22.0	19.5
Somewhat oppose	12.3	10.9

TABLE 2.9 (*cont.*)

	Anglos	*Hispanics*
Taxes (cont.)		
Strongly oppose	10.9	9.3
Neither favor nor oppose	3.5	2.2
N	32,936	3,039
Balancing the federal budget: federal government should do. . .		
More	81.4	76.6
Same	13.7	12.6
Less	1.3	2.5
Nothing	0.9	1.8
N	3,035	286
Best way for federal government to reduce budget deficit		
Increase taxes	12.0	13.2
Reduce spending	77.7	70.9
Reduce Social Security	1.4	6.2
Something else is best	6.3	3.4
N	4,005	357
Jobs		
Jobs availability in community. . .		
Plenty	28.0	26.7
Difficult to find	61.8	66.9
Depends on the type of job	5.7	3.3
N	7,645	758
Favor more trade agreements		
Strongly favor	15.1	36.9
Somewhat favor	31.3	31.0
Somewhat oppose	19.1	12.8
Strongly oppose	28.6	15.6
Neither favor or oppose	6.0	3.7
N	43,720	4,262

Source: 2004 National Annenberg Election Survey.

than were Anglos. This difference in attitudes follows previous research indicating that Hispanics' trust in government is higher than those of Anglos or African Americans. In turn, this attitude may impact their trust and faith in government to improve economic conditions.

Turning to evaluations of their own pocketbook finances, clear distinctions exist between the Anglo and Hispanic respondents, with Hispanics tending to view their personal economic situations more negatively than Anglos. While the plurality of Anglos, 44.7 percent, rated their own economic situation as "good," the plurality of Hispanics, 47.2 percent, evaluated their economic situation as "fair." In fact, only 27.3 percent of Hispanics considered their personal finances to be "good." Moreover, approximately one out of five Hispanics perceived their economic situation as "poor," whereas only about one in ten Anglos held this view. In light of Hispanics' lower socioeconomic standing when compared to Anglos, it is understandable why their assessments of their own finances tend to be bleaker than those of Anglos.

Respondents were also asked to evaluate Bush's economic performance and efforts at improving the state of the economy. Here, we see divergent opinions from Hispanics and Anglos. While the majority of Hispanics, 53 percent, disapproved of Bush's handling of the economy, almost a majority of Anglos, 49 percent, approved of Bush's handling of the economy. Likewise, when asked to assess whether Bush's economic policies were improving the economy, more Anglos, at 34.4 percent, believed that his policies were making the economy better than did Hispanics, at 24.8 percent. Instead, the largest number of Hispanic respondents, 39.6 percent, replied that Bush's policies had actually made the economy worse. Hispanic perceptions of the economic performance and policies put forth by the Bush administration appear to have been more critical than the perceptions held by Anglos.

The NAES also included several other questions pertaining to the economy. With regard to the issue of taxes, the study found that Hispanics are slightly more in favor of reducing taxes than are Anglos: 73.7 percent of Hispanics responded that they "strongly favored" or "somewhat favored" reductions in federal taxes, while 69.9 percent of Anglos responded in this way. Moreover, an overwhelming majority of Americans support more government efforts to balance the budget, with little variation based on race.

And when asked the best way to reduce the budget deficit, both Anglos and Hispanics felt that a reduction in spending was the ideal solution, followed by an increase in taxes. In terms of unemployment and job opportunities, Anglos and Hispanics also shared similar viewpoints. When asked about jobs available in one's community, the majority of respondents (regardless of ethnicity) believed that jobs were difficult to find. But more Hispanics than Anglos, 66.9 percent versus 61.8 percent, felt this way. Finally, respondents were asked for their opinions on trade agreements. With regard to this issue, we see significant differences in the opinions of Hispanics and Anglos. While 36.9 percent of Hispanics were strongly in favor of trade agreements, only 15.1 percent of Anglos were. On the other hand, almost twice as many Anglos as Hispanics, 28.6 percent versus 15.6 percent, were strongly opposed to trade agreements. While Anglos may view these trade agreements as responsible for sending American jobs overseas, Hispanics may perceive them as beneficial to their homelands (e.g., North American Free Trade Agreement [NAFTA] and Mexico).

Finally, we focus on Anglos and Hispanic opinions on other domestic issues, namely health care, social security, and poverty. The results are presented in table 2.10. On the issue of more federal spending on health insurance, Hispanics tended to favor government spending on health care more than Anglos by a margin of approximately 10 percent (81.7 percent versus 70.1 percent). Considering that approximately one-third of all Hispanics in the United States lack health insurance, this is one issue where we would expect Hispanics to support higher levels of government involvement.

On the question of whether Social Security funds should be invested in the stock market, Hispanic and Anglo opinions also differed to some extent. While the plurality of Hispanics, 31 percent, strongly favored the proposal to invest Social Security in the stock market, the plurality of Anglos, 27.3 percent, only somewhat favored this proposal. Thus, it appears as if Hispanics were more supportive of Bush's initiative for Social Security reform than were Anglos.

The final domestic policy issue that we examine pertains to government efforts to reduce income differences. Here, we see that Hispanics were overwhelmingly more supportive of government efforts to reduce income inequality than were Anglos: 68.6 percent of Hispanics favored such policies, while only 56.9 percent of Anglos did. This preference of Hispanics is under-

TABLE 2.10
Anglo and Hispanic Opinions on Other Domestic Issues

	Anglos	Hispanics
Health care		
Favor government spending more on health insurance		
More	70.1	81.7
Same	20.4	13.2
Less	5.3	3.1
Social Security		
Favor investing Social Security in stock market		
Strongly favor	25.7	31.0
Somewhat favor	27.3	26.3
Somewhat oppose	13.6	13.2
Strongly oppose	25.2	19.5
Neither favor or oppose	4.1	3.2
N	19,714	1,856
Poverty		
Favor government trying to reduce income differences		
Strongly favor	38.1	48.1
Somewhat favor	18.8	20.5
Somewhat oppose	14.2	12.2
Strongly oppose	24.6	16.7
Neither favor or oppose	4.3	2.5
N	30,767	2,826

Source: 2004 National Annenberg Election Survey.
Note: Cell entries are column percentages.

standable given that, according to the U.S. Census, approximately one in five Hispanics (22.5 percent) lives in poverty.

Explaining Hispanic Partisanship

Many important political values and predispositions help individuals understand the political world, allow them to filter and deal with incoming political information, and also structure their political behavior. For example, important values like moral traditionalism, authoritarianism, or equal opportunity no doubt are important factors to consider when studying Hispanic political behavior; unfortunately, the sorts of complex survey batteries that are typically used to study these attitudes in survey research are not generally available in the large-sample surveys of Hispanics that we use in our study. Other political values, like ideology and partisanship, are often included in large-sample Hispanic surveys, so in this section we focus on these political values, especially partisanship, since it has been previously studied in the research literature (e.g., Cain, Kiewiet, and Uhlaner 1991; Alvarez and García Bedolla 2003).

Identification with a political party is one of the most critical political attitudes that an individual develops. Because one's party identification plays such a significant role in explaining an individual's vote decisions (Campbell et al. 1964), understanding the factors that influence one's acquisition of partisanship is critical. This is especially true for an immigrant group such as Hispanics, since the traditional way that individuals acquire their partisan preferences is through their parents (Vaillancourt 1973). But since this type of socialization and learning is unavailable to many Hispanics, understanding which factors affect a Hispanic's decision to become a Democrat, Republican, or an independent becomes that much more important. And perhaps the long-term nature and stability of partisanship, as asserted in the *American Voter* (Campbell et. al 1964), may not hold for a group of individuals whose socialization into American politics follows a different path. To this end, tables 2.11 and 2.12 offer a number of different insights on the acquisition of partisanship for the Hispanic community.

In table 2.11, we look at self-reported responses from the 2006 LNS on partisanship, by a respondent's ethnicity and political ideology. Hispanics could have identified as a Democrat, Republican, an independent, don't care, or don't know. In terms of ideology, they were offered the choice of liberal, conservative, middle of the road, don't think of self in these terms, and don't know. Among those Hispanics who identify as Democrats, the plurality of respondents, 30.7 percent, do not consider their political ideology in terms of the conservative and liberal. In fact, we see the same pattern holding for Mexicans and Puerto Ricans who report

TABLE 2.11
Hispanic Party Identification, by Ethnic Group and Ideology

	Democrat	Republican	Independent	Don't care	Don't know
Ideology, all Hispanics					
Conservative	22.7	45.9	22.2	16.3	16.2
Liberal	18.5	9.0	16.5	7.0	5.8
Middle of the road	21.4	17.2	24.5	8.1	9.5
Don't think of self in these terms	30.7	23.0	28.9	41.4	29.6
Don't know	6.7	5.0	7.8	27.2	39.0
N	3085	970	1435	1410	1734
Mexicans					
Conservative	21.9	42.2	21.7	15.2	14.6
Liberal	16.9	10.3	16.9	6.5	5.5
Middle of the road	22.7	16.8	24.9	9.2	10.5
Don't think of self in these terms	32.2	26.0	28.7	40.5	30.0
Don't know	6.4	4.8	7.8	28.6	39.4
N	1938	524	1088	1013	1256
Cubans					
Conservative	17.5	51.0	26.6	15.9	15.5
Liberal	22.3	4.0	18.8	4.6	8.6
Middle of the road	26.2	14.6	35.9	4.6	3.5
Don't think of self in these terms	22.3	23.2	14.1	40.9	27.6
Don't know	11.7	7.3	4.7	34.1	44.8
N	103	151	64	44	58
Puerto Ricans					
Conservative	25.5	51.2	17.8	18.8	14.4
Liberal	21.0	8.4	14.9	7.8	3.6
Middle of the road	20.5	15.3	26.7	7.8	9.0
Don't think of self in these terms	27.7	19.9	36.6	45.3	36.0
Don't know	5.3	5.3	4.0	20.3	36.9
N	415	131	101	64	111

Source: 2006 Latino National Survey.
Note: Entries are column percentages.

being Democrats. The only deviation from this pattern is for Cuban Democrats; their modal ideological category is moderate.

Thus, while the conventional wisdom is that individuals who identify as Democrats typically think of themselves as liberal, this association is not borne out among Puerto Ricans and Mexicans who self-identify as Democrats. Nearly twenty-eight percent of Puerto Rican Democrats do not think of themselves in terms of the liberal-conservative scale, 25.5 percent consider themselves to be conservative, 21 percent as liberal, and 20.5 percent as middle of the road. Likewise, among Mexican Democrats, 32.2 percent do not think of themselves in these ideological terms, 22.7 percent as moderates, 21.9 percent as conservative, followed by 16.9 percent as liberal. These two examples suggest that the correlation between ideology and Democratic partisanship does not appear to be as strongly related as it is for the rest of the American electorate. These results support the contentions asserted by Hajnal and Lee (2008), who question the linear model of partisanship, as developed in the *American Voter* (Campbell et al. 1964), when explaining the acquisition of partisanship among immigrants.[4]

But when we look at the relationship between partisanship and ideology among all Hispanics who self-identify as Republicans, they more closely adhere to the linear model of partisanship. Among all Hispanic Republicans, 45.9 percent consider themselves to be conservative, and, similarly, 42.2 percent of Republican Mexicans think of themselves as being ideologically conservative. An even stronger association between partisanship and ideology occurs for Cuban and Puerto Rican Republicans; 51 percent of Cubans and 51.2 percent of Puerto Ricans consider themselves as conservatives.

Among Hispanics who choose independence versus Democratic or Republican affiliation, its relationship to ideology and ethnicity is more varied. For instance, for the total Hispanic population, 28.9 percent do not think of themselves in these ideological terms, while roughly a quarter, 24.5 percent, consider themselves to be ideologically moderate. Among Mexican and Puerto Rican independents, we see a similar pattern emerge. For Cuban independents, however, 35.9 percent are ideologically moderate. And for Hispanics who do not care about their party identification, approximately 41 percent, irrespective of ethnic groups, do not conceptualize their political ideology in terms of the liberal-conservative scale.

While these data help us to understand the relationship between party identification and ideology, they also show that ideology and partisanship may not be as closely related for Hispan-

[4]The linear model of partisanship assumes that individuals conceptualize partisanship on a left-to-right continuum, with the left denoting Democrats, center as independents, and the right as Republicans.

ics as they are for the rest of the electorate. As we discussed in the introduction, part of this difference can be attributed to the lack of political socialization experienced by many Hispanics in the United States, as well as variations in the political system of their homeland when compared to the United States. To further explore the determinants of Hispanic party identification, we estimate a statistical model of partisanship, with the estimates presented in table 2.12. This model identifies the factors affecting a Hispanic's decision to identify with one of the two major political parties or as an independent. In line with the analysis of Hispanic partisanship by Alvarez and García Bedolla (2003), this model of Hispanic partisanship accounts for one's income and education level, gender, generational status, ethnicity, and media usage. We also account for Hispanics' political ideology, as well as their position on six issues that we have established to be important to Hispanics: immigration, school vouchers, government-sponsored health insurance, and government involvement in school funding and income redistribution.[5]

The likelihood of identifying as a Democrat is influenced by a Hispanic's age, education, generational status, ethnicity, political ideology, and the individual's position on the issue of abortion. More educated, liberal, and older Hispanics are more likely to identify as Democrats than as Republicans or independents. Second-generation Hispanics also have a greater probability of being a Democrat than are first-generation Hispanics. And consis-

[5]The model of partisanship was estimated using probit analysis, where the dependent variable was coded as 1 for the party label identified in the column, 0 otherwise. Income was coded as a categorical variable, ranging from low to high. Education was coded in a similar manner. Age is was a continuous variable, ranging from low to high. Female was a dummy variable, with a 1 indicating a female respondent and 0 a male respondent. Catholic was also coded as a dummy variable. Both the generational status variables are dichotomous, with the baseline category being first-generation Hispanics. The three variables on ethnicity (Mexican, Puerto Rican, and Cuban) are also dummy variables, with the reference category being respondents of Central or South American descent. News usage is also a dummy variable, where 1 indicates that the respondent uses English-language news, 0 for Spanish-language news. Both of the political variables, conservative and liberal, are also dummies, and the reference category is moderates and those who do not think of themselves in these terms. The issue variables are categorical, with the direction of the variable indicated by its label in table 2.12.

TABLE 2.12
A Model of Hispanic Party Identification

	Democrat	Republican	Independent
Constant	−1.20***	−1.83***	−.45
	(.37)	(.47)	(.43)
Demographics			
High income	.04	.04	.03
	(.02)	(.03)	(.04)
Education	.05**	-.00	−.04
	(.02)	(.03)	(.03)
Age	.01***	.00***	−.01*
	(.00)	(.00)	(.00)
Female	.05	−.13	−.17*
	(.08)	(.10)	(.09)
Catholic	−.26	.15	.45*
	(.26)	(.30)	(.27)
Second generation	.48**	.14	−.25*
	(.11)	(.15)	(.14)
Third generation	.07	.12	−.13
	(.13)	(.16)	(.17)
Mexican	−.17*	.05	.02
	(.10)	(.14)	(.12)
Puerto Rican	−.44***	.44**	.18
	(.16)	(.20)	(.19)
Cuban	−.77**	.77***	.33
	(.20)	(.22)	(.21)
Use English-language news	−.05	.39***	−.11
	(.10)	(.13)	(.12)

(continued)

TABLE 2.12 *(cont.)*

	Democrat	Republican	Independent
Political			
Conservative	−.12	.39***	−.01
	(.09)	(.11)	(.11)
Liberal	.18*	−.31**	.25**
	(.11)	(.16)	(.12)
Issue attitudes			
Abortion should be illegal	−.10**	.16***	−.10*
	(.05)	(.06)	(.05)
Support vouchers	−.04	.12**	−.00
	(.04)	(.05)	(.04)
Support government redistribu-tion of income	.05	.02	.01
	(.05)	(.06)	(.06)
Support government spending on schools	.07	−.07	−.06
	(.05)	(.07)	(.06)
Support government sponsored health insurance	.01	−.14**	.09
	(.05)	(.06)	(.06)
Illegal immigration benefits economy	.17	−.15	.03
	(.14)	(.17)	(.17)
N	1176	1176	1176
Log-likelihood	−736.187	−397.21	−511.1

Source: 2006 Latino National Survey.

Note: Models were estimated using probit analysis. The dependent variables are coded as 1 for the party identification listed in the column and 0 otherwise. Entries not in parentheses denote the probit coefficients; entries in parentheses are the corresponding standard error estimates for the given coefficient.

*Estimate significant at $p < .10$ level; ** Estimate significant at $p < .05$ level; *** Estimate significant at $p < .01$ level.

tent with the findings of Alvarez and García Bedolla (2003), one's ethnic group also influences one's choice of a political party. Both Mexicans and Puerto Ricans are less likely to be Democrats than are Central and South Americans. Finally, we see that Hispanics who are against making abortion illegal reduce their likelihood of becoming a Democrat.

Hispanics choosing to affiliate themselves with the Republican Party are influenced by some of the same factors as discussed earlier. For example, Cubans and Puerto Ricans have a higher likelihood of identifying as a Republican than Central and South Americans. Three of the six issues also affect a Hispanic's decision to become a member of the Republican Party. Those who believe that abortion should be illegal, favor school vouchers, and are against government-sponsored health insurance are more likely to identify as Republicans than as Democrats or independents. One factor that impacted the decision to identify as a Republican, but not a Democrat, pertains to media usage. Hispanics who mainly use English-language news also increase their probability of identifying as a Republican.

Among Hispanics who view themselves as independents, demographics and issue positions continue to play a role in this decision. In particular, older Hispanics as well as females are less likely to identify as independents than with the two major parties. While religious affiliation did not affect a Hispanic's likelihood of identifying as a Republican, Catholics, as opposed to other religious groups, are more likely to identify as independents. Moreover, generational status once again helps to explain the acquisition of partisanship, so that second-generation Hispanics are less likely to identify as independents than are first-generation Hispanics. Given that second-generation Hispanics have been in the United States for a longer period of time than their first-generation counterparts, they have had more time to familiarize themselves with the ins and outs of American politics, as well as being able to differentiate between the two major political parties in the United States. Finally, as in the case of identifying with either of the two major parties, a Hispanic's position on abortion influences the individual's likelihood of being an independent. Hispanics who are against making abortion illegal are less likely to identify as an independent than as a Democrat or Republican. Interestingly, while income has been an

71

important factor in explaining partisanship in previous studies (e.g., Green and Palmquist 1990), no such association exists for Hispanics.

Overall, our model of Hispanic party identification provides us with numerous insights into the factors that influence one's decision to become a Democrat, Republican, or an independent. We saw how generational status, ethnicity, and demographics, as well as attitudes toward issues, particularly on the issue of abortion, played a role in explaining this decision. While some of these factors mattered to Hispanics in their likelihood of being a Democrat, some of these attributes were not as important to Hispanics in their likelihood of identifying as a Republican or an independent. As we have stressed throughout this book, the heterogeneity of the Hispanic population means that the factors contributing to the formation and acquisition of political attitudes come from a variety of different sources, with no single explanation that can readily explain how Hispanics acquire their party identification.

CONCLUSION

Consistent with other aspects of political behavior, Hispanics' opinions on certain policy issues, as well as their acquisition of partisanship, differ to some extent from those of the rest of the American electorate. As we hypothesized in this chapter, most of these differences may be explained by different patterns in available political information, predispositions, and values; however, we should also note that the distinct opinions of Hispanics might be the result of their political involvement and incorporation. On issues that directly relate to Hispanics, such as immigration reform, undocumented immigrants, and bilingual education, we see that Hispanic public opinion dramatically differs from that of other Americans. On the other hand, on issues such as jobs, education, and the economy, Hispanics share many of the same attitudes and opinions as Anglos and Blacks. And because foreign policy issues have dominated the American political landscape in recent years, we also have an understanding of how Hispanics' views on the war in Iraq compare with those of non-Hispanics: overall, we find that Hispanics' attitudes toward the war tend to be more pessimistic and critical of the Bush administration than those of Anglos. Moreover, we find that the acquisition of partisanship among Hispanics is influenced by a host of factors, ranging from subgroup differences such as generational status and country of origin, but is also influenced by their issue positions and political ideology.

Understanding these variations in public opinion and party identification is important for several reasons. First, they give us a more nuanced understanding of American public opinion and partisanship, particularly in light of the demographic shifts that are changing the composition of the American electorate. An individual's race and ethnicity can no longer be treated simply as another demographic variable, given that Hispanics are projected to become one-quarter of the American population in the next several decades. This means that Hispanic public opinion and party identification *is* part of American politics: knowing on which policies Hispanics' attitudes differ and what explains these variations will allow elected officials to act in ways that best serve their electorate. And understanding how Hispanics acquire their partisanship is crucial if political parties wish to gain the allegiance of this coveted group of voters.

Turnout and Political Participation

IN RECENT DECADES, the United States has been swept by a new wave of immigration. The U.S. Census Bureau, which keeps track of demographic changes in the United States, found that between the two most recent decennial censuses in 1990 and 2000, the foreign-born population of the United States increased by 57 percent, from 19.8 to 31.1 million. During this period, the native U.S. population increased by 9.3 percent. Also, the percentage of foreign-born who were naturalized American citizens increased by 56 percent, from 8 million to 12.5 million (Malone et al. 2003). As of March 2003, when the Census Bureau most recently updated these estimates, it found that the U.S. foreign-born population had increased to 33.5 million, and there is little reason to believe that those trends have changed considerably in the few years since this latest census report (Larsen 2004). The 2003 census study found that a majority of these new foreign-born residents of the United States were from Central or South America and the Caribbean, and thus they can be classified as primarily Hispanic immigrants.

These immigration trends are one of the main mechanisms fueling an increase in the American Hispanic population. Again looking at what happened between the 1990 and 2000 decennial censuses, the U.S. Census Bureau found that the Hispanic population of the United States increased by 50 percent in that decade alone, from 22.4 million to 35.3 million (Guzman 2001). Updates, provided most recently in the 2004 Current Population Survey, show that the Hispanic population grew in just four years (2000 to 2004) to over 40 million.[1] No matter how you slice the demographic data, Hispanics are a rapidly expanding component of American society.

While the Hispanic population in the United States is still heavily concentrated in just a handful of states, with over three-

[1]Table 1.1, "Population by Sex, Age, Hispanic Origin, and Race: 2004," http://www.census.gov/population/socdemo/hispanic/ASEC2004/2004CPS_tab1.1a.html.

quarters of Hispanics in the 2000 census found to be living in seven states (California, Texas, New York, Florida, Illinois, Arizona, and New Jersey), it is clear that the Hispanic population is also growing in many parts of the country that are not traditionally considered to be Hispanic settlement states. Such changes may also fail to be picked up in data like that collected by the U.S. Census Bureau. During a visit in the summer of 2007 to Harrodsburg, a historically Anglo town in the bluegrass region of central Kentucky, for example, one of the authors of this book was surprised to see a small Hispanic food market along one of the major thoroughfares running through the center of Harrodsburg. Observational data like these have been cited in a number of recent popular works (e.g., Kotlowitz 2007; Tobar 2005).[2]

In this chapter, we focus on the political participation of Hispanics in American national elections, especially in recent presidential elections. Little research has been done on the political participation of Hispanics in the United States.[3] We first look at the overall levels of participation in presidential elections by Hispanics as compared to Black Americans to better understand the dilemma of Hispanic turnout. We then look in more detail at data from recent presidential elections, and there we see that the dynamics of Hispanic turnout are unique, a fact that has not been addressed well in the research literature on voter participation in the United States. Finally, to consider the full spectrum of Hispanic involvement in American politics, we turn to an analysis of forms of political participation by Hispanics outside of the ballot booth.

Hispanic and Black Participation in Recent Presidential Elections

The study of voter participation in the United States has long been based on the use of data from the U.S. Census Bureau, especially

---

[2]The documentary *Farmingville* (2004) also exemplifies this phenomenon, focusing on the Hispanic population in the small town of Farmingville, which is located in Long Island, New York.

[3]The published studies examining Hispanic voter turnout are few. Some prominent exceptions include the studies by Uhlaner, Cain, and Kiewiet (1989), DeSipio (1996), Leighley and Vedlitz (1999), Shaw, de la Garza, and Lee (2000), and Highton and Burris (2002).

the Current Population Survey (CPS) data on voting behavior collected following each federal election since the late 1960s. Originally used in the seminal work of Wolfinger and Rosenstone (1978), CPS data have been used in most published academic studies of voter participation because of the broad scope of each CPS survey: they typically include the reported behavior of tens of thousands of registered voters throughout the nation. The large sample size allows researchers to study how policy and procedural differences across states influence registration and turnout rates; it also enables researchers to study subsamples of the population (like Blacks and Hispanics) that, in a typical academic survey with a sample size of perhaps a thousand to fifteen hundred adults, may not be well represented. Also, the CPS surveys have a relatively low misreporting rate, a problem that appears to plague some of the other survey datasets that might be used to study voter participation, such as the American National Election Survey (see Burden 2000). For these reasons, we concentrate on the CPS voter supplement data in this chapter.

In figures 3.1a and 3.1b, we provide population, registration, and participation estimates, expressed in terms of the actual number of individuals in each classification, from each of the presidential election CPS studies since 1972. We show in figure 3.1a statistics for Hispanics and in the bottom panel, figure 3.1b, statistics for Blacks. In each figure, we give the estimated size of the voting-age population, the citizen voting-age population (for 2000 and 2004), the population of registered voters, and finally the estimated number who voted in each election.

Focusing only on the data for Hispanic participation since 1972, we see a number of important trends. First, it is very clear that the potential Hispanic electorate has grown considerably since 1972. While the population of Hispanics of voting age was just over 5 million in 1972 (and, of course, the actual voting-eligible population would have been lower than that by some unknown factor due to some Hispanics' lack of citizenship), it was well over 25 million by 2004. When we look at data from the two most recent CPS studies, which include estimates for the actual voting-eligible population of Hispanics (the citizen voting-age population), we see that while the potential electoral population is clearly smaller than the voting-age population would suggest for both 2000 and 2004, it is still considerable, and it in-

A.

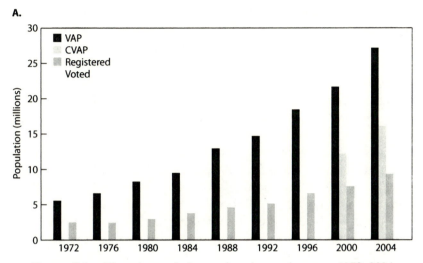

FIGURE 3.1A: Hispanic population, registration, and turnout, 1972–2004

B.

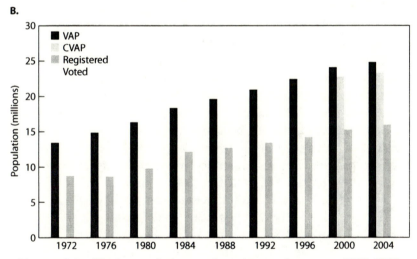

FIGURE 3.1B: Black population, registration, and turnout, 1972–2004

creased in size between just these two years, from over 12 million in 2004 to more than 16 million in 2004.

But we also see in figure 3.1a that the Hispanic registration and voting-age population lags considerably behind its electoral potential, as defined by either the voting-age or citizen voting-age populations. Also, the registration and turnout levels for Hispanics have increased since 1972, but not at the same apparent rate as the level of either the Hispanic voting-age or citizen voting-age populations have. In 1972, approximately 2.5 million Hispanics were registered to vote, and 2.1 million of them reported voting. By 2004, there were just over 9.3 million registered Hispanics and 7.6 million Hispanics who reported voting.

Figure 3.1b provides identical statistics for the Black population since 1972. There, we see, first, that the size of the Black voting-age population was considerably greater than that of Hispanics in 1972: there were nearly 13.4 million Blacks of voting age in the United States in 1972, compared to 5.6 million Hispanics of voting age. But looking at 2004, we see that the growth of the Black voting-age population has been much slower than that of Hispanics: in 2004, the size of the Hispanic voting-age population was about 2.2 million greater than the size of the identical Black population. When we look at the 2000 and 2004 data, where we have estimates of citizen voting-age population for Blacks and Hispanics, we see an important issue regarding citizenship: virtually all Blacks of voting age in the United States are citizens, while only around 60 percent of Hispanics of voting age are citizens. This is one factor that keeps the number of Hispanics who are registered and voting lower than we might expect when we look at the growth in the voting-age population of Hispanics.

In comparison with Blacks, it is also clear that the relative size of the Hispanic electorate, measured by either the number registered or the number voting, is smaller. In 1972, about 8.8 million Blacks reported being registered to vote, and about 7 million voted in that presidential election. By 2004, nearly 16 million Blacks were registered and 14 million voted. As we have already discussed, only 2.5 million Hispanics were registered in 1972, with 2.1 million voting; these numbers increased to 9.4 million registered Hispanics in 2004, with 7.6 million voting. Yet while the sheer number of Hispanics who are registered and participating is lower than the number of Blacks, the data in figure 3.1 demonstrate that the change over time has been quite different for the participation of these two minority groups in the presidential election process: while Black registration and turnout in presidential elections has doubled between 1972 and 2004, Hispanic registration and turnout has increased nearly fourfold during this same period of time.

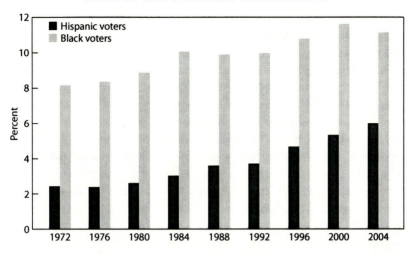

FIGURE 3.2: Hispanic and Black voters of total electorate, 1972–2004

Figure 3.2 presents comparative participation statistics in a different manner, allowing us to see from an alternative perspective the variations in Black and Hispanic participation in presidential elections. Here we graph, again between 1972 and 2004, the fraction of voters from each minority group as a share of the entire electorate, using data from the CPS. This comparison is quite enlightening, since it helps to document three key results that may help us understand the potential for these two minority groups to score increased political representation gains in the near future.

First, in figure 3.2, we see that during this entire period of time, Blacks have always made up a greater share of the presidential electorate than have Hispanics. In 1972, Blacks made up 8.2 percent of the total electorate relative to the 2.5 percent Hispanic share of the electorate in that year. In 2004, Blacks still made up a larger share of the presidential electorate than did Hispanics, at 11.2 percent versus 6.0 percent.

Second, we see little evidence in figure 3.2 that the difference between the Black and Hispanic shares of the presidential electorate has changed much since 1972. While there is some year-to-year fluctuation in the difference between 1972 and 2004, generally the difference is right around 5 percent in each year. In 1972, the difference was 5.7 percent, and by 2004, it was 5.1 percent. So while both groups are clearly increasing in size as a share of the overall electorate, it does not appear from these data that Hispanic voters are gaining ground on Black voters, despite the demographic increases in the Hispanic population.

A third important implication flows from the first two, and that is the observation that even though both the Black and Hispanic shares of the overall electorate are increasing at roughly the same rate, together their share of the electorate has increased significantly since 1972. At the beginning of the series reported in figure 3.2, these two minority groups combined made up 10 percent of the overall share of the electorate. By 2004, they made up 17 percent of the electorate. If the growth in the relative share of the presidential election vote by these two minority groups continues in the next few presidential elections—growth that we expect to see especially for Hispanic voters—then soon Blacks and Hispanics will together make up one-fifth of the presidential electorate. And as we will discuss later in this book, we expect that if the composition of the electorate continues to change in this way, it will likely result in different messages and issue emphases from presidential candidates.

WHERE ARE THE HISPANIC VOTERS?

While Hispanic voters may not yet make up a large percentage of the American presidential electorate (and may not do so for some time), their political significance in national elections, and in many state and local elections, is magnified because of their geographic concentration. Any observer of the demographic distribution of the Hispanic population in the United States would quickly be able to rattle off the few states in which the vast bulk of the Hispanic population lives, and that list would no doubt include California, Texas, Florida, New York, New Mexico, and Arizona. Yet the demographic distribution of the Hispanic population may not be directly reflective of the demographic distribution of the Hispanic electorate, so in this section we examine the question of where the Hispanic voters are in the United States.

We begin in figure 3.3 by plotting the state-by-state distribution of the percentage of each state's citizen voting-age population that was Hispanic in 2004, using CPS data. In this national map, colors that are closer to light gray are states with only a

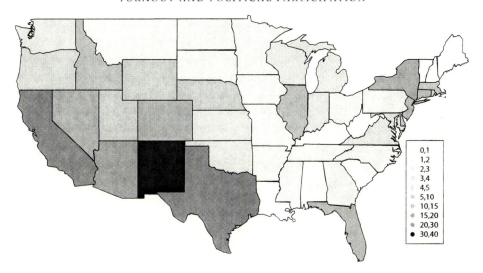

	0,1
	1,2
	2,3
	3,4
	4,5
	5,10
	10,15
	15,20
	20,30
●	30,40

FIGURE 3.3: Hispanic citizen voting-age population by state, 2004

small Hispanic potential electorate, while colors close to black represent states in which a large fraction of the potential electorate is made up of Hispanics. States with sizeable populations of citizen voting-age Hispanics are many of the "usual suspects," listed here in the order of the relative sizes of their Hispanic citizen voting-age population: New Mexico, Texas, California, Arizona, Florida, New York, and Nevada. In the first three of these states, the Hispanic citizen voting-age population is quite sizeable, at 37 percent of the state electorate in New Mexico, 27 percent in Texas, and 21 percent in California. Arizona's Hispanic citizen voting-age population makes up 18 percent of its electorate, and the other states in the list just given are all at 10 percent or slightly more.

But there are several states that might surprise some readers as having larger Hispanic citizen voting-age populations than one might have anticipated. Colorado is one such state, where in 2004 the Hispanic citizen voting-age population was nearly 12 percent of the state electorate; New Jersey (8.5 percent), Illinois (7 percent), and Idaho (6 percent) are three others. Clearly, in a number of states the potential size of the Hispanic electorate has become politically significant, and some of these states are not those that casual observers of American politics might predict.

81

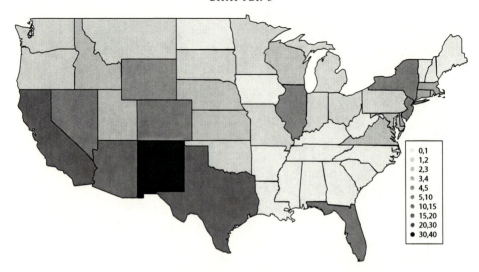

⊙	0,1
⊙	1,2
⊛	2,3
⊛	3,4
⊛	4,5
⊛	5,10
●	10,15
●	15,20
●	20,30
●	30,40

FIGURE 3.4: Hispanic turnout by state, 2004

Next, in figure 3.4, we provide another spatial depiction of the Hispanic electoral population in the United States, this time mapping Hispanic turnout as a fraction of each state's overall turnout in the 2004 presidential race (using CPS data). This portrait of the Hispanic electorate is very much like that seen in figure 3.3; that is, states with relatively large Hispanic citizen voting-age populations tend to be states in which Hispanics make up a larger share of overall turnout. Thus, Hispanic turnout figures are highest in New Mexico, at 32 percent of the citizen voting-age population; Texas (19 percent); and California (16 percent). Other states with relatively large Hispanic turnout rates are Arizona (13 percent) and Florida (11 percent), followed by Colorado, Nevada, New York, New Jersey, and Illinois. Throughout the South, Upper Northeast, and parts of the Midwest, Hispanic turnout is slight.

Importantly for Hispanic political representation, many of these same states have traditionally figured as prominent presidential battleground states, including, for example, Illinois and Florida. Others, such as New Mexico, have been close in recent presidential elections. And some of the other states in which Hispanics make up a sizeable fraction of the electorate are ones that some think might be "in play" in upcoming presidential elections, especially states in the "mountain West" like Colorado, Arizona, and Nevada. Clearly, depending on the configuration of candidates and continued demographic changes in the United States, the geographic concentration of Hispanic voters in a handful of politically important states may very well help magnify Hispanic political representation, at least in presidential elections.

ATTRIBUTES OF THE HISPANIC ELECTORATE

There are competing explanations for why Hispanics participate in presidential elections at lower rates than both Anglo and Black voters. One set of explanations focuses on demographics, while the other examines the procedural and legal barriers to participation and how they may affect Hispanics. Unfortunately, at this point in time there is simply not enough rigorous research in the academic literature that tests these competing explanations (Bailey and Alvarez 2007); the methodological issues associated with testing the competing explanations are profound, due especially to the fact that Hispanic voters are so heavily concentrated in only a few, primarily southwestern, states. The geographic concentration of Hispanic voters makes it difficult to study legal and procedural barriers, which exist at the state level—since Hispanic voters live in so few states, there is little variation in those procedural and legal barriers that would allow their effect on Hispanic voters to be studied precisely, making this a critical question for future study.

At this point, we focus on looking primarily at the demographic attributes of Hispanic voters in this section, and in the next section we explore why Hispanic voters themselves say they do not vote—and discuss research that hints at some reforms that might make it easier for Hispanics to register and vote. We show in table 3.1 the demographic profile of the Hispanic electorate as compared to those of the Black and Anglo (non-Hispanic) electorate, using data from the 2004 CPS. We provide data for the age, education, income, and residential stability of these three racial and ethnic groups; for Hispanics, we provide percentages based both on the voting-age population and on the citizen voting-age population.

What we see in table 3.1 are profound differences between the Hispanic voting population and the Black and Anglo voting populations. First, we see that Hispanic turnout is lower irrespective

TABLE 3.1
Demographic Correlates of Turnout, 2004

	Percentages of voting-age population		
	Hispanic	Anglo, non-Hispanic	Black
Age			
18 to 24	20.4	48.5	44.1
25 to 44	23.0	61.6	54.0
45 to 64	38.5	72.0	62.6
65 to 74	46.8	74.5	66.3
75 and over	44.7	69.7	60.9
Education			
Less than 9th	11.9	37.4	38.5
9th to 12th	16.3	40.0	43.1
High school grad	27.8	57.2	52.4
Some college	45.0	70.6	63.6
College degree	48.1	78.5	68.7
Advanced degree	60.3	83.7	72.6
Income			
Less than $10K	18.8	37.8	49.4
$10K–$14.9	15.1	48.7	52.0
$15K–$19.9	21.0	55.3	56.1
$20K–$29.9	21.8	59.4	55.2
$30K–$39.9	24.5	63.4	62.7
$40K–$49.9	29.4	70.9	61.0
$50K–$74.9	44.4	73.3	69.4
$75K–$99.9	51.7	78.8	73.7
$100K–$149.9	55.0	82.0	74.4
Greater than $150K	53.5	82.0	72.8
Duration of residence			
Less than 1 month	14.4	44.2	48.6
1–6 months	15.9	53.0	48.7
7–11 months	20.8	56.3	50.6
1–2 years	20.3	64.5	55.5
3–4 years	31.3	71.8	67.7
5 years or longer	46.7	77.5	73.9

Source: 2004 Current Population Survey.

of age; while nearly 50 percent of non-Hispanic Anglos (and 44 percent of Blacks) who are eighteen to twenty-four voted in 2004, only 20 percent of eighteen- to twenty-four-year-old Hispanics voted in 2004. And for older voters, the picture does not improve, since less than majorities of sixty-five- to seventy-four-year-old Hispanics, and of Hispanics older than seventy-five, voted. This finding is striking when we note that 70 percent or more of non-Hispanic Anglos in each of those two age groups voted in 2004.[4] Finally, more than 60 percent of Blacks in this age group also reported voting in this election year.

Turning to education and income, we again see major differences between Hispanics, non-Hispanic Anglos, and Blacks. Of those Hispanics with the lowest levels of educational attainment, less than a high school degree, very few turn out to vote: 12 percent of Hispanics with a ninth-grade education or lower voted in 2004, while only 16 percent of those with some high school education voted. Nearly four of ten non-Hispanic Anglos or Blacks in the same educational attainment categories voted. A similar result is true for income, as evidenced in table 3.1.

Residential mobility is a key factor for understanding Hispanic voter turnout, and in table 3.1 we see that Hispanics who have not lived at their current residence for long are much less likely to vote than Anglos in a similar residential situation: 14 percent of voting-age Hispanics who have lived at their residence less than a month voted in 2004, compared to 44 percent of non-Hispanic Anglos and 49 percent of Blacks. When we move to those who would by any measure be considered residentially stable—eligible individuals who have been at their current residence five years or more—we see that large percentages of such individuals who are non-Hispanic, Anglo, or Black turn out to vote, since roughly three-quarters of voting-age non-Hispanic Anglos or Blacks in this group voted in 2004. But the same is not true of Hispanics: less than a majority of voting-age Hispanics who have lived at their current residence for five years or more voted in 2004.

The analysis so far indicates that two factors need to be taken into account when we think about Hispanic voter participation

---

[4]When we examine these percentages as a function of the citizen voting-age population, the differences persist.

in presidential elections. Age and residential mobility appear to account for why Hispanics are less likely to participate in presidential elections. Even when controlling for citizenship, Hispanics, especially those who are very young and those who have not been at their current residence for long, are less likely to vote than their Anglo or Black counterparts.[5]

WHY HISPANICS SAY THEY DON'T VOTE

In recent versions of the CPS Voter Supplement, the Census Bureau has included a question asking registered voters who did not vote why they did not vote. We provide in table 3.2 the responses to this question for Hispanics, non-Hispanic Anglos, and Blacks. What we see here is quite interesting: concentrating on Anglo registered nonvoters first, we see that they claimed they did not vote because they were too busy (19 percent) or ill (16 percent) or because they were not interested or did not like the candidates (each around 10 percent of the responses). Black voters had a similar set of reasons for not voting.

But for Hispanics, it is important to note that nearly one-quarter of the Hispanic registered nonvoters said they were too busy to vote, and 11 percent said they had registration problems. The latter percentage is clearly higher than those for non-Hispanic Anglos (6 percent) and Blacks (7 percent). These results indicate that registered Hispanics who do not vote have reasons that differ somewhat from those of non-Hispanic Anglos and of Blacks.

These results also hint at some possible procedural changes that might make it easier for Hispanics to vote. Two types of reforms have been proposed: one set of reforms would make the registration process easier to navigate. Such changes have been ongoing since the mid-1990s, when the National Voter Registration Act (NVRA, or "Motor Voter") became law; the Motor Voter law sought to expand the availability of voter registration materials into public agencies and to make the by-mail registration process easier and more readily available to eligible citizens (among many other reforms). More recently, the Help America

---

[5]We performed the same analysis on the Hispanic citizen voting-age population, and the results hold.

TABLE 3.2
Reasons for Not Voting

Reason for not voting	Hispanic	Anglo, non-Hispanic	Black
Illness or disability	10.7	16.2	16.5
Out of town	6.3	9.9	5.5
Forgot to vote	6.1	3.0	3.9
Not interested	10.5	10.8	10.0
Too busy	23.5	18.9	20.7
Transportation problems	1.6	1.9	4.2
Did not like candidates or issues	7.3	11.1	6.4
Registration problems	10.9	6.2	7.2
Bad weather	0.2	0.5	0.3
Inconvenient polling place	1.5	3.2	2.6
Other	11.6	10.8	9.8
Don't know	9.8	7.6	13.0

Source: 2004 Current Population Survey.

Vote Act (HAVA) sought further reforms in the voter registration process, mainly by requiring that states develop centralized voter registration systems and use provisional ballots for voters whose names do not appear in the voting rolls when they go to vote.

It is hard to precisely document how these reforms may have helped ease the registration process for eligible Hispanic citizens, in part because some of these reforms are relatively recent, but also because the geographic concentration of Hispanic voters in only a few key states makes studying the effects of reform on their registration patterns difficult. This is even more distressing because in the 2004 election, Hispanic registered voters reported in greater percentages that they had registration problems that kept them from voting, and 2004 was the first presidential election in which provisional ballots were used nationally. Given the widespread availability of "fail-safe" voting and the high rate at which Hispanic registered voters continued to report problems with registration, it would seem that more needs to be done to simplify the registration process for Hispanic voters.

A number of intriguing reforms have been proposed, three of which might help alleviate the registration problem for Hispanic voters. One idea is to move to a system of "universal registration" (Overton 2006, chap. 6). Overton describes what this would entail: "Every high school student who is a U.S. citizen could be automatically registered when he or she turns eighteen, and the government could register the remainder of Americans who are not on the voting rolls during the U.S. census count every ten years" (166–67). This would turn the American registration process into something like that used in many other industrial democracies, and it would place the burden for affirmative action in the registration process on the government, not on the voter.

Another idea that has recently been discussed is similar, since it also places the burden of registration on the shoulders of the government, not the voter. As we have seen in this chapter, residential mobility is highly correlated with failure to vote among Hispanics; thus, a system of automatic reregistration for eligible and previously registered voters might ease the burden somewhat for Hispanics and other eligible citizens. For example, state governments could be required to search their voter registry when a citizen changes his address, most likely when he moves within the state and seeks to change the address on his driver's license. If the state finds a match in the voter registry for the citizen at his former address, it can automatically reregister the citizen at his new address and send mailings to the individual in question at both the old and new addresses. Procedures like these, in which the state would take the burden of reregistering voters who move within the state, are possible with the new statewide voter registration databases required under HAVA.[6]

A third reform proposes to allow voters to register on election day in their polling places; this reform is typically called "Election Day Voter Registration," or EDR. This process has been used in seven states (as of 2006): Maine, Minnesota, and Wisconsin have used EDR since the 1970s; Idaho, New Hampshire, and Wyoming have used it since the 1990s; and Montana began using it in 2006. Iowa has adopted EDR recently, and North Carolina is now implementing a variant of EDR in which voters go to one-

[6]They are possible both because states will have access to the statewide voter registry and because these registries are required under HAVA to be integrated into the state's database of driver's license holders. In the future, it might be possible for procedures like these to be expanded across state lines, as states seek to make their voter registries interoperable with those of other states (Alvarez and Hall 2005).

stop registration and voting sites. Research has shown that EDR states consistently have higher registration and turnout rates relative to non-EDR states, and, more importantly, EDR boosts turnout among those who have the most difficulty getting and staying registered, including Hispanics (Alvarez and Ansolabehere 2002; Alvarez, Nagler, and Wilson 2004; Alvarez and Nagler 2007a, 2007b).[7]

A second impediment to voting for Hispanics is revealed in the response that the greatest number of nonvoters gave when asked why they did not vote: nearly one-quarter of registered Hispanics said they were "too busy" to vote. This implies that the many reforms proposed to make the voting process more convenient and easier for registered voters to use may also help boost voter turnout. In particular, efforts to expand access to the ballot outside the traditional confines of geographic, precinct-based balloting might make it easier for busy Hispanic voters to participate. The continued push to expand both vote-by-mail and "early" in-person voting may make it easier for eligible citizens, especially Hispanics, to participate, since many of these reforms are now being implemented in the states with high concentrations of Hispanic voters. As Berinsky (2005) has argued, however, the evidence to date is ambiguous about whether the effort to expand voting by mail and early voting really does change the basic composition of the electorate; more research on this important policy issue needs to be done.

Political Participation Outside the Ballot Booth

Of course, going to the polls and voting in a presidential election is only one form of political participation. Past research has been critical of the academic focus on presidential election turnout, instead advocating an examination of the broader range of ways in which Americans are involved in political activities (Verba et al. 1995). Observers of American political behavior have long noted the willingness of Americans to be involved in their communities

[7] EDR's effects on voter turnout and on the turnout propensities of different subpopulations of the electorate have been examined in a variety of published studies: Fenster 1994; King and Wambeam 1995; Highton 1997; Brians and Grofman 1999, 2001; Knack and White 2000; and Knack 2001.

and local organizations, including Alexis de Tocqueville, who discussed his observations of American participatory behavior in the mid-1800s (1904). Recent debate in both academic and nonacademic circles has revolved around whether the proclivities of Americans to be involved in their communities has declined in past decades in what some consider a decline in "social capital" (e.g., Putnam 2000).

Here, we present a snapshot of recent data on the nonelectoral forms of political participation by Hispanics in the United States, drawing upon survey data collected by the National Annenberg Election Survey (NAES) and the Pew Hispanic Center in 2004. Both of those surveys asked respondents, including in the case of the NAES a reasonably sized sample of Hispanics, about a variety of political activities. The NAES data allow us to compare Hispanic political activities to those of both Anglos and Blacks; the Pew data give us the chance to study a broader range of political and nonpolitical activities of Hispanics outside of the presidential election ballot box.

We begin in figure 3.5 with the comparative data available from the 2004 NAES. That survey asked respondents whether they had volunteered in a political campaign, attended any political meetings, donated money to political candidates or causes, worn a political button or posted a political sign in their yards, or engaged in other forms of political behavior. These questions revealed that a considerable amount of political activity exists among Hispanics. Nearly 25 percent of Hispanics in the 2004 NAES sample said they had volunteered to work on a campaign, and more than 10 percent also said they had worn a political button or put a sign in their yard. Smaller percentages of Hispanics—just over 5 percent in each case—had attended a political meeting or donated money to a political campaign.

The 2004 NAES data also allow us to compare Hispanic political activity with that of Anglos and Blacks. Generally speaking, we find that the dimensions of political activity that figure prominently for Hispanics were also prominent for Anglos and Blacks, especially volunteering for campaigns and wearing buttons or putting up political signs. But despite that correlation, there were clearly vast differences between the political activity of Anglos, Blacks, and Hispanics in 2004.

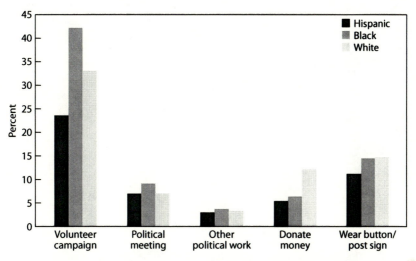

FIGURE 3.5: Rates of political participation, 2004 NAES

While the most frequently cited form of political behavior for all three racial or ethnic groups was volunteering for a campaign, over 40 percent of Blacks said they did volunteer work, and nearly 35 percent of Anglos said the same. This again is compared to just under 25 percent of Hispanics. Furthermore, both Anglos and Blacks were more likely to have worn buttons or posted signs in their yards, with 15 percent of both Anglo and Black respondents saying they had posted a sign or worn a button, slightly greater than the proportion of Hispanics who cited the same type of political activities. And finally, Anglos were more likely than either Blacks or Hispanics to have donated money to political causes.

The NAES data also enable us to look at the overall number of participatory acts by Hispanics compared to both Anglos and Blacks. To do that, we simply add the number of mentioned political activities for each respondent in the NAES and then plot in a histogram the percentages of each racial or ethnic group who said they had participated in no political acts or who participated in one through four political participatory acts. We provide this histogram in figure 3.6.

Note in figure 3.6 that the vast proportion of survey respondents of all races and ethnic groups reported having engaged in

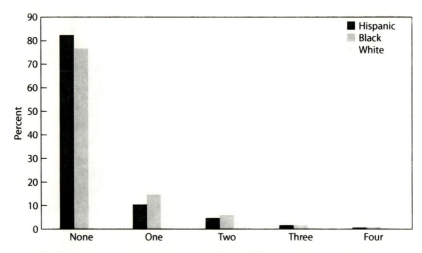

FIGURE 3.6: Rates of political involvement, by racial/ethnic group

no participatory acts at all: approximately 75 percent of Anglo and Black respondents said they participated in no political activity, as compared to over 80 percent of Hispanics. Roughly 15 percent of Blacks and Anglos reported one participatory act, while 10 percent of Hispanics reported a single political act. Many fewer reported engaging in more than one act. The overall picture suggested by figure 3.6 is that Hispanics reported engaging in fewer participatory acts in the NAES survey than did Anglos or Blacks.

The data collected by the Pew Hispanic Center in 2004 give us a chance to examine in more detail a broader array of political and nonpolitical activities by Hispanics. This survey asked respondents whether they had contacted an official, contacted a Hispanic official, attended a political meeting, or volunteered in their church, school, neighborhood, for a candidate, or for a Hispanic/Latino group. We present in figure 3.7 the frequency distribution of responses. The participation questions here break down into three types, involving contacting officials, attending meetings, and volunteer activities. Of the three types of activities, by far the most prevalent were volunteer activities, followed by meeting attendance and contacting officials. Note especially that in terms of volunteer activities, Hispanics are heavily involved in their communities: 35 percent volunteered in their church, over 25 percent volunteered in a school, and nearly 25

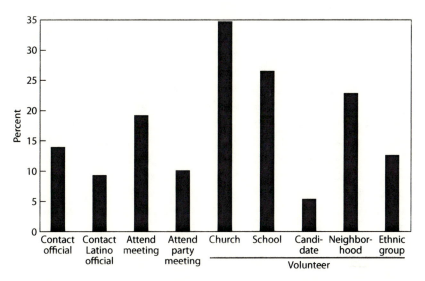

FIGURE 3.7: Hispanic political and nonpolitical participation, 2004 Pew Hispanic Survey

percent volunteered in their neighborhood. Volunteer work for candidates or ethnic groups was much lower, about 5 percent.

Other forms of community activities, like attending meetings or contacting officials, were not as widespread among Hispanics in this 2004 sample. But for both contacting and attending meetings, we see that nonpolitical activities were more widespread than direct political activities, especially meeting attendance. Almost one in five Hispanics said they had attended a meeting, but only about one in ten said they had attended a party meeting.

DIRECT POLITICAL ACTION: PROTESTS IN 2006

Another way to gauge Hispanic political participation is to study instances in which direct collective action is possible. Collective action has been the subject of a great deal of research in political science; social movements and protest politics have been of critical importance at many points in American political history, especially in the quest by racial and ethnic minority groups for economic and political rights. Salient moments of such collective action in American political history include events like the March on Washington in August 1963 and the farmworker strikes in 1965 and 1966 in California and Texas.

A similar salient political moment arose in late 2005, when the U.S. House of Representatives passed H.R. 4437, a bill that its sponsors argued would control illegal immigration into the United States. The House passage of this bill generated a grassroots movement of protest among Hispanics throughout the United States, which was picked up by the Spanish-language media, especially radio stations, in many of the larger cities in the nation. In early March 2006, rallies, marches, and protests began in a number of cities. By April and May, these marches and protests swelled to the point where hundreds of thousands of Hispanics (along with many non-Hispanics) marched in large cities like New York and Los Angeles. Then the mass media began to pay attention to these protests, and many pondered what the long-term implications of this mass mobilization might be for the future of Hispanic political participation in America.

These large-scale protests are of interest to political scientists not just because of their potential political significance but also because of their analytic importance. The problem of collective action has been a perplexing one for political scientists, especially since Mancur Olson published his critique of analytic theories about collective action (1971). Olson's argument, based on "rational choice theory," asserted that outside of very special circumstances involving very small groups, mobilizing rational individuals for collective purposes is difficult if not impossible. The dilemma, of course, is that while Olson's logic of collective action is convincing, we still do see instances, like that in 2006, in which collective action arises on a sweeping scale. Cases like the 2006 protests raise many interesting questions, such as how individuals become involved in these collective actions, who is involved, what they get out of their involvement in the collective action, and what the long-term consequences of their participation in the collective action might be.

Such questions would require a book-length treatment of their own to answer. Here, we are most interested in exploring the basic question of how widespread involvement in the 2006 protests was in the Hispanic community and, within the community, who was involved. The longer-term consequences of their involvement will play out in the 2008 election and beyond and are thus questions for future research. To study our more immediate questions, we use data from a survey conducted by Democracy Corps of 984 Hispanic likely voters, fielded May 18–June 4, 2006.[8] One important caveat in our use of these data is that the population surveyed was one of likely voters, and those are of course Hispanics who closely follow politics and who are potentially more likely to be involved in political activity than Hispanics who are registered but participate infrequently, who are not registered to vote, and so on.

The Democracy Corps survey contained a series of questions asking these Hispanic likely voters about the demonstrations; the one we use here asked, "Have you personally participated in any of the demonstrations held in many cities on the immigration issue? (If no) Do you have a close friend, relative or neighbor who participated in any of the demonstrations held in many cities on the immigration issue?" We start our analysis by presenting in figure 3.8 the responses to this survey question by the Hispanic likely voters in the sample; their responses are also broken down by partisanship and ideology. In this figure and those that follow in this chapter, we plot all of those who said that they had themselves participated or knew someone who had participated as "Yes" and those who did not participate and did not know someone who participated as "No."

We find among Hispanic likely voters in this sample that participation in the 2006 protests was widespread: 43 percent said they participated or knew someone who had participated, and 56 percent said they did not participate or did not know of anyone who participated. While not presented in figure 3.8, in the original survey data, 19 percent of the Hispanic likely voter respondents polled reported that they had participated themselves, while 24 percent knew of someone who had participated. As is apparent in figure 3.8, participation in the demonstrations had a partisan and ideological skew: roughly half of the Democratic Hispanic likely voters participated or knew someone who participated in the demonstrations, while around 40 percent of independent Hispanic likely voters participated or knew someone who participated; less than 30 percent of Republican Hispanic

[8]For more information about this survey, see http://archive.democracycorps. com/reports/surveys/Democracy_Corps_May_18-June_4_2006_Survey.pdf.

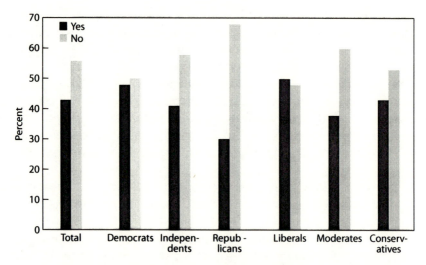

FIGURE 3.8: Participation in 2006 immigration marches,
by partisanship and ideology

likely voters participated or knew someone who participated.
We also see that liberals were more likely to participate or know
someone who participated than were moderates or conservatives.

Next, we turn to some demographic dimensions and examine
the extent to which they might be associated with participation
in these collective actions: gender, age, and income. These are
presented in figure 3.9. We see only a slight gender gap in participation, with female Hispanic likely voters marginally more
likely to have participated or to know of someone who participated than males. There is, however, quite a dramatic association
between age and participation: over 60 percent of likely voters
age eighteen to twenty-nine participated or knew of someone
who participated, falling to only 21 percent of those over sixty-
four. Furthermore, in figure 3.9 an association between income
and participation also seems to exist, though the pattern seems
somewhat nonlinear, with the highest levels of participation
coming from those in the $30,000 to $50,000 income range.

In figure 3.10 we shift attention to questions associated with
Hispanic identity, looking at national origin and the use of Spanish language at home. Here, we see that the greatest levels of
participation came from those of Mexican background (over 50
percent of the Mexican Hispanic likely voters participated in the

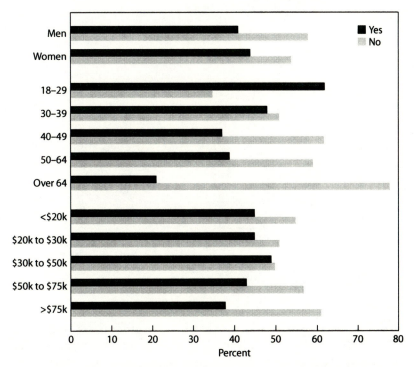

FIGURE 3.9: Demonstration participation and demographics

demonstrations or knew someone who participated), with the second highest level of participation from those with Central or South American backgrounds. When we look at Spanish language use and protest participation, Hispanic likely voters who spoke at least some Spanish at home (those who spoke both Spanish and English or who only spoke Spanish at home) were most likely to participate or know someone who participated in the protests.

Finally, in figure 3.11, we look at nativity and participation: was the likely voter born in the United States or in another country, and were the individual's parents born in the United States or another nation? Here, we see only a slight association between the likely voter's nativity and participation, but we do see that 50 percent of those with one parent born outside the United States, and 52 percent of those with both parents born outside the United States, participated or knew of someone who participated in the demonstrations.

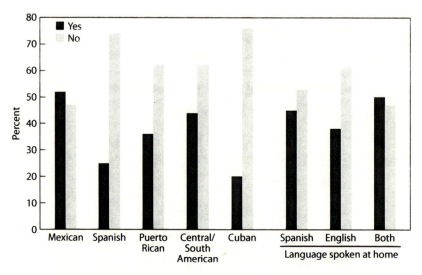

FIGURE 3.10: Demonstration participation and identity

Much more research is needed on the 2006 demonstrations, looking in more detail not just at those Hispanics who participated (who we can say based on our analysis here were more likely to be young people of Mexican, Central American, or South American descent who spoke at least some Spanish at home, who had at least one parent born outside the United States, and who were Democratic and liberal in political orientation) but also at why they participated. What did they get out of participation in this collective action? And, probably more important, did their participation in this collective action fuel heightened interest in politics, and will it lead them to be more likely to participate in political action in the future?

CONCLUSION: WHITHER HISPANIC POLITICAL PARTICIPATION?

As we view the current political landscape, we draw a number of important conclusions regarding Hispanic political participation—and the implications of their participation for how their concerns and preferences are reflected in political representation and public policies. First, a central theme in our research is that the

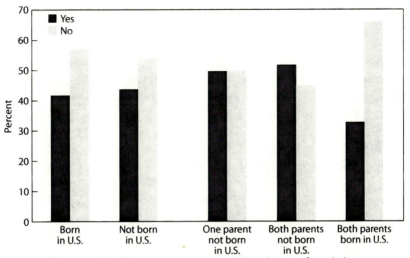

FIGURE 3.11: Demonstration participation and nativity

Hispanic population is growing at an incredible rate and that all predictions expect this population growth to continue into the foreseeable future. Yet when we look at the most common and easy-to-measure metric of political participation, voting in a presidential election, we find that Hispanics are not turning out to vote as frequently as Blacks or Anglos. Partly, this is due to demographic issues: the noncitizenship rate is much greater for Hispanics than for non-Hispanics, and the Hispanic population is younger and poorer than the non-Hispanic population. Thus, more Hispanics are not eligible to vote, and more Hispanics find it difficult to register and get out to vote on election day. Unless some of these demographic differences between Hispanics, Anglos, and Blacks lessen, and until procedural changes make the registration and voting process easier, it is likely that the participation of Hispanic voters in presidential elections will continue to lag behind that of Anglos and Blacks.

These particular dynamics may not be fixed in the near future, and much will depend on the political context at both the national and the state level. Becoming a regular participant in the electoral process is a many-staged process. For many resident Hispanics in the United States, the first step is naturalization; thereafter, it is a matter of registering to vote and keeping that registration up-to-date. Once correctly registered, participation depends critically on resources (political information and interest, which we will discuss in later chapters), but it can also hinge on mobilization efforts. Much recent research has studied get-out-the-vote efforts and has shown that they can be very important determinants of whether registered voters participate (Gerber and Green 2000a, 2000b); some studies have also begun to look at the effectiveness of these mobilization efforts for Hispanics (e.g., de la Garza, Abrajano, and Cortina 2008; Sinclair, McConnell, and Michelson 2008; Michelson 2003; Ramirez 2005) as well as the amount of Hispanic electoral representation that exists for a given Hispanic voter (Barreto 2007; Barreto, Segura, and Woods 2004). Further, some studies have found that context can be an important factor regarding whether newly naturalized Hispanics participate in subsequent elections (Pantoja, Ramirez, and Segura 2001). All of this implies that conditions exist in which we might see Hispanic participation in future presidential elections grow dramatically if resources are devoted to registering and mobilizing Hispanics and if the political context is focused on issues that might be of great importance to Hispanics (for example, education and health care) or that might be seen as a threat to Hispanics (for example, immigration reform).

As our analysis of the 2006 demonstrations showed, however, there are conditions under which many Hispanics can be mobilized to engage in collective political activity outside the traditional avenues of political participation. Exactly what the prerequisites for massive mobilization might be has yet to be studied. Whether the 2006 demonstrations can help to explain the increase in Latino turnout rates in the 2008 presidential election is unclear, as is the answer to the related question regarding whether the demonstrations will mobilize Hispanics for other forms of political action, especially future collective actions like marches and demonstrations.

Our studies here confirm that outside the ballot box, Hispanics are highly involved in nonpolitical activities, especially in their communities, volunteering in their churches, neighborhoods, and schools (García Bedolla 2005; Pardo 1997). They are also active in direct forms of political activity, including working on campaigns and helping candidates get out their messages, though at lower rates than Anglos and Blacks. Strong community involvement and strong political participation no doubt operate to improve Hispanic social, economic, and political representation. Whether nonpolitical activity and political activities other than voting will themselves help improve Hispanic turnout rates in the future is unknown, and is clearly an area crying out for future research.

Political Knowledge, Efficacy, and Awareness

EVERYDAY EXPERIENCE brings home the reality that there are some people who are highly knowledgeable about political affairs and contemporary politics—academics, journalists, political activists, and others. And it is likely that every reader of this book knows someone who professes ignorance about politics and who might take pride in his or her lack of political knowledge. But most people fall somewhere in between these extremes: we are all aware that our friends, family members, and colleagues at work know bits and pieces of information about politics and that they tend to accumulate more of these bits and pieces of political information at points in time when they need those data and when an abundance of political information happens to be in circulation—right around the time of a major election, for example, or during periods of political controversy or crisis.

Academic researchers have known for many years that individuals' political knowledge helps explain a wide array of their political behaviors, from turnout (Delli Carpini and Keeter 1993, 1996) and voting (Krosnick 1990; Kinder and Sanders 1990) to susceptibility to campaign messages (Zaller 1992; Alvarez 1997). Politically knowledgeable individuals behave differently from those who are less knowledgeable, because they possess a more tightly connected cognitive structure that allows them to organize their political beliefs and ideology (Krosnick 1990; Kinder and Sanders 1990). For a growing segment of the American population, however, the process by which individuals learn and become knowledgeable about politics differs from the process traditionally experienced by the rest of the American electorate (at least in the modern era, when much of this research on political knowledge has been conducted). As we have emphasized, demographic changes in the American landscape have resulted in more than 20 percent of the total U.S. population being made up of immigrants, a majority of whom were born outside of the

United States (Guzman 2001). Thus, while traditionally people learn about politics from their parents (Hyman 1959; Campbell et al. 1964; Easton and Dennis 1969; Greenstein 1965; Valentino and Sears 1998), it may be the case that a sizeable portion of the U.S. electorate is acquiring political knowledge in ways that do not conform to this long-held standard.

The aim of this chapter is to examine the pathways to political knowledge for Hispanics and for Anglos. Considering how important political knowledge is to the political behavior of individuals, it is crucial to know what differences exist between these groups and if these variations can be attributed to the manner in which each group is socialized politically. Next, we explore the different factors that contribute to political knowledge from both a behavioral and a structural standpoint and then discuss the political implications of these findings.

WHY POLITICAL INFORMATION MATTERS

One of the strongest forms of political socialization, the acquisition of partisanship through one's parents (Campbell et al. 1964), is largely unavailable to foreign-born immigrants with respect to the country to which they immigrate. Although scholars have questioned the long-term effects of preadult socialization (Vaillancourt 1973), especially in terms of partisanship, its long-term stability cannot be overlooked (Petrocik 1996). The potential implications of differences in political socialization processes are great, since an individual's knowledge of politics influences almost every aspect of that person's political and civic life. Understanding the political knowledge of Hispanics—many of whom are themselves immigrants or who are recently descended from immigrants—requires new research and sensitivity to the possibility that common academic perspectives on the acquisition of political knowledge and its effects on voting behavior may not perfectly apply to Hispanics in contemporary American politics.

While European immigrants at the turn of the century also became socialized to U.S. politics differently than did the native-born, political parties and ethnic politicians at that time took on the responsibility of fostering immigrant political socialization (DeSipio 2001). Urban political machines, as well as ethnic

103

politicians and their organizations, saw to it that the newcomers were involved in and recruited to the political process (Erie 1988). But with the rise of candidate-centered politics, political parties are no longer as powerful or influential as they once were, and their roles and responsibilities have changed, shifting particularly toward an emphasis on serving their candidates (Aldrich 1995). As DeSipio (2001) observes, contemporary immigrants' exposure to government and political institutions is largely restricted to the state and local level; thus, the extent to which immigrants learn about and become familiar with politics depends largely on where they live. Today's immigrants are faced with even greater challenges in becoming politically incorporated than were their predecessors.

Unlike European immigration, moreover, which tapered off by the mid-nineteenth century, Hispanics' rates of immigration have steadily increased from 1970 through 2000 and are predicted to increase further (Malone et al. 2003). While 19.9 percent of the Hispanic population in 1970 was foreign-born, by 2000 this figure had reached 45.5 percent. This means that a considerable portion of this immigrant group is constantly being replenished with individuals who are politically socialized in a manner that differs from the socialization of both U.S.-born Hispanics and U.S.-born Anglo Americans.

We know that formal education facilitates political knowledge and learning.[1] Thus, the children of foreign-born Hispanics could potentially substitute for their lack of U.S.-relevant political knowledge (with which their parents cannot provide them) through formal education. However, a large number of Hispanic students face substandard educational opportunities (Orfield and Lee 2004), which in turn affects their ability to become politically informed and aware individuals (Niemi and Junn 1998). School districts with large minority populations differ considerably from school districts serving majority Anglo students on a host of indicators—from federal funding and resources to teacher qual-

---

[1]See the discussion regarding the determinants of political information in Alvarez and Brehm (2002), pages 45–51. Delli Carpini and Keeter (1996) also discuss the role of formal education in structuring political education, stating that "formal education is a key determinant of how knowledgeable citizens are about politics," and "schooling promotes the acquisition of political knowledge" (278).

ity and course curriculum (Meier et al. 2005; Orfield and Lee 2004). This is troubling, since formal education "is a key determinant of how knowledgeable citizens are about politics," and "schooling promotes the acquisition of political knowledge" (Delli Carpini and Keeter 1996, 278). The financial constraints faced by majority–minority school districts have led many to eliminate civics and government courses in favor of vocational courses, such as sewing and hairdressing (Kozol 2005). Such a shift makes it more difficult for the children of immigrants to learn about American politics.

Differences in political socialization could affect the development of political knowledge for Hispanics due to their influence on the nature of political communications. One of us has developed a theory of information-based advertising which contends that a Hispanic's level of political knowledge guides the political communication decisions made by parties and candidates as they compete for votes (Abrajano 2010). This theory's central prediction is that more politically knowledgeable individuals will be targeted with advertisements containing policy messages requiring a strong background in politics and current events, while less knowledgeable voters will be more likely to be targeted with political spots that contain simple issue appeals or culturally based themes. Abrajano studies the content of thousands of commercials produced by presidential, congressional, and gubernatorial contenders in the 2000–2004 election cycles, and finds that candidates generally behaved according to this theory of information-based advertising. This finding suggests that Hispanics may possess political knowledge that is qualitatively different from the political knowledge of other voters, in part as a result of the way in which campaigns target their political communication strategies to Hispanics.

Along with political knowledge, citizens' attitudes toward government and feelings of political efficacy can also influence their overall interest in government and the political process. Those who feel they have little impact on the political process or that their participation is of little significance may be expected to have little interest in politics. Furthermore, if political campaigns are pitching messages to Hispanics that are laden with symbolic content instead of issue content, that approach could affect the perceptions of political efficacy and general political interest of

Hispanics. Finally, if Hispanics live in communities that are not highly politicized or active in incorporating Hispanics into politics, this may also influence their attitudes toward government and politics.

DEFINING POLITICAL KNOWLEDGE

Political knowledge could simply mean the amount of information one possesses with respect to government, current events, and public policies, or it could also include one's level of political interest and rate of political participation. Delli Carpini and Keeter (1996) provide a more comprehensive measure of political knowledge that accounts for both behavioral and structural factors. In explaining this concept, they develop what they refer to as a "simple path model of political knowledge." Their model, presented in figure 4.1, indicates that the first set of variables along this path is related to demographics. This includes an individual's racial or ethnic identity, region of residence, age, and gender. The demographic factors go on to influence the second stage in this path, labeled as the "structural" variables: these include one's formal years of education, income, and occupational opportunities.

Racial or ethnic background plays an important role in the types of structural opportunities available to individuals, especially in terms of education. As we discussed earlier, ample evidence indicates that the types of schools that racial minorities and Anglo students attend dramatically differ from one another (Kozol 2005; Orfield and Lee 2006; Fry 2007). Schools with high minority enrollments receive approximately $1,000 less per student per year than schools with the lowest minority or poverty enrollments.[2] Moreover, schools with high enrollments of Hispanics receive greater levels of Title 1 funding, are constrained by a higher teacher-student ratio, and receive more free lunches (one measure used to gauge the poverty rate in schools) than those schools with low enrollments of Hispanics (Fry 2007).[3]

[2]Kevin Carey, "The Funding Gap," *Education Trust*, October 29, 2003.
[3]Title 1 funds are formula grants sponsored by the federal government. These grants are available to school districts with a high percentage of poor children.

Orfield and Lee (2004) estimate that in public schools in which 80 to 90 percent of the population is Hispanic or Black, 85 percent of the students are living in poverty. Thus, being Hispanic or Black often leads to the structural disadvantage of attending schools that are underfunded and underresourced (Kozol 2005; Orfield and Lee 2004). Other research studying racially and ethnically diverse school districts in California (where direct comparisons between Hispanic, Black, and Anglo students are possible) has documented substantial differences in the math and reading test scores of Hispanic and Black students relative to Anglo students in the same districts (Bali and Alvarez 2003, 2004; Betts, Zau, and Rice 2003). All of these strands of research produce a highly disconcerting portrait, because as we have discussed earlier, formal education is associated with political knowledge (Delli Carpini and Keeter 1996; Alvarez and Brehm 2002).

One of the major consequences arising from these inequalities is that Hispanic and Black high school students tend to exhibit lower levels of political knowledge than Anglo students. Using a 1988 survey conducted by the National Assessment of Education Progress of more than four thousand high school students, researchers found that Anglo students' average score on measures of civic knowledge (measured as the number of correct answers to civics questions) was 69 percent, compared to 58 percent for Hispanics and 56 percent for Blacks. This means that a gap of 11 percent exists between Anglo and Hispanic students, and a slightly greater gap (13 percent) between Black and Anglo students, in their knowledge of government and politics. The other findings from this survey, which included 150 questions related to civic engagement and knowledge of U.S. politics, revealed that Hispanic and Black students systematically knew less about the structure and function of the U.S. government, political parties, lobbying, state and local government, and the basic rights of citizens when compared to Anglo students.[4]

These differences in political knowledge cannot be attributed to a lack of political interest on the part of Hispanic and Black high school students. The survey reveals that a greater percentage of Hispanic students (51.2 percent) find government interesting to study than do Anglo students (40.2 percent); Black students

[4]Refer to Niemi and Junn 1998, 111, for the specific questions.

also report higher rates of interest in government (44.1 percent) when compared to Anglo students (Niemi and Junn 1998). Niemi and Junn find that the most important determinant of learning for Hispanic students is related to the civics curriculum of a given school. The extent to which current events and a large variety of issues are offered as part of the school's curriculum best predicts a Hispanic student's knowledge of politics. Even when controlling for a student's home environment, such as household structure and parents' education level, and for individual achievement, including plans to go to a four-year college, a school's civics curriculum is still the strongest predictor of students' political knowledge. Although Niemi and Junn do not directly account for the institutional discrepancies in the types of schools that Anglos and Hispanics attend, variations in course offerings can be considered as suitable proxies, since schools with more funding can typically provide a wider array of classes than schools with less funding.

In addition to race determining the educational opportunities of many Hispanics, the composition of the Hispanic population also dictates how structurally advantaged or disadvantaged Hispanics will be relative to other racial groups. By "composition," we refer to Hispanics' nativity, or place of birth. As of 2000, the U.S. Census estimates that 45.5 percent of the Hispanic population was foreign-born (Campbell and Lennon 1999). The percentage of the foreign-born population has continually increased from 1970 through 2000. In 1970, 19.9 percent of the Hispanic population was foreign-born; this figure reached 28.6 percent in 1980 and 35.8 percent in 1990. Having such a significant portion of the population born outside of the United States means that Hispanics' rates of acculturation and socialization into American society and politics will be markedly different from those of populations born in the United States (Portes and Rumbaut 1992; García Bedolla 2005). While the percentage of foreign-born in the Asian population in the United States is also quite high, Asians' socioeconomic status is typically much higher than that of Hispanics (DeSipio 2001).

Again, as we discussed earlier, the two primary ways in which political socialization occurs are through formal education and through informal education by friends and family. But a majority of foreign-born Hispanics (70 percent) arrives in the United States as adults and is not exposed to any of the civic learning that would occur in high school or college in the United States. The remaining one-third of the foreign-born Hispanic population is under the age of eighteen, and they are faced with numerous challenges in the public education system.

One's place of employment could also provide an opportunity to discuss and learn about politics (Delli Carpini and Keeter 1996). But the reality is that many Hispanics who immigrate to the United States do so to work primarily in the service or agricultural sectors (Smith 2001). This being the case, their occupational status does little to foster any sort of political discussion, dialogue, or network. The language barrier is yet another hurdle that foreign-born Hispanics face in the political socialization and learning process: unless their workplace is one in which Spanish is spoken, the possibility of interacting in political discourse at work is unlikely.

Altogether, these factors present a rather troubling picture for Hispanics. First, they suggest that almost half of the Hispanic population faces considerable barriers to becoming incorporated into the American political system. Yet American-born Hispanics do not really fare any better, since they, too, are faced with similar challenges by way of substandard educational systems. Thus, the path of political knowledge, as presented by Delli Carpini and Keeter (1996), suggests that becoming as politically knowledgeable and aware as the rest of the American population will be a struggle for the majority of Hispanics. The amount of political interest and knowledge of the foreign-born population may be lower than it is for U.S.-born Hispanics, but since the foreign-born population makes up almost half of the Hispanic population in the United States, it is also going to drive down the political knowledge rates for the entire group.

STRUCTURAL INDICATORS

The status of Hispanics in America's racial paradigm makes it difficult to ignore how instrumental race is in determining an individual's structural opportunities. While we have focused only on the structural factors that are believed to be significant influences on Hispanic political knowledge, other structural indicators, such as differences in household structures, levels of wealth, and occupation, also exist; these are closely linked to one's education levels and nativity. As figure 4.1 depicts, structural indicators are critical because they go on to directly and indirectly impact an individual's level of political knowledge. The direct impact of structural variables on political knowledge is evident in the strong correlation between years of formal education and levels of political knowledge (Delli Carpini and Keeter 1996; Niemi and Junn 1998; Nie, Junn, and Stehlik-Barry 1996). Indirectly, one's schooling and occupation significantly influence one's likelihood of becoming involved and interested in politics ("behavioral" variables). Education is key to developing an individual's political behavior and attitudes. In particular, how interested one is and how often one pays attention to politics, the extent to which one discusses politics with family and friends, and one's feelings of political efficacy and civic duty are all influenced by these structural variables. Those with higher levels of education and income are more likely to be involved in and attentive to politics and be part of social networks than those with lower levels of education (Verba, Schlozman, and Brady 1995; Delli Carpini and Keeter 1996). So either directly or indirectly, one's racial or ethnic background, gender, age, years of education, and interest in politics are all important factors in determining one's overall knowledge of politics.[5]

Estimates from the U.S. Census indicate that while just over half of Hispanics over the age of twenty-five have graduated from high school, at least 80 percent or more of the Anglo, Black, and Asian population over the age of twenty-five has completed high school. The research discussed earlier also documents that in primary and secondary public schools, Hispanic students score lower than their Anglo counterparts on student achievement tests. These differences are consistent with the educational opportunities available to Hispanic and Anglo students in the United States. A comparison of the household income levels of

---

[5]Some may argue that race directly influences the behavioral variables. This argument is best exemplified through the Black community. We discuss this issue at greater length later in this chapter.

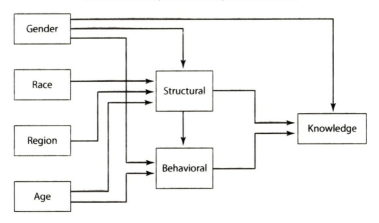

FIGURE 4.1: Delli Carpini and Keeter's (1996) Simple Path of
Political Knowledge

Hispanics relative to those of Blacks and Anglos reveals a similar pattern. Survey data from a 2002 study by the Pew Hispanic Center and Kaiser Family Foundation indicate that half of Hispanic survey respondents made less than $30,000, compared to only 29 percent of Anglo and 44 percent of Black survey respondents. In contrast, Anglos were concentrated in the highest income category (42 percent), more so than Hispanics (17 percent) or Blacks (22 percent). Moreover, 2000 U.S. Census estimates indicate that Hispanics have a lower median family income than Anglos, Blacks, and Asians. More Hispanics also live in poverty (29 percent) relative to the three other racial groups (23.7 percent for Blacks, 10.7 percent for Asians, and 8 percent for Anglos). While the proportion of Hispanics who own a home is just slightly lower than it is for Blacks (45.7 versus 46.6 percent), it is considerably lower when compared to home ownership rates of Asians and Anglos, at 53.3 and 72.5 percent, respectively. So, as Delli Carpini and Keeter's model predicts, race helps determine how structurally advantaged or disadvantaged a particular group will be; in this case, because of hardships that Hispanics face in the educational system and the size of the foreign-born population, their educational attainment levels are lower than those of non-Hispanics, a disadvantage which then spills over into differences in their household and median income, poverty, and home ownership levels.

BEHAVIORAL INDICATORS

Moving on to the next path in the model, behavioral factors, we present several measures of political interest, activity, trust, and efficacy by race/ethnicity in table 4.1. As we discussed in chapter 3, Hispanics' overall levels of political involvement are moderately lower than that of Anglos and Blacks, as measured by the number of activities in which they participated. The other behavioral components that we focus on pertain to political interest, efficacy, and political knowledge. We use data from the 2000 and 2004 National Annenberg Election Surveys (Romer et al. 2006). Political interest is measured as the frequency with which individuals pay attention to politics, as well as the number of times in a given week they discuss politics with their family and friends. As table 4.1 demonstrates, across these measures of political interest, Hispanics are less politically inclined than are Anglos. In both 2000 and 2004, a much smaller percentage of Hispanics reported following politics on a regular basis than did non-Hispanics. In 2000, 36.6 percent of Anglos said that they followed politics "most of the time," while only 19.8 percent of Hispanics responded in this manner. Likewise, we see that in 2004, 41 percent of Anglos followed politics "most times," whereas only 23 percent of Hispanics did. At the other end of the scale, we see that a greater percentage of Hispanics hardly follow politics when compared to Anglos. In 2000, approximately one out of five Hispanics responded that they "hardly at all" pay attention to politics; the percentage of Anglos that responded in this fashion was lower, at 10.7 percent.

The frequency of an individual's engagement in political discussion with family and friends is another strong indicator of political interest and awareness. Using this measure, we once again see that a greater proportion of Anglos routinely talk about politics with friends and family when compared to the Hispanic population in the United States. Of the Hispanic respondents in 2004, only 12.2 percent discussed politics six or seven times a week, while a moderately larger percentage of Anglos, 20.9 percent, reported having political discussions with this frequency, creating a gap of 8.7 percent. A larger percentage of Hispanics than Anglos reported in both 2000 and 2004 that they never or rarely discuss politics. These two measures of political interest demonstrate that, on average, Hispanics are less engaged in politics and less likely to discuss politics than are Anglos. These results are in keeping with Delli Carpini and Keeter's model due to the structural discrepancies between Hispanics and Anglos.

Next, we examine several indicators of political efficacy and attitudes toward government, particularly trust in the federal government and trust in the honesty of elected officials. The political efficacy question asks respondents whether they feel that politics is "too complicated for people like me" and that "people like me have no say over who gets to be president." Consistent with previous research (Abrajano and Alvarez, forthcoming), Hispanics tend to be more trusting of government than Anglos. For instance, in 2004, 6.5 percent of Hispanics responded that they always trust government to do what is right, whereas only 1.6 percent of Anglos felt this way. Moreover, a larger percentage of Hispanics, 7.4 percent, have a great deal of trust in the honesty of elected officials than do Anglos, at 3 percent. Despite these slightly more positive attitudes toward government, Hispanics feel that they are less politically efficacious than Anglos. In 2000, 25.4 percent of Hispanics strongly agreed with the statement that politics is too complicated for them, whereas only 18.6 percent of Anglos strongly agreed with this statement. A similar pattern emerges for Hispanics and Anglos interviewed in 2004. Interestingly, a larger percentage of Anglos are strongly opposed to the notion that politics is too complicated for them than are Hispanics (26.1 versus 19.2 percent in 2000; 25.9 versus 18.5 percent in 2004). So while Hispanics are more trusting in the federal government than Anglos, they are less likely to feel that they can make a difference in politics and that their involvement matters. Perhaps the reason for these differences stems from Hispanics' lower socioeconomic status and standing in society relative to Anglos: this may lead many to feel that they play less of a role in the American political system. Another explanation could be their relative inexperience and lack of awareness of U.S. government and politics, especially for those who recently immigrated to the United States.

As Delli Carpini and Keeter's model clearly demonstrates, structural differences account in part for why these behavioral indicators differ for Hispanics and Anglos. Therefore, the structural disadvantages that Hispanics face pose a challenge for

TABLE 4.1

Levels of Political Trust, Activity, and Interest: 2000 and 2004 Elections

	2000		2004	
	Hispanics	Anglos	Hispanics	Anglos
Political interest				
Follow politics. . .				
Most times	19.8	36.6	22.8	41.2
Sometime	30.0	35.1	32.3	36.2
Now and then	26.8	17.6	30.9	16.2
Hardly at all	23.4	10.7	12.7	6.1
N	2,611	28,112	6,155	67,851
Number of times politics is discussed with family/friends in a week. . .				
0–1	61.3	45.5	47.9	33.6
2–3	24.7	29.2	26.5	28.7
4–5	8.0	12.9	12.4	16.3
6–7	6.1	12.4	12.2	20.9
N	2,611	28,112	6,155	67,851
Political trust				
Trust government to do what is right. . .				
Always	9.7	2.9	6.5	1.6
Most times	28.5	24.9	27.1	26.1
Sometime	59.0	68.7	58.6	65.4
Never	2.7	3.4	7.9	6.9
N	1,286	14,033	1,388	14,956
Trust in the honesty of elected officials				
Great deal	—	—	7.4	3.0
Fair amount	—	—	46.4	45.3
Not much	—	—	35.2	42.6
None	—	—	8.1	7.9
N			619	7,222

enabling them to become involved and interested in politics. Referred to largely in the political participation literature as a resource-based explanation, the idea is that one has to have the ability, time, and resources to participate in political activities (Verba, Schlozman, and Brady 1995). Also, because most Hispanics are not

TABLE 4.1 *(cont.)*

	2000		2004	
	Hispanics	*Anglos*	*Hispanics*	*Anglos*
Political efficacy				
Politics too complicated[a]				
Strongly agree	25.4	18.6	32.0	22.2
Somewhat agree	31.5	31.3	30.3	31.4
Neither agree/disagree	—	—	0.3	0.5
Somewhat disagree	20.2	23.1	17.2	19.2
Strongly disagree	19.2	26.1	18.5	25.9
N	1,321	14,159	3,672	41,060
Political knowledge				
General political knowledge[b]	0.8	2.4	3.7	4.1
Knowledge of candidates' issue positions[c]	2.5	6.0	2.5	2.9
N	1553	8924	486	6535

Source: 2000 and 2004 Annenberg National Election Survey.

Note: With the exception of the political knowledge cell entries, cell entries are column percentages.

[a]In the 2000 survey, the question was phrased as "people like me have no say over who gets to be president."

[b]General political knowledge is measured as the number of correct answers a respondent provides on questions pertaining to one's general knowledge of politics (e.g., identifying Cheney's position, number in Congress required to overturn a veto).

[c]Knowledge of candidates' issue positions is measured as the number of correct answers a respondent provides on questions asking them to identify Bush and Gore's positions on several policy areas.

considered to be "likely voters," and in fact many are first-time voters with no voting record, they are not likely to be contacted or mobilized by candidates or political parties. Finally, the fact that almost half of the Hispanic population is foreign-born further decreases their likelihood of participating in politics (Leal 2002).

Before turning to the last stage of the path model, political knowledge, we need to discuss one important matter. Blacks face many of the same structural disadvantages as Hispanics, yet their rates of political participation are higher than those of Hispanics (Verba, Schlozman, and Brady 1995). The main reason for this difference rests in their unique political and historical experience in the United States. Blacks' history of slavery, segregation, and discrimination created a powerful collective or group identity that has been expressed in their political behavior (Dawson 1994). Blacks have a long history of using politics as a means to protect and advance their interests. While Hispanics have also suffered from discrimination and segregation (Hero 1992; Gutierrez 1995), their experiences are not comparable to the African American experience.

Thus, despite the structural barriers that both Blacks and Hispanics face, the political participation rates of Blacks are higher than those of Hispanics (and sometimes comparable to those of Anglos), due to the distinct racial experiences defining Black and Hispanic political identity in the United States. This difference presents Hispanics with yet another challenge: not only do they face structural disparities that are most apparent in the public education system and the labor market, but also they lack a strong and cohesive political identity based on race. Hispanics certainly did not undergo the same historical experiences as Blacks, so they do not share a long and unified history that produced a system of closely knit social and political networks or a definitive set of political elites and leaders that they can turn to. Unlike Blacks, most Hispanics do not use the pan-ethnic label of "Hispanic" as a shortcut in their political evaluations, decisions, and assessments.

POLITICAL KNOWLEDGE OF HISPANICS
AND ANGLOS IN 2000 AND 2004

Delli Carpini and Keeter's model culminates with the main variable of interest—that of political knowledge. The various indicators examined thus far lead us to predict that Hispanics' levels of political knowledge may be lower than those of Anglos. We begin with two different measures of political knowledge, using data from the 2000 and 2004 National Annenberg Election Surveys. These datasets allow us to quantify political knowledge and to look at how it differs for Hispanics relative to other racial and ethnic groups.[6] Our first measure of political knowledge is based on survey questions that asked respondents about "hard" political facts (e.g., Zaller 1992). For instance, respondents were asked to identify the office held by Dick Cheney, that a two-thirds majority is required in Congress to overturn a presidential veto, and so forth.[7] While this measure does not directly capture the behavioral aspects that Delli Carpini and Keeter include in their conceptualization of political knowledge, it indirectly captures them, since individuals who are politically interested and involved would also be more likely to know that Dick Cheney is the vice president of the United States than would those with little interest in politics.

As we see in the bottom panel of table 4.1, this measure of political knowledge depicts Anglos' political information scores as somewhat higher than those of Hispanics in both 2000 and 2004. In 2000 the general political knowledge score for Hispanics was 0.8 relative to the Anglo score of 2.4; but in 2004 the gap narrowed considerably, with the average political information score at 4.1 for Anglos and 3.7 for Hispanics. These findings are consistent with previous scholarship that highlights the fact that the American electorate is not very knowledgeable about politics in general (e.g., Delli Carpini and Keeter 1996), and while this measure indicates that Anglos' knowledge in 2004 was greater than Hispanics', it was only marginally so.

Our second approach to measuring political knowledge using the NAES 2000 and 2004 data is to examine the number of times

[6]There is a lively academic literature on the measurement of political knowledge. For some reviews of the literature, see Zaller 1992 (especially his "Measures Appendix"), Delli Carpini and Keeter 1993, Mondak 1999, and Barabas 2002. However, there has not been a great deal of study about whether generic measures like these are adequate for studying the political knowledge of subpopulations of the electorate like Hispanics; this is an area ripe for new research.

[7]Specifically, we use the following questions from the 2004 Annenberg survey: cMC01 ("Do you happen to know what job or political office is now held by Dick Cheney?"); cMC03 ("Who has the final responsibility to determine if a law is constitutional or not? Is it the president, the Congress, or the Supreme Court?"); cMC05 ("How much of a majority is required for the U.S. Senate and House to override a presidential veto?"); cMC07 ("Do you happen to know which party has the most members in the United States House of Representatives?"); and cMC09 ("Which one of the parties would you say is more conservative on the national level?").

that a respondent was able to correctly identify a candidate's issue position on seven possible issues (e.g., Bartels 1986; Alvarez 1997). These policy areas include George W. Bush's and John Kerry's positions on health care, social security, tax cuts, and so on.[8] Exhibiting the same pattern as our other measure of political information, we find that in both 2000 and 2004, the mean political knowledge scores of Hispanics are lower than those for Anglos. Consistent with the other measure as well, we find that in 2000 the gap between the political knowledge of Hispanics and Anglos is greater than in 2004. In 2000, political knowledge as measured by the number of correct answers regarding the positions of the two presidential candidates was 2.5, relative to the Anglos' score of 6.0. But in 2004, Anglos' mean scores are somewhat higher than those of Hispanics (2.9 versus 2.5). Again, while Anglos' overall scores are greater than those of Hispanics, the difference in 2004 is quite modest. Notice that the number of Hispanics interviewed in 2000 is almost three times as large as the number of Hispanics interviewed in 2004; this may have also contributed to the difference in political knowledge from these two time periods. Moreover, perhaps measuring political knowledge in this factual manner goes above and beyond what the "average" voter knows about politics, regardless of the individual's racial/ethnic background. A better measure might combine factual knowledge of politics and the candidates' issue positions with rates of political activity and interest. Such a measure might suggest that Hispanics are less politically knowledgeable than Anglos.

[8]Our political knowledge variable is based on a respondent's ability to correctly identify the presidential candidate's issue position based on sixteen questions. Respondents were asked whether Kerry or Bush favors: (1) reducing the number of frivolous lawsuits; (2) stem cell funding; (3) an assault weapons ban; (4) making abortion more difficult; (5) the Patriot Act; (6) spending on Iraq and Afghanistan; (7) investing Social Security in the stock market; (8) Medicare prescription law; (9) reimporting drugs from Canada; (10) negotiating with drug companies; (11) making union organizing easier; (12) cutting the deficit in half; (13) eliminating overseas tax breaks to cut taxes for companies that create jobs; (14) eliminating overseas tax breaks to cut corporate taxes; (15) eliminating the estate tax; and (16) making Bush's tax cuts permanent. Anglos' responses ranged from zero to seven correct answers, while Hispanics' responses ranged from zero to six correct answers.

The 2000 NAES panel data also contained a detailed set of questions about the backgrounds of Bush and Al Gore, as well as their ideological positions. The 2000 NAES panel survey data allow for comparison of political knowledge, using these additional measures, across both race/ethnicity and time of the campaign. In other work, Abrajano (2010) has analyzed these data in detail; instead of reproducing that analysis here, we simply wish to focus on some of the important findings, because those results reinforce the analysis in this chapter.

When Abrajano looks at the knowledge of candidate backgrounds by race and ethnicity, typically the pattern that emerges is that Hispanics are generally less likely to answer these questions correctly, and are more likely to express no opinion than are either Anglos or Blacks. One excellent example of this phenomenon regards a question focused on a highly publicized event in the 2000 presidential campaign, when Bush gave a speech at Bob Jones University during the primary season. In the preelection wave of the NAES, most Anglos (52 percent) said that Bush was the candidate who spoke at Bob Jones University, as did 36 percent of Blacks. But 28 percent of Hispanics said that Bush gave that speech, 14 percent said it was Gore, and 43 percent of Hispanics did not give an answer to the question (32 percent of Anglos did not answer, and 38 percent of Blacks did not answer). None of these percentages changed much in the pre- and postelection comparison presented by Abrajano.

The data on candidate ideological placement in Abrajano (2010) are also of interest; as we discussed earlier, a variety of scholars have used candidate spatial placements to develop measures of voter knowledge of candidate issue and ideological positions (Bartels 1986; Alvarez 1997). Focusing only on the percentages of Hispanics, Anglos, and Blacks, Abrajano shows first that Hispanics were more likely to not provide a placement: in the preelection survey, 11.2 percent of Hispanics did not place Bush, and 12.2 percent did not place Gore. This compares to 5.4 percent for Anglos (for both Bush and Gore) and 4.7 percent for Blacks (again, for both Bush and Gore). In the postelection survey, the nonresponse rate for Hispanics regarding Bush drops to 3.6 percent, but the nonresponse rate for Gore rises to 10.5 percent. Abrajano (2010) shows that for both Anglos and Blacks, the nonresponse rate falls slightly with respect to the placement of both Bush and Gore.

MORE ANALYSIS OF HISPANIC POLITICAL KNOWLEDGE IN 2006

Since political knowledge has been found to be such an important mediating variable in political behavior, we provide in this section a more detailed analysis of Hispanic political knowledge using the most recent data available. The 2006 Latino National Survey lets us update the political knowledge and interest analysis, though only for Hispanics. In table 4.2 we provide an analysis of the 8,634 respondents in the LNS who answered the factual political knowledge and political interest questions in this survey.

Beginning with the factual political information questions, of which there are three in the LNS, we see a picture that is consistent with what we have shown in earlier analyses in this chapter: Hispanics in general are not well informed about politics. The first factual political question in table 4.2 asked Hispanic respondents which political party had a majority in the U.S. House; recall that the LNS survey was in the field from November 2005 through August 2006, and that it was only after the November 2006 election that the Democratic Party held a majority of seats in the U.S. House. With that in mind, we see that less than a majority of the Hispanic respondents in this survey (almost 41 percent) were correct in their answer; nearly 46 percent did not know the answer, and almost 14 percent said that the Democrats controlled the House.

The next factual question asked respondents which presidential candidate received the most votes in the 2004 presidential election. Again, only a minority was able to provide the correct answer to this question, with 37.7 percent saying that Bush won that election. Nearly 37 percent did not know the answer, and 21 percent said that Kerry won the 2004 election (the wrong answer).

Finally, the third factual political question we examine using the 2006 LNS asked which political party is more conservative. Here we take the correct answer to be the Republican Party, an answer provided by 36 percent of respondents. Thirty-eight percent said they did not know the answer, and 26 percent were of the opinion that the Democrats are the more conservative political party.

The 2006 LNS also included a series of political interest questions, and we provide the responses to those questions in the lower half of table 4.2. Here we see that nearly one-third of the respondents report not being interested in politics, around one-quarter report that they almost never or very infrequently watch television news, and 45 percent almost never read a newspaper. Clearly these data indicate that many Hispanics have little interest in politics and that many Hispanics are not exposed to mass media coverage of politics in the television news or newspapers. Finally, we also provide in table 4.2 data on whether respondents rely on English- or Spanish-language media sources; 45 percent of respondents rely on Spanish-language media only, while 24 percent rely upon both Spanish- and English-language media.

Unfortunately, at this point we really cannot compare the 2006 LNS data to any similar data for Anglos or Blacks. But even without the comparisons that we were able to produce for 2000 and 2004 using the Annenberg survey data, the 2006 LNS data do seem consistent with what we have seen throughout this chapter. Many Hispanics lack some important preconditions for being politically informed—many are simply not interested in politics, and many are not exposed to media news sources. Furthermore, when Hispanic respondents were asked factual political questions, the 2006 LNS data revealed that consistently at least one-third of the respondents did not know the answer, and even when they ventured an answer, another 15 to 25 percent provided the incorrect response.

CONCLUSION

When we use both census and survey data to assess Delli Carpini and Keeter's model of political knowledge, both point to the conclusion that Hispanics' levels of political knowledge are systematically lower than those of Anglos. These findings are also consistent with research from Verba, Schlozman, and Brady (1995), which finds a similar pattern in the rates of political participation

TABLE 4.2
Hispanic Political Knowledge and Interest

	% Hispanics Responding
Factual political knowledge*	
Which party has the majority in the U.S. House of Representatives?	
Democrats	13.7
Republicans	40.7
Don't know	45.6
Which presidential candidate had the most votes in 2004?	
Bush	37.7
Kerry	21.2
Don't know	36.6
Which political party is more conservative?	
Democrat	26.0
Republican	36.0
Don't know	38.0
Political interest	
Interest in politics and public affairs	
Not interested	30.0
Somewhat interested	44.7
Very interested	20.9
Don't know/refused	4.4
Frequency of watching television news	
Daily	62.5
Most days	12.9
Once or twice a week	16.8
Almost never	7.8
Frequency of reading the newspaper	
Daily	20.5
Most days	6.2
Once or twice a week	28.2
Almost never	45.1

TABLE 4.2 *(cont.)*

	% Hispanics Responding
Political interest *(cont.)*	
News source for information on politics and public affairs	
English	30.2
Spanish	45.0
Both	23.8
Other	0.9
N	8,634

Source: 2006 Latino National Survey.

*Of these respondents, 12 percent correctly answered one or more of these questions.

and knowledge for Anglos and Hispanics. As such, it is apparent that variations do exist in the levels of political knowledge of Hispanics and Anglos.

Because an individual's racial identity, structural opportunities, and levels of political knowledge are so closely linked to one another, Hispanics face several barriers in their ability to become as politically informed and aware as their Anglo counterparts. In 2000 and 2004, Anglos were more knowledgeable about Bush and Kerry's positions on such issues as abortion, gun control, and health care than were Hispanics. They were also more aware of "hard" political facts when compared to Hispanics. Our analysis of Hispanic responses to factual political questions in the 2006 LNS, as well as their responses to political interest and media exposure questions, further confirmed these findings. This is a troubling set of results, since political knowledge influences one's political behavior in a variety of ways—from an individual's ability to evaluate candidates to conditioning his or her susceptibility to political messages. While other research has shown that information shortcuts or heuristics are effective substitutes for large amounts of stored political knowledge when making political decisions (Popkin 1994; Lupia 1994; Lupia and McCubbins 1998), this result is contingent on shortcuts being readily available and useful. But as Abrajano (2010) points out, Hispanics

were exposed to a smaller proportion of meaningful and substantive informational shortcuts by way of Spanish-language
televised campaign advertisements than were non-Hispanics in
the 2000 campaign. And the most effective shortcut used by voters,
partisanship, might not work for Hispanics as it does for Anglos,
given that the research shows that the means by which Hispanics
acquire partisanship seem quite distinct (Alvarez and García
Bedolla 2003).[9] Thus, for Hispanics, any gains in political knowledge would be beneficial, since they are the ones who are most in
need of substantive political information. Better political information not only would allow them to increase their stored levels of
political knowledge, but also would enable them to behave in a
manner that is consistent with their political beliefs and values.

On a more positive note, Abrajano (2010) finds that personal
contact from campaigns positively affects Hispanics' political
knowledge levels. Considering that Hispanics' stored levels of
political information are lower than those of Anglos, information
provided by campaigns may be a good substitute for Hispanics'
lack of stored political information. However, it may not be a
perfect proxy, since parental socialization and formal education
are considered to have long-term effects (Converse 1961), whereas
campaign effects are found to be more short-term. As such, the
education system needs to be reformed in order to incorporate a
greater amount of civics and government classes into the curriculum, particularly for Hispanics who attend schools that predominantly comprise racial and ethnic minorities. From a political perspective, candidates and their campaigns would be well
served by devoting more of their efforts to personally contacting Hispanics and providing them with substantive information
about their policy platforms and positions.

While it is true that the political socialization process for recent
immigrants differs from the process experienced by their predecessors as well as nonimmigrants, this research suggests that alternative sources of political information may improve Hispanics' levels of political knowledge. The existing research on the
determinants of political knowledge may therefore need to be
reassessed as a result of the background and experiences of the
most recent additions to the American public.

[9]We discuss this point in much greater depth in chapter 6.

Voting Behavior

As WE HAVE DISCUSSED thus far, candidates and political parties are vying to understand and capture the Hispanic vote. Hispanics will make up 25 percent of the population by 2050, and because the rate of Hispanic immigration has been steadily increasing since 1975 (U.S. Census 2007), the preferences and political orientation of this particular electorate are constantly changing and emerging. Hispanics are concentrated not only in key battleground states but also in those with the largest number of electoral votes. Public opinion and survey research reveals that Hispanics' policy and issue concerns differ from those of non-Hispanics in ways that make them potentially subject to political messages from both the left and the right (Abrajano, Alvarez, and Nagler 2008); thus, how candidates campaign and reach out to Hispanics requires careful thought and evaluation.

The intersection of these factors reveals why recent presidential candidates of both major political parties have tried to understand the Hispanic vote—and why they have also placed special emphasis in recent presidential elections on developing specific Hispanic messages. Political parties also stand to benefit from understanding the factors that influence the way Hispanics cast their ballots, as Hispanics' allegiance to one particular party may not be as deeply rooted as the partisan affiliations of other racial and ethnic groups in American electoral politics, as the exit poll data we present in this chapter reveal.

As we have noted in earlier chapters, an important increase in the amount of research on Hispanic politics has taken place in the United States in the last two decades, driven to some extent by the strong growth of the Hispanic population in the United States. Little of this research has focused on how Hispanics vote in presidential elections. Other than our work with Jonathan Nagler, no other study has used typical theories of voting behavior to study Hispanic presidential voting behavior. Two studies (Welch and Sigelman 1993; Leal et al. 2005) have examined Hispanic voting behavior but have failed to include issue preferences in their analyses. The existing research has focused instead on elections at the state and local levels (Graves and Lee 2000; Cain and Kiewiet 1984; Abrajano, Alvarez, and Nagler 2005; Falcon 1989; Hero and Beatty 1989; Hill and Moreno 2005; Hajnal, Gerber and Louch 2002). A series of edited volumes also focuses on the Hispanic vote (de la Garza and DeSipio 1992, 1996, 2000, 2005), but these are state-by-state analyses that mainly look at mobilization and turnout.[1]

Despite the lack of studies of Hispanic voting behavior at the presidential level, the research literature on Hispanic partisanship gives us some leverage in understanding how issues may influence Hispanic political behavior. As we have noted in other work, in every presidential election for the past thirty years, the Democratic Party has won a solid majority of the votes of Hispanics and other racial minorities (Schmal 2004; Abrajano, Alvarez, and Nagler 2008). Hispanics might be more amenable to Democratic Party appeals for several reasons, one being the hypothesis that Democrats have traditionally been more sympathetic to minority groups and their interests (Cain, Kiewiet, and Uhlaner 1991). But even though Hispanic voters have generally supported the Democratic Party (De Sipio 1996; de la Garza and DeSipio 1992; Garcia and de la Garza 1977), scholars have argued that the partisan differences that exist in the Hispanic electorate are rooted in their country of origin. The historical experiences of Mexicans and Puerto Ricans in the United States has resulted in

[1]Moreover, recent reviews in the *Annual Review of Political Science* on Hispanic politics and ethnic politics (Segura 2006; de la Garza 2004) really only touch upon Hispanic voting behavior in the context of Hispanic voter willingness to support candidates based on shared ethnic identity, and these findings are limited to statewide samples. In our paper with Jonathan Nagler (Abrajano, Alvarez, and Nagler 2008), we conducted a comprehensive literature search on Hispanics or Hispanic voting using the Worldwide Political Science Abstracts (1972–2006). We found only eight refereed articles focusing on Hispanic voting behavior in presidential (1), Senate (1), congressional (1), mayoral (3), and statewide elections (2). We searched for the terms "Hispanic" or "Hispanic and Voting" and found 160 matches. Out of these articles, 8 focus on Hispanic voting behavior. There are three additional nonrefereed articles on the 2004 presidential election (Leal et al. 2005), the 2004 Los Angeles mayoral election (Sonenshein and Pinkus 2002), and the 2003 gubernatorial recall election in California (Barreto, Segura, and Woods 2004).

their support of the Democratic Party (Pycior 1997), while the experiences of Cubans has led to their support for the Republicans (Garcia 1996; Moreno 1997).

In addition to these historical and sociological theories, studies by Cain, Kiewiet, and Uhlaner (1991) and Alvarez and García Bedolla (2003) look to other hypotheses that can shed light on Hispanic party identification. Cain, Kiewiet, and Uhlaner (1991) find that Hispanic partisanship is best explained by the "minority group status hypothesis," which suggests that perceived economic discrimination experienced by Hispanics makes them more inclined to support the Democratic Party, since Democrats have traditionally advocated the interests of minority groups. They find little support for the "economic advancement" hypothesis, which contends that as Hispanics' economic status increases, the second and third generations are more likely to become Republicans than are first-generation Hispanics. Studying the 2000 presidential election, Alvarez and García Bedolla (2003) examined how political issues factor into Hispanic partisanship; they found little support for the hypothesis that Hispanic Democrats would "convert" to the Republican Party based on their pro-life position on abortion. But this does not imply that abortion, combined with other social issues, may not play a role in the vote decisions of Hispanics, either in the 2004 presidential election or in future elections. We also explore these issues briefly later in our postscript, where we discuss some preliminary results regarding the 2008 presidential election.

In this chapter, we explore Hispanic voting patterns in national general elections from 1992 through the most recent 2006 midterm election. We use exit poll data from each election, as these data provide us with a large number of observations based on interviews with real voters as they left the polling places on election day. Importantly, the large sample size of these exit polls also allows us to study large samples of Hispanic voters, as well as compare them with large samples of Anglo, Black, and Asian voters. Exit polls, unfortunately, do not typically include many of the detailed questions regarding issue preferences or political values that we use in other chapters. But for the purposes of this chapter, the exit poll data provide a wealth of information on the nature of Hispanic voter choice in recent national general elections.

Hispanic Voting Patterns, 1992–2006

To understand Hispanic voting preferences over the past decade, we present exit poll data on Hispanic, Anglo, Black, and Asian American voting behavior in presidential and midterm elections from 1992 through 2006. These surveys are conducted as registered voters leave the polling booths on election day and are sponsored by several news media organizations (e.g., ABC News, CBS News, NBC News, CNN).[2] Using these exit polls, we can study a consistent set of variables over a broad range of recent national elections in the United States. We examine voter choice by race/ethnicity, as well as by ideology, partisanship, evaluations of personal finances and the state of the national economy, and level of education. We present this information in tables 5.1–5.8.

Voting Patterns by Race and Ethnicity

To give us a general sense of the voting behavior of the major racial/ethnic groups in the United States, figure 5.1 presents voters' level of support for the Democrats (either presidential or congressional candidates) from 1992 through 2006 by race/ethnicity.

Hispanics, with the exception of the 2004 presidential election, over this broad sweep of recent political history ranked second in their support for Democratic candidates. While Hispanic support for the Democrats remained fairly constant over this period of time, at an average of 61.8 percent, Hispanic support for the Democratic Party is clearly not on par with that of Blacks: in the 1992 presidential election, a gap of approximately 20 percent exists in the amount of support Hispanics and Blacks provided to Bill Clinton. By 1996, Hispanic support for Clinton increased by more than 10 percentage points to 71.7 percent, and he won the Hispanic vote over Bob Dole by a margin of more than 50 percent. Hispanics were also willing to support the Reform Party candidate, H. Ross Perot, though the percentage of Hispanics

[2]From 1992 through 2000, Voter News Service sponsored and conducted the exit poll surveys. From 2002 through 2006, Edison Media Research and Mitofsky conducted the surveys for the National Election Pool. For additional discussion of using exit poll data to study Hispanic vote choice in presidential elections, see Abrajano, Alvarez, and Nagler 2008.

supporting him dropped from 14.1 percent in 1992 to 5.5 percent in 1996.

In the 2000 presidential race, many were hopeful that Gore and the Democrats would be able to capitalize on Clinton's increased share of the Hispanic vote in 1996 and attract even more support from them. This, however, was not the case; Gore's share of the Hispanic vote dropped by 10 percentage points to 61.6 percent. Several academics, as well as the popular media, attributed this drop in support to the Elian Gonzalez affair of June 2000 and the manner in which the Clinton administration handled it (Hill and Moreno 2005). Prior to this event, Clinton had made significant inroads within the Cuban population in Florida. However, following what many believed to be a poorly executed plan by then attorney general Janet Reno and the U.S. Immigration and Naturalization Service to return Gonzalez to his family in Cuba, Cuban Americans supported Bush over Gore by a decisive margin. Hill and Moreno (2005) aptly characterized this election as a referendum on the Clinton administration's foreign policy decisions toward Cuba.

After the 2004 election, much debate ensued about the exact share of the Hispanic vote that went to Bush and to Kerry. According to the National Election Pool results, Bush won the support of 44 percent of the Hispanic electorate, marking the first time that any Republican presidential candidate had received more than 40 percent of the Hispanic vote. Additionally, an independent national exit poll conducted by the *Los Angeles Times* reported 45 percent of the Hispanic vote going to Bush. And while the National Annenberg Election Survey estimated this figure slightly lower at 41 percent, this still represented an increase of approximately 6 percentage points over the 2000 Annenberg estimate. Only the William C. Velasquez Institute's 2004 exit poll produced significantly distinct results from these three polls: it estimated Bush's share of the Hispanic vote to be approximately 35.1 percent.[3] These varying estimates have led to different interpretations

---

[3] Also adding fuel to the controversy was the fact that preelection telephone surveys had found Hispanic support for Bush to be below 40 percent. For example, a *Washington Post* survey from July 2004 had the race at 60 percent Kerry, 30 percent Bush, 2 percent Nader, and 8 percent undecided (Richard Morin and Dan Balz, "Kerry Has Strong Advantage Among Latino Voters," *Washington Post*, Thursday, July 22, 2004, A01, http://www.washingtonpost.com/wp-dyn/articles/A3368-2004Jul21.html [accessed July 8, 2008]).

TABLE 5.1
1992 Presidential Election Results, by Race/Ethnicity and Demographics

1992	White			Black			Hispanic			Asian		
	Clinton	Bush	Perot	Clinton	Bush	Perot	Clinton	Bush	Perot	Clinton	Bush	Perot
Overall	39.0	40.5	20.5	83.1	10.2	6.8	60.8	25.1	14.1	30.6	54.7	14.7
Ideology												
Liberal	34.0	7.4	19.3	31.6	26.1	29.7	31.3	18.9	24.7	23.2	9.1	17.0
Moderate	54.6	41.4	53.2	53.3	26.6	57.8	51.5	55.3	42.5	49.7	35.3	81.4
Conservative	11.4	51.2	27.5	15.1	47.3	12.6	17.1	25.8	32.8	27.1	55.6	1.6
Partisanship												
Democrat	64.9	9.1	25.9	84.0	32.9	37.7	74.9	9.4	27.8	67.2	20.6	11.3
Republican	9.4	68.3	32.1	2.6	38.6	18.4	4.9	68.0	21.0	1.6	55.4	9.5
Independent	25.6	22.6	42.0	13.3	28.5	43.9	20.3	22.6	51.2	31.2	24.0	79.3

Personal finances

Better	13.9	40.6	18.7	11.6	35.7	8.0	17.3	35.5	5.2	22.7	46.0	25.0
Worse	47.1	44.5	44.5	51.9	23.5	46.2	41.8	16.9	41.4	45.8	8.6	32.4
Same	39.1	36.8	36.8	36.6	40.8	45.7	40.9	47.6	53.4	31.6	45.5	42.6
National economy												
Excellent	1.1	0.9	0.4	1.3	3.8	3.3	2.2	0.0	0.0	0.0	0.0	15.9
Good	3.3	41.1	9.1	3.3	28.7	8.5	5.4	35.8	8.0	0.0	40.5	8.2
Not so good	47.8	47.9	50.0	42.1	50.2	41.3	51.5	55.0	59.7	52.4	44.6	34.4
Poor	47.9	10.1	40.5	53.3	17.3	46.9	40.9	9.2	32.3	47.6	14.9	41.5
Education												
No high school	7.9	5.1	6.7	10.5	5.6	6.3	20.9	4.1	3.3	5.5	5.4	15.9
High school degree	25.3	24.5	26.6	25.3	22.4	32.5	23.7	40.5	47.6	2.5	12.8	36.6
Some college or beyond	66.8	70.4	66.8	64.2	72.0	61.3	55.5	55.1	49.1	92.0	81.8	47.5
N	13,214			1,231			354			150		

Source: 1992 Voter News Service National Election Day Exit Poll, conducted by the Voter News Service.

Note: Cell entries that examine vote choice by ideology, partisanship, personal finances, views of the national economy, and education are weighted column percentages. Cell entries that present overall vote choice are weighted row percentages. Percentages may not add to 100 percent because of "don't know" or no responses.

TABLE 5.2
1994 Midterm Election Results (U.S. Senate and House),
by Race/Ethnicity and Demographics

1994	White		Black		Hispanic		Asian	
	Dem	Rep	Dem	Rep	Dem	Rep	Dem	Rep
Overall	41.9	55.9	88.7	10.0	60.6	33.9	59.9	37.8
Ideology								
Liberal	31.5	6.0	31.5	25.0	34.4	6.2	39.3	5.8
Moderate	53.4	37.3	49.8	36.2	44.5	41.4	53.3	50.5
Conservative	15.1	56.7	18.7	38.8	21.1	52.5	7.4	43.8
Partisanship								
Democrat	63.5	8.9	86.3	13.4	77.6	11.5	65.0	3.9
Republican	9.6	61.7	1.4	48.4	3.3	65.6	9.9	71.8
Independent	27.0	29.4	12.3	38.3	19.1	22.9	25.1	24.3
Personal finances								
Better	31.7	18.8	36.5	29.6	23.5	25.2	25.5	11.3
Worse	17.6	28.9	18.3	38.0	26.2	36.8	21.4	30.0
Same	50.7	52.3	45.2	32.3	50.3	38.0	53.1	58.7
National economy								
Excellent	3.5	0.7	3.5	0.0	1.7	0.0	4.7	0.0
Good	52.5	29.7	43.2	17.7	49.3	35.6	49.4	33.3
Not so good	38.6	54.9	44.8	66.4	35.0	57.3	30.8	43.6
Poor	5.4	14.7	8.5	15.8	14.0	10.8	15.1	23.1
Education								
No high school	6.0	4.3	8.4	24.8	19.7	7.4	4.0	4.8
High school degree	21.7	22.7	22.2	20.9	31.5	10.1	4.0	1.5
Some college or beyond	72.2	73.0	69.4	54.3	48.8	82.6	92.1	93.7
N	5723		481		202		97	

Source: 1994 Voter News Service National Election Day Exit Poll, conducted by the Voter News Service.

Note: Cell entries that examine vote choice by ideology, partisanship, personal finances, views of the national economy, and education are weighted column percentages. Cell entries that present overall vote choice are weighted row percentages. Percentages may not add to 100 percent because of "don't know" or no responses.

of the 2004 presidential election: did the Republicans make significant inroads with the Hispanic electorate, or was their apparent progress largely an artifact of their candidate, George W. Bush, and his relationship with Hispanics? Others have attributed these varying election results to the nonrepresentative sample of exit polls: Cubans may have been overrepresented in the sample, as may have Texan Hispanics.[4]

Hispanic support for the Democrats in the midterm elections does follow the same pattern as we see in presidential elections. Hispanics in the 1994 and 2006 elections were second only to Blacks in their level of support for the Democrats, but their level of Democratic support dropped in 1998 and 2002. While 60.6 percent of Hispanics in 1994 supported the Democrats, 56.4 percent voted for the Democrats four years later. This means that support for the Republicans increased to 36.3 percent in 1998. By the 2002 midterm election, we saw an increase in the amount of Democratic support from Hispanics, up 6.4 points to 62.8 percent.

As we discussed in earlier chapters, 2006 brought the issue of immigration reform to the forefront of the national debate, as a result of lawmakers' efforts to overhaul existing U.S. immigration laws. The bill put forth by House Republicans, H.R. 4437, drew considerable controversy, since it would have made assisting undocumented immigrants a felony with which the members of nonprofit organizations and charitable church groups would have been chargeable. Moreover, the proposed bill would have charged those who entered the United States illegally with having committed a felony.

Both political pundits and the media predicted that Hispanic participation in the immigration marches would boost their rates of turnout in the 2006 midterm election.[5] The results from this election suggest that this may have been the case. Democrats took 67.1 percent of the Hispanic vote, the largest percentage the

[4]This claim arose after the 2004 election, when a representative from NBC (a member of the exit poll media consortium) asserted at a public event that the national exit poll might have overrepresented Cubans in Miami-Dade County. An excellent overview of this debate appears in Suro, Fry, and Passel (2007), pages 11–15.

[5]Pew Hispanic Center Fact Sheet, "The Latino Electorate: An Analysis of the 2006 Election," July 24, 2007, http://pewhispanic.org/factsheets/factsheet.php?FactsheetID=34.

TABLE 5.3
1996 Presidential Election Results, by Race/Ethnicity and Demographics

1996	White			Black			Hispanic			Asian		
	Clinton	Dole	Perot	Clinton	Dole	Perot	Clinton	Dole	Perot	Clinton	Dole	Perot
Overall	43.4	45.6	9.2	83.7	12.0	3.6	71.7	21.0	5.5	43.0	47.8	7.8
Ideology												
Liberal	31.2	4.8	16.3	30.0	20.3	26.8	32.5	11.3	13.1	39.3	10.3	17.7
Moderate	56.3	37.0	51.5	52.5	38.3	45.9	51.6	37.5	62.7	55.1	58.2	78.1
Conservative	12.5	58.3	32.2	17.5	41.4	27.4	15.9	51.2	24.2	5.5	31.6	4.2
Partisanship												
Democrat	63.8	8.9	22.0	81.5	26.0	40.4	77.4	18.9	22.5	62.4	8.9	38.4
Republican	10.7	68.8	25.2	5.6	50.9	17.7	7.4	69.4	24.0	14.3	67.4	3.5
Independent	25.6	22.4	52.8	13.0	23.2	41.9	15.2	11.7	53.5	23.3	23.7	58.1
Personal finances												
Better	45.5	21.2	25.2	47.1	29.3	21.7	43.8	18.8	19.2	53.4	17.3	0.0
Worse	11.8	29.0	31.1	10.7	29.5	34.0	13.6	32.6	36.2	11.4	31.0	41.2
Same	42.8	49.8	43.7	42.2	34.0	44.3	42.7	48.6	44.6	35.2	51.7	58.8

National economy												
Excellent	6.5	1.4	1.1	5.8	9.0	7.8	2.3	6.9	6.5	7.1	5.4	0.0
Good	68.8	41.3	32.2	55.1	43.0	24.4	62.4	20.0	38.5	61.7	49.1	13.6
Not so good	22.1	48.0	49.2	32.2	37.5	35.0	31.9	52.6	45.6	31.2	41.5	86.4
Poor	2.6	9.4	17.4	6.9	10.5	32.8	3.4	20.6	9.4	0.0	4.0	0.0
Education												
No high school	7.0	4.2	7.1	8.2	9.6	8.5	13.0	10.3	8.1	6.3	2.2	16.0
High school degree	23.6	20.9	32.2	27.2	27.7	32.4	32.6	21.1	41.5	19.7	4.5	20.8
Some college or beyond	69.4	74.9	60.7	64.6	62.7	59.1	54.4	68.6	50.4	74.0	93.5	63.2
N	13,414			1,639			730			180		

Source: 1996 Voter News Service National Election Day Exit Poll, conducted by the Voter News Service.

Note: Cell entries that examine vote choice by ideology, partisanship, personal finances, views of the national economy, and education are weighted column percentages. Cell entries that present overall vote choice are weighted row percentages. Percentages may not add to 100 percent because of "don't know" or no responses.

TABLE 5.4
1998 Midterm Election Results (U.S. Senate and House),
by Race/Ethnicity and Demographics

1998	White		Black		Hispanic		Asian	
	Dem	Rep	Dem	Rep	Dem	Rep	Dem	Rep
Overall	42.3	55.3	78.3	11.9	56.4	36.3	59.5	37.7
Ideology								
Liberal	31.7	5.9	31.2	16.5	34.4	11.3	48.5	11.8
Moderate	57.1	88.5	53.9	42.1	53.9	42.4	40.4	46.4
Conservative	11.3	49.9	14.9	41.4	11.6	46.3	11.1	41.8
Partisanship								
Democrat	61.8	9.7	81.3	24.2	72.6	16.5	62.3	14.2
Republican	10.7	64.4	1.3	46.1	9.7	49.9	7.8	60.8
Independent	27.6	25.9	17.4	29.7	17.8	33.7	29.9	25.1
Personal finances								
Better	48.9	31.9	55.3	44.9	53.5	46.3	61.9	43.1
Worse	11.1	15.1	9.2	14.4	13.4	23.6	3.9	11.8
Same	40.0	53.0	35.5	40.7	33.1	30.0	34.2	45.1
National economy								
Excellent	21.6	8.4	21.6	8.4	27.7	10.2	23.5	19.3
Good	67.4	61.4	67.4	61.4	59.9	58.8	74.0	56.4
Not so good	9.5	20.5	9.5	20.5	11.2	26.3	2.5	23.1
Poor	1.5	9.7	1.5	9.7	1.3	4.7	0.0	1.2
Education								
No high school	5.5	4.6	7.3	8.8	6.5	7.0	0.0	0.0
High school degree	22.5	21.4	18.8	16.1	22.8	34.3	23.1	3.1
Some college or beyond	72.1	74.0	73.9	75.1	70.7	58.7	76.9	96.9
N	6786		793		436		112	

Source: 1998 Voter News Service National Election Day Exit Poll, conducted by the Voter News Service.

Note: Cell entries that examine vote choice by ideology, partisanship, personal finances, views of the national economy, and education are weighted column percentages. Cell entries that present overall vote choice are weighted row percentages. Percentages may not add to 100 percent because of "don't know" or no responses.

party won in the entire 1994–2006 period. In 1994, 60.6 percent of Hispanics voted for the Democrats. This figure dropped to 56.4 percent in 1998 and rose to 61.4 percent in 2002. So from 2002 to 2006, Democrats saw their support from the Hispanic electorate increase by approximately 6 percent. Whether this shift can be directly attributed to the immigration debate and the Republicans' proposals cannot be answered with this information alone. Overall, these patterns suggest that the Democrats' advantage among Hispanics is neither guaranteed nor consistent, particularly in light of Hispanics' decreased support for the Democratic candidate in the 2004 presidential election.

Turning to the voting patterns of Blacks, we see that they have consistently provided nearly universal support to the Democrats, reaching or exceeding 80 percent, across these eight election cycles. For example, in the 1992 presidential election, 83.1 percent of Blacks supported Clinton, and four years later, Blacks' support for Clinton increased to 83.7 percent. Al Gore captured an even larger share of the Black vote in 2000, with 89.9 percent supporting him. Little changed in the 2004 general election; 88.3 percent of Black voters cast their ballots for the Democratic candidate, John Kerry. Likewise, in midterm elections, 88.9 percent of Blacks supported the Democratic candidate in 1994, 78.3 percent in 1998, 88.5 percent in 2002, and 86.5 percent in 2006. Thus, more than any other racial/ethnic group, Blacks are clearly the strongest and most loyal supporters of Democratic candidates.

Asian American voters' support for Democratic candidates has ranged from a low of 30.6 percent in 1992 to a high of 59.9 percent in 1994. While Clinton gained a much larger share of the Asian American vote in the 1994 election, at 43 percent, than he did in 1992 when he won 30.6 percent, a plurality of Asian Americans still preferred Dole over Clinton and Perot in both of these presidential elections. But from 1998 through 2006, Asian American support for the Democrats has been constant at over 50 percent. In particular, note that their support for Democrats remained almost identical across the midterm election years (at approximately 59 percent), and that more than a majority of Asian Americans in 2004 cast their ballots for Kerry. This bodes well for the future of the Democratic Party, as the number of Asian immigrants to the United States has also been steadily increasing in the past twenty-five years (Wong 2006). If

TABLE 5.5
2000 Presidential Election Results, by Race/Ethnicity and Demographics

2000	White			Black			Hispanic			Asian		
	Gore	Bush	Nader	Gore	Bush	Nader	Gore	Bush	Nader	Gore	Bush	Nader
Overall	42.2	54.1	2.6	89.9	8.5	0.7	61.6	35.1	2.4	54.6	41.1	3.0
Ideology												
Liberal	35.4	5.1	44.4	29.9	7.0	25.8	35.4	9.2	42.4	37.7	4.9	41.5
Moderate	55.3	45.4	48.0	55.3	53.6	67.8	50.9	41.3	48.0	55.2	50.9	25.8
Conservative	9.3	49.5	27.6	14.8	39.4	6.5	13.7	49.5	9.6	7.1	44.2	32.7
Partisanship												
Democrat	63.9	8.5	23.3	86.0	20.2	44.3	79.1	14.9	23.0	72.3	6.1	31.1
Republican	6.7	65.9	12.1	2.5	39.6	23.8	5.0	62.9	18.8	0.9	66.9	10.2
Independent	25.1	12.1	51.7	9.0	31.3	22.6	11.7	18.5	42.0	21.1	21.5	39.1
Personal finances												
Better	64.0	36.7	43.2	64.3	48.2	26.5	60.2	35.6	42.8	71.4	58.0	8.7
Worse	7.3	13.7	13.7	5.2	20.1	11.8	12.5	15.1	21.4	4.2	4.8	18.7
Same	43.2	9.5	42.1	29.0	31.7	61.7	24.9	48.7	28.3	19.8	35.2	72.7

National economy												
Excellent	31.1	10.4	17.4	18.2	6.3	5.7	28.3	10.1	20.1	32.7	22.8	29.7
Good	61.9	72.2	63.4	63.1	59.4	82.5	54.2	57.6	58.0	56.3	60.8	70.3
Not so good	5.4	14.1	13.7	14.6	26.3	11.8	13.8	29.1	17.0	4.6	16.3	0.0
Poor	0.6	2.2	4.5	2.8	5.3	0.0	2.8	2.3	4.9	3.0	0.0	0.0
Education												
No high school	4.8	3.6	1.6	7.2	2.9	2.9	12.5	8.0	0.0	4.5	0.0	12.3
High school degree	21.3	21.8	9.8	23.5	21.2	29.4	25.4	24.7	13.4	5.6	4.9	26.4
Some college or beyond	73.8	74.5	88.6	69.3	75.9	67.7	62.1	67.3	86.6	89.9	95.1	61.3
N	10443			1255			842				224	

Source: 2000 Voter News Service National Election Day Exit Poll, conducted by the Voter News Service.

Note: Cell entries that examine vote choice by ideology, partisanship, personal finances, views of the national economy, and education are weighted column percentages. Cell entries that present overall vote choice are weighted row percentages. Percentages may not add to 100 percent because of "don't know" or no responses.

TABLE 5.6
2002 Midterm Election Results (U.S. Senate and House), by Race/Ethnicity and Demographics

1998	White		Black		Hispanic		Asian	
	Dem	Rep	Dem	Rep	Dem	Rep	Dem	Rep
Overall	39.5	57.3	88.5	9.0	62.8	34.7	61.4	35.8
Ideology								
Liberal	29.7	5.3	21.1	18.1	30.7	10.4	33.5	5.7
Moderate	57.1	40.0	58.8	50.9	56.3	41.7	54.0	57.3
Conservative	13.2	54.7	20.1	31.0	13.0	47.9	12.5	37.0
Partisanship								
Democrat	63.8	8.1	85.7	42.0	78.2	11.9	65.2	8.1
Republican	8.8	72.0	3.1	29.5	5.5	71.9	8.3	69.4
Independent	27.3	19.9	11.2	28.5	16.3	16.3	26.4	22.5
Personal finances								
Better	19.2	37.7	23.1	31.5	28.2	43.3	23.1	31.9
Worse	40.3	21.7	30.7	36.6	31.9	22.5	41.4	6.2
Same	40.0	40.0	44.9	31.6	39.8	34.1	35.4	62.0
National economy								
Excellent	1.0	1.7	0.8	1.1	3.7	1.9	0.0	0.0
Good	23.6	54.1	17.6	31.3	25.6	56.4	12.9	55.8
Not so good	56.2	39.7	61.9	58.6	55.4	34.0	71.7	43.4
Poor	18.1	3.5	18.7	9.1	14.0	7.1	13.2	0.8
Education								
No high school	3.3	5.6	6.5	4.8	16.9	7.2	4.1	0.0
High school degree	24.0	21.2	25.7	16.7	23.7	25.4	7.2	3.3
Some college or beyond	72.7	73.2	67.8	78.5	54.5	67.4	88.7	96.7
N	6728		920		478		49	

Source: 2002 National Election Pool.

Note: Cell entries that examine vote choice by ideology, partisanship, personal finances, views of the national economy, an education are weighted column percentages. Cell entries that present overall vote choice are weighted row percentages. Percentages may not add to 100 percent because of "don't know" or no responses.

TABLE 5.7
2004 Presidential Election Results, by Race/Ethnicity and Demographics

2004	White		Black		Hispanic		Asian	
	Kerry	Bush	Kerry	Bush	Kerry	Bush	Kerry	Bush
Overall	40.9	58.1	88.3	11.0	53.3	44.0	56.0	43.7
Ideology								
Liberal	39.6	4.8	31.6	13.6	38.4	10.7	36.1	9.2
Moderate	52.2	39.9	51.7	39.1	44.1	37.4	55.4	32.0
Conservative	8.2	55.3	16.7	47.7	17.5	51.9	8.5	58.8
Partisanship								
Democrat	63.5	6.6	83.2	30.7	69.4	12.6	51.8	5.8
Republican	5.7	69.4	2.4	35.5	5.2	63.2	9.7	62.3
Independent	26.6	20.4	11.9	26.2	19.0	16.5	33.5	29.0
Personal finances								
Better	12.5	49.7	12.0	38.9	17.8	56.9	16.3	69.9
Worse	45.0	10.5	47.7	21.1	39.5	9.8	42.4	6.7
Same	41.0	38.9	38.1	37.8	41.3	30.6	38.0	23.5
National economy								
Excellent	0.4	6.7	1.4	12.4	3.3	8.2	5.4	15.5
Good	11.3	72.9	15.2	48.7	6.5	70.0	8.4	41.3
Not so good	53.0	16.9	49.8	30.0	63.1	19.7	55.7	40.0
Poor	33.9	1.9	33.4	7.9	26.4	2.1	25.0	3.2
Education								
No high school	3.3	3.5	5.7	5.4	8.3	9.7	3.2	0.0
High school degree	20.2	21.8	27.8	24.7	21.3	27.1	12.6	15.5
Some college or beyond	76.5	74.7	66.5	69.9	70.4	63.3	84.2	84.5
N	10,417		1547		1121		207	

Source: 2004 National Election Pool, conducted by Edison Media Research and Mitofsky International.

Note: Cell entries that examine vote choice by ideology, partisanship, personal finances, views of the national economy, and education are weighted column percentages. Cell entries that present overall vote choice are weighted row percentages. Percentages may not add to 100 percent because of "don't know" or no responses.

TABLE 5.8
2006 Midterm Election Results (U.S. Senate and House), by
Race/Ethnicity and Demographics

2006	White		Black		Hispanic		Asian	
	Dem	Rep	Dem	Rep	Dem	Rep	Dem	Rep
Overall	47.3	45.9	86.5	11.0	67.1	27.7	61.2	31.9
Ideology								
Liberal	34.6	4.4	27.5	10.3	34.1	11.0	33.3	10.4
Moderate	56.2	39.4	40.6	37.2	51.4	35.5	59.1	34.6
Conservative	10.4	56.2	17.3	52.5	14.5	53.5	7.6	55.1
Partisanship								
Democrat	60.3	5.3	81.9	24.4	76.8	10.0	51.3	6.8
Republican	8.2	72.2	2.2	47.7	4.6	67.9	6.3	69.5
Independent	26.8	19.0	13.4	23.8	14.8	17.5	36.4	23.7
Personal finances								
Better	15.7	47.0	14.0	38.1	15.8	52.5	19.6	39.9
Worse	35.2	11.1	43.3	21.9	34.7	11.2	23.2	16.8
Same	48.7	41.2	42.0	38.6	49.1	35.8	54.6	43.3
National economy								
Excellent	1.8	17.7	2.5	18.2	5.5	17.4	1.2	19.1
Good	26.2	58.8	15.2	48.5	24.3	47.2	33.0	46.4
Not so good	51.6	19.3	57.2	23.7	51.2	21.5	44.6	34.6
Poor	19.4	3.3	23.9	9.1	17.8	8.5	18.5	0.0
Education								
No high school	2.7	2.1	6.7	6.7	11.8	5.8	0.0	3.4
High school degree	20.2	19.4	27.1	17.4	26.2	13.1	6.4	6.6
Some college or beyond	77.1	78.5	66.2	75.9	62.0	81.1	93.6	90.0
N	7609		915		873		183	

Source: 2006 National Election Pool Survey, conducted by Edison Media Research and Mitofsky International.

Note: Cell entries that examine vote choice by ideology, partisanship, personal finances, views of the national economy, and education are weighted column percentages. Cell entries that present overall vote choice are weighted row percentages. Percentages may not add to 100 percent because of "don't know" or no responses.

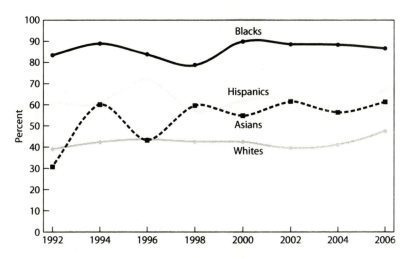

FIGURE 5.1: Democratic vote share of the two-party vote, by
race and ethnicity (1992–2006)

immigration remains a salient issue in upcoming years, and if
Democrats continue to take a strong stand in support of liberal
immigration policies, they may be able to secure the allegiance of
Asian American voters.

Finally, we see that Anglo support for Democratic candidates
has consistently been the lowest among the racial/ethnic groups
in this time period. In fact, the Anglo share of the Democratic
vote has never exceeded 50 percent in these eight election cycles.
For example, in the 2004 presidential election, 58.1 percent of Anglos supported Bush, while 40.9 of Anglos voted for Kerry. In the
election cycles that we examine, in only one other instance—the
1992 race, in which 39.5 percent of Anglos voted for Clinton—
was Anglo support for the Democratic presidential candidate
lower. These levels of support give the Democratic Party even
more reason to mobilize and secure the votes of Hispanics and
Asian Americans. Considering the rapid and continuing growth
of these two immigrant groups, Democrats may consider investing in a campaign strategy that targets these voters and estab-
lishes them as a solid base of the Democratic Party that can be
expected to vote reliably Democrat, as African Americans have
been for the past fifty years.

Voting, Political Ideology, and Partisanship

Early models of voting behavior focused on the political party that individuals affiliate themselves with, along with voters' political ideology, as the main variables guiding voters' decisions in national elections in the United States (e.g., Downs 1957; Campbell et al. 1964). Though a sizeable segment of both the Hispanic and Asian American populations are recent newcomers to the United States, which means that their political socialization process differs from native-born Americans, their voting patterns based on their partisanship and political ideology are quite similar to those of Anglos and Blacks. That is, individuals who identify as Democrats and Republicans lend the majority of their support to their respective candidates, while liberals tend to favor Democrats and conservatives support Republican candidates.

We find such patterns to be true in both the presidential and midterm elections. For instance, in the 1992 election, 84 percent of Black Democrats supported Clinton, compared to 74.9 percent of Hispanic Democrats and 67.2 percent of Asian American Democrats. With respect to support for Republicans, we see that Anglo Republicans were most supportive of Bush, followed by Hispanics, Asians, and Blacks. In this same election, H. Ross Perot drew considerably more support from Hispanic independents than did Clinton and Bush combined (51.2 percent versus 44.9 percent). This was true also for Anglos, Blacks, and Asian Americans who considered themselves independent. Among Anglos, a larger percentage of those who thought of themselves as liberals supported Bush (54.6 percent) than did the other racial/ethnic groups. In this same vein, a much greater percentage of Anglo conservatives, 51.2 percent, supported Bush than did Black conservatives (47.3 percent). We also see a gap in support for Bush between Anglo conservatives and Hispanic conservatives (25.4 percent). This finding suggests that Hispanic conservatives may not link ideology as closely to presidential vote choice as do Anglos or Blacks. Note that Bush's share of votes from Hispanic moderates was larger than it was for Clinton and Perot. Among Anglos, Clinton gained more support from moderates than did Bush or Perot, yet among Blacks and Asian

Americans, Perot gained more support from moderates than did Bush or Clinton.

The 1994 midterm election revealed many of the same patterns of voter preferences as did the election of 1992. More than 60 percent of Hispanics and 88.7 percent of Blacks supported the Democrats, while only 41.9 percent of Anglos voted for the Democratic candidates. Asian Americans also favored Democrats over Republicans, at 59.9 percent versus 37.8 percent. Consistent with their traditional voting patterns, Blacks supported Democratic candidates to a much greater extent than did Anglos, Hispanics, and Asian Americans. Blacks and Hispanics who identified as Democrats voted for the Democratic candidate at higher rates than did Asian American and Anglo Democrats. Anglos, Hispanics, and Asian Americans who identified as Republicans supported Republican candidates to a greater degree than did Republican-identified Blacks or other Republicans. Ideological preferences also guided voters' support for either the Democratic or Republican candidates, with moderates casting more of their votes for the Democrats, irrespective of their race or ethnicity. Moderate Hispanics were almost evenly divided in their support of Republicans and Democrats, with a slight edge going to the Democrats, at 44.5 percent versus 41.4 percent. But among Black, Anglo, and Asian American voters who considered themselves moderates, Democratic candidates gained a much wider share of the vote.

Voting preferences in 1996, based on ideology and partisan preferences, were consistent with traditional theories of voting behavior: Democrats favored Clinton over Dole, while most of the conservative voters supported Dole to a greater extent than Clinton or Perot. Among Anglos who identified themselves as independents, 52.8 percent voted for Perot, while 41.9 percent of Black independents, 53.5 percent of Hispanic independents, and 58.1 percent of Asian American independents supported Perot. Thus, irrespective of their racial or ethnic background, independents primarily supported the independent candidate, Ross Perot.

Turning to consider the 2000 election results sorted in terms of voters' ideological and partisan preferences, we see that Gore received a greater share of moderates' votes, regardless of their racial/ethnic background, than did Bush. Gore also captured a larger percentage of support from moderate Anglos, Asian Americans, and Hispanics than did Ralph Nader. Black voters who identified themselves as moderates, however, tended to cast their ballots for Nader: 67.8 percent voted for Nader, while only 55.3 percent of Black moderates supported Gore. These patterns suggest that Anglos, Hispanics, and Asian American voters who registered as independents were more supportive of Nader than Gore or Bush. But a larger percentage of Black independents supported Bush (31.3 percent) than Nader (22.6 percent). This pattern implies that the correspondence between party identification and choice of candidate may be slightly weaker for Blacks than for the rest of the American electorate.

If we take a closer look at 2004 Hispanic voting preferences as shaped by political orientation and economic attitudes, we find that a larger percentage of Hispanic moderates supported Kerry than did Hispanic liberals, at 44.1 percent versus 38.4 percent. But for those who cast their ballots in favor of Bush, the majority considered themselves to be conservatives (51.9 percent), and more than one-third, 37.4 percent, identified as moderates. Hispanics' partisan preferences once again corresponded to their vote choice, with 69.4 percent of Hispanic Democrats voting for Kerry and 63.2 percent of Hispanic Republicans supporting the incumbent, Bush. Among Hispanic independents, Kerry had a slight edge over Bush: 19 percent of Kerry's vote share was from independent Hispanics, while only 16.5 percent of Bush's share of the Hispanic vote came from Hispanics registered as independents.

Hispanics' partisan and ideological differences also continued to have an important impact on their voting behavior in 2006. Democrats won the majority of their support from Hispanic moderates, while 53.5 percent of Republican supporters considered themselves to be ideologically conservative. Party affiliation also dictated voters' decision to vote for either the Democrats or Republicans: of those Hispanics who cast their ballots for the Democrats, more than three-fourths registered as Democrats, whereas 67.9 percent of Hispanics who were registered as Republicans voted for Republican candidates. Republicans had a slight edge among independent Hispanics, with 17.5 percent supporting them and 14.8 percent of Hispanic independents voting for the Democrats.

VOTE CHOICE AND PERSONAL FINANCES

How did voters' assessments of their personal finances and the national economy factor into their vote decision? Like the rest of the American electorate, and in line with the theory of retrospective voting, Hispanics reward the incumbent administration so long as they evaluate the state of the national economy positively, but they punish it when they feel that the economy is not performing very well (e.g., Kiewiet 1983). The same pattern occurs with respect to one's pocketbook, or personal finances, so that individuals with improved personal finances generally supported the incumbent administration/party, while those who perceived their personal economic situation as worse tended to support the challenger. Notice that in the 2000 presidential election, Hispanics who viewed their pocketbook finances to be better than they had been a year before rewarded the incumbent administration by casting a larger percentage of votes for Gore; this was the case for all four racial/ethnic groups. For example, 60.2 percent of Hispanics who considered their personal finances to have improved from the year before supported Gore, whereas only 35.6 percent and 42.8 percent of Hispanics with improved finances voted for Bush and Nader, respectively. Evaluations of the national economy were generally positive in this election year. A strong majority of Anglos ranked the national economy as "good," with a larger percentage of those holding this view supporting Bush over Gore and Nader (72.2 versus 61.9 and 63.4 percent, respectively). A majority of Hispanics shared this same economic assessment with Anglos, but 28.3 percent of Hispanics who perceived the national economy as excellent cast their ballots in support of Gore, 20.1 percent for Nader, and only 10.1 percent supported Bush. And Hispanics who viewed the economy as "not so good" preferred Bush to Nader and Gore.

In cases in which individuals were more pessimistic about their personal finances or the national economy, the incumbent administration typically suffered. For those elections in 1992, 1996, 2000, and 2004, the nonincumbent candidate won over a larger percentage of Hispanic voters who saw their personal finances as worse than they had been a year before. We observe the same pattern for Anglos, Blacks, and Asian Americans. As exemplified by the 1992 presidential race, Clinton won a larger percentage of Hispanic votes from those who thought that the national economy was poor (40.9 percent) than did Perot (32.3 percent) and Bush (9.2 percent). We see the same trend for the other racial/ethnic groups in this election year.

But in 2004, less optimistic evaluations of the economy led Hispanics to cast a larger percentage of their ballots for Kerry than for Bush. Of those Hispanics who supported Bush, more than a majority (56.9 percent) felt that their personal finances had improved from the previous year. In comparison, only 17.8 percent of those who voted for Kerry evaluated their personal finances in this manner. Instead, most of Kerry's Hispanic supporters felt that their personal finances were the same as they had been in the previous year (41.3 percent). In terms of Hispanics' opinions about the national economy, we see that Bush gained most of his support from Hispanics with good economic evaluations, whereas Kerry's support largely came from Hispanics who felt that the economy was "not so good." This pattern is similar to those for the past two presidential elections.[6]

In a more detailed analysis of similar exit poll data, we have studied the voting decisions of Hispanic voters relative to Anglo voters in the 2004 presidential election and reached similar conclusions (Abrajano, Alvarez, and Nagler 2008). There, we found that retrospective economic evaluations played an important role in the 2004 presidential election for Hispanic voters, as did traditionally important issues like health care and education. But we also found that Hispanic voters were strongly affected in their voting behavior by both moral value issues (like abortion and gay marriage) and by foreign policy issues (the Iraq War and national security). In fact, it may be that this unique set of issue appeals was what drove the observed increase in the percentage of Hispanic voters who cast ballots for the Republican presidential candidate in the 2004 presidential election.

Perceptions of the national economy during midterm elections also affected the way in which individuals cast their ballots. To illustrate this point, voters in 1994 who viewed the national economy as being good supported the incumbent administration, the

[6]One exception worth mentioning pertains to Asian Americans in the 1996 presidential election: of those who supported Perot, 86.4 percent perceived the national economy as being "not so good."

Democrats, to a much greater extent than they supported the Republicans. Those who perceived the national economy as "not so good," however, were more supportive of the Republicans than of the Democrats. In terms of the effect of pocketbook finances, a greater percentage of Anglos, Blacks, and Asian Americans who perceived their personal finances as better than they had been a year earlier supported the Democratic over the Republican candidate. But Hispanics who felt that their finances had improved from the previous year threw their support to Republican candidates to a slightly greater extent (25.2 percent) than to Democratic candidates (23.5 percent). Interestingly, a majority of Anglos and Asians who felt their financial situation was the same as it had been a year earlier lent their support to the Republicans, while similarly situated Hispanics and Blacks voted for the Democrats.

Voters' perceptions of the national economy in the 1998 election, however, did not dictate their vote choices as much as they had in 1994. Among Anglos, for instance, 60.4 percent of those who supported the Democrats rated the national economy as good, while an almost equal number of those who voted for Republicans, 61.4 percent, also evaluated the national economy as good. But in the previous midterm election, the majority of Anglos (54.9 percent) who supported the Republicans had felt that the economy was not doing well, while the majority of Anglos voting for the Democrats had rated the national economy as good (52.5 percent). We see a similar pattern for both African American and Hispanic voters. With respect to the impact of personal finances on the vote, though, the same trend held in 1998 as in the previous midterm election, as well as in the presidential elections: the majority or plurality of those whose personal finances had improved from the previous year supported the incumbent administration, but those whose financial picture had darkened tended to support the Republicans.

In the most recent midterm elections of 2006, economic evaluations at both the national and pocketbook level also influenced Hispanic voters. Hispanics who felt that the national economy was not doing very well favored the Democrats over the Republicans by more than 25 percent. On the other hand, Hispanics who perceived the national economy to be healthy provided more support to Republican than to Democratic candidates. With respect to personal finances, almost a majority of Hispanics who voted for the Democrats viewed their finances to be the same as they had been in the previous year. More than a majority of Hispanics who supported the Republicans, 52.5 percent, assessed their personal finances as being better than they had been the year before.

Vote Choice and Education

Demographic attributes, such as education, have long been argued to be an important factor in explaining vote choice (e.g., Lazarsfeld, Berelson, and Gaudet 1944). Here, we are particularly interested in understanding the relationship between race and education on vote choice from 1992 through 2006. Overall, a number of notable patterns emerge. Prior to the 2004 presidential election, the exit poll data typically show that of those Hispanic voters supporting Democratic candidates, they usually possessed lower levels of educational attainment than Hispanic voters supporting Republican candidates (who tended to have higher levels of educational attainment). The 2004 presidential election is the one election where we do not see this particular pattern, suggesting again that specific Republican appeals to certain segments of the Hispanic electorate might have been particularly effective. When we look at Anglo, Black, and Asian voters across this span of elections, it appears that the association between educational attainment and partisan vote choice is quite similar across all of the racial and ethnic groups.

Conclusion

Our analysis of the presidential and midterm elections taking place from 1992 through 2006 provided several important insights. Hispanic voters, just like the rest of the American electorate, cast their ballots according to the major theories of voting behavior: that is, partisanship and political ideology matters, as do voters' evaluations of both the national economy and their own personal finances. Thus, when assessing the voting behavior of Hispanics, we can say with certainty that their voting patterns follow the same general trend as those of Anglos, African

Americans, and Asian Americans. Nonetheless, some subtle variations in the factors influencing the way Hispanics cast their ballots exist. For instance, Hispanic moderates tend to be more supportive of Democratic candidates than Anglos who identify as moderates. Moreover, while Hispanics are most definitely partisans, their partisanship does not appear to be as strong as that of Blacks and Anglos. In particular, given the manner in which Hispanics are being socialized into American politics, their partisan attachments may not be as stable as those of the Anglo electorate (Campbell et al. 1964; Miller and Shanks 1996). Thus, short-term forces such as campaigns and direct issue appeals may shape Hispanic partisanship to a greater extent than for other voters.

What does the future hold for Hispanic voters? Will one party gain a strong foothold with Hispanic voters, or will future elections be up for grabs? The answers to these questions depend on the way in which both presidential and congressional candidates campaign and appeal to the Hispanic electorate, and on which issues they choose to emphasize. Currently, it appears that the issue of immigration is not disappearing from the national debate. Thus, if Republicans continue to be perceived as anti-immigrant, Democrats may be able to secure 60 percent or more of the Hispanic electorate in the years to come.

On the other hand, Republicans may be able to overcome their party's position on immigration by appealing to Hispanics on other issues, such as social and moral values—particularly in light of the growing number of Protestant evangelicals within the Hispanic community (Pew Hispanic Center 2007). While it is virtually impossible to predict the outcome of the future of immigration policy in the United States, it is clear that Hispanic voters will remain key players in both presidential and midterm elections.

Intergroup Relations and Coalition Building

THE EMERGENCE of minority candidates onto the urban political scene has occurred only within the last thirty to forty years in the predominantly large urban centers of Chicago, New York, Philadelphia, San Antonio, and Los Angeles (Betancur and Gills 2000a; Sonenshein 1997; Munoz and Henry 1986). Hispanic mayors have been elected in important large cities like Denver, Los Angeles, and San Antonio; Blacks have been successful in Chicago, New York, Philadelphia, and Los Angeles. Electing Blacks and Hispanics into office has been achieved through what Browning, Marshall, and Tabb (1984) and others refer to as a "rainbow coalition." The classic view of a rainbow coalition (Browning, Marshall, and Tabb 1984) holds that the likelihood of electing ethnic and racial minorities into office improves with the formation of coalitions with minority groups (e.g., Blacks and/or Hispanics) and liberal Anglos. Given that Blacks and Hispanics share many commonalities in terms of their life circumstances—e.g., both are economically disadvantaged when compared to Anglos—the assumption is that their political interests will also overlap (Kaufman 2003).

Creating these rainbow coalitions enables Hispanics and Blacks to increase their electoral presence as well as promote policies salient to racial and ethnic minorities. Scholars have cautioned that the decision not to form such coalitions may disadvantage racial and ethnic minorities, because it runs the risk of government coalitions being dominated by conservative Anglo politicians, which could result in policies adverse to minority interests.

With the growth of other immigrant groups in the United States, particularly those of Asian origin, minority coalitions can no longer be conceived of as those that occur only between Blacks and liberal Anglos, or among Blacks, Hispanics, and liberal Anglos. In certain U.S. cities, the most feasible minority coalitions are between Hispanics and Asian Americans or a combination of Hispanics, Asian Americans, and liberal Anglos. For example, in

Monterey Park, California, a city just east of Los Angeles and known to many as America's first suburban Chinatown (Horton 1995), Asian Americans make up the majority of the city's inhabitants (61.8 percent), while Hispanics make up almost one-third of the population, 28.9 percent.[1] In a city in which more than 90 percent of its residents are non-Anglo, it would seem that a political coalition based on minority group interests would be relatively easy to develop and maintain. Yet as we will discuss in greater depth later on this chapter, such matters are not that easy or straightforward.[2] Because politics is inextricably linked to power, sacrificing or compromising one's share of the political pie becomes a contentious issue, particularly if a group is a relative newcomer to the political scene (García Bedolla 2005). Moreover, the concept of "perceived social distance" (Bogardus 1928) contends that the extent to which racial and ethnic minorities interact and socialize with one another depends on their perceptions and attitudes of the group in question. The research applying social distance theory to racial and ethnic groups finds that Hispanics feel the most socially compatible with Anglos, and the least socially compatible with Blacks (Dyer, Vedlitz, and Worchel 1989).[3] So despite the theoretical appeal and simplicity of the rainbow coalition, in practice, intergroup relations and minority coalitions are more complex affairs.

Our aim in this chapter is to examine the conditions under which minority coalitions are likely to form and endure. As Kaufmann (2003) contends, racial and ethnic groups must share a similar set of political beliefs and experiences, such as encounters with discrimination and identifying as a minority group, in order to sustain a political coalition. We draw on recent survey data to determine Hispanics', Blacks', Anglos', and Asian Americans' attitudes toward one another, particularly with respect to issues of

---

[1] These percentages are from the U.S. Census Bureau (2000) estimates.

[2] See Horton (1995) for an extensive discussion of the political dynamics in Monterey Park, California.

[3] These attitudes, however, can vary according to a group's socioeconomic status. When Anglos and Hispanics share similar socioeconomic conditions, the likelihood of forming a coalition with Blacks is low (Meier and Stewart 1991; Kaufmann 2003). Likewise, Blacks may find it more advantageous to form coalitions with Anglos in situations in which Hispanics' socioeconomic capital is low (Randall and Delbridge 2005).

group commonality. Again, this comparative perspective advances the existing work on intergroup relations, because much of the previous work has typically focused on biracial political coalitions (e.g., Blacks and Hispanics). In our increasingly multiracial and multiethnic society, understanding the prospects for racial and ethnic political cooperation is an important and salient issue not only for today but also for years to come.

HISPANIC–BLACK RELATIONS

Traditionally, Blacks and Hispanics have been viewed as "natural" coalition partners in both the electoral and the political arena. This expectation primarily stems from their relatively similar status in terms of socioeconomics and life chances. The classic study by Browning, Marshall, and Tabb (1984) of ten California cities finds evidence of such coalition-based Black and Hispanic minority representation in seven of the ten cities. Moreover, "whereas no Blacks or Hispanics served on city councils in 1960, by the late 1970s, minority council representation, on the average over all ten cities, was 55 percent of the minority population, with Blacks closer to parity than Hispanics" (242). Browning, Marshall, and Tabb also accounted for minority members participating in the coalitions that dominated city policymaking on minority-related issues. Mollenkopf (1994), however, is skeptical of this classical view and argues that broader and more complex coalitions, as opposed to the simple biracial coalitions discussed by Browning, Marshall, and Tabb, are necessary to ensure minority representation.

The increasing political and socioeconomic competition between Blacks and Hispanics has also generated friction between these groups in cities across the United States (Vaca 2004; Betancur and Gills 2000b; Sonenshein 1997; McClain and Karnig 1990; Munoz and Henry 1986). These political dynamics have led Blacks and Hispanics to be particularly vulnerable to the manipulations of those in power, who are typically Anglo (Betancur and Gills 2000b). To illustrate this point, Betancur and Gills suggest that Chicago's current mayor, Richard Daley, "visibly replaced disloyal Blacks with Hispanics who are royal to his regime." They continue: "Many Blacks think that Hispanics are being incorporated into government at their expense. Tensions are particularly high among Hispanic and Black elites competing for attention and benefits from local government" (34–35).

In addition to these political tensions, competition exists between Blacks and Hispanics at the socioeconomic level for public assistance, limited job opportunities, and control of local institutions (Betancur and Gills 2000a). As McClain and Karnig's (1990) study of forty-nine cities with sizeable Black and Hispanic populations reveals, Hispanics tend to be less successful both socioeconomically and politically when they reside in cities in which Blacks are either the majority or the plurality of the population. On a more positive note, however, Oliver and Wong (2003) find that Asian Americans, Anglos, Blacks, and Hispanics who reside in racially diverse neighborhoods are more racially tolerant than those living in less diverse communities. Individuals who live in these racially heterogeneous areas are also more likely to express shared and common goals with other racial groups than those who live in more homogeneous areas.

Despite the sources of tension just discussed, instances of successful biracial coalition building between Hispanics and Blacks have taken place. One case resulted in the election of Chicago's first Black mayor, Harold Washington. Betancur and Gills (2000b) point out, however, that this alliance was temporarily inspired by the "experience of exclusion and feeling of alienation and anger caused by years of monopoly power and racism by the local Democratic machine" (64). And since this alliance was based only on an electoral connection, a lasting coalition built on shared substantive interests did not endure. Thus, the main problem with Black–Hispanic coalitions, especially those that are created for electoral purposes, is that they can be temporary and are useful only when they serve the interests of each of the minority groups.

Hispanic–Asian American Relations

While less attention has been devoted to examining the relations between Hispanics and the other prominent minority group in the United States, Asian Americans, this relationship has become more important and relevant, particularly on the issue of immigration reform.

The existing work on Hispanic–Asian coalitions focuses on the electoral arena. Lai (1999) examines the voting patterns of Hispanics and Asians in the 1994 election of California's Forty-ninth Assembly District, which includes the city of Monterey Park, and as we mentioned in the introduction to this chapter, comprises mostly Hispanics and Asian Americans. The election pitted a Latina incumbent, Diane Martinez, against an Asian American challenger, Judy Chu. Although Chu possessed both strong name recognition and a previous record in the area, the incumbent won. Lai attributes Martinez's victory to the strong patterns of racially polarized voting between Hispanics and Asian Americans. Moreover, the Hispanic voting-age population was larger than the Asian American voting-age population.

In contrast, Saito's (1993) examination of Asian Americans and Hispanics in the same Los Angeles area provides a more optimistic picture of coalition building. He analyzes an Asian American organization that was established around the issue of redistricting and reapportionment. In this situation, Asian American and Hispanic organizations agreed to plans that protected the political interests of both ethnic groups; considering that this was a mutually beneficial agreement, it is not surprising that both Hispanics and Asian Americans were willing to work together. The studies by Lai and Saito point out two important realities of coalition building: coalitions are successful when shared interests are at stake, but they can suffer when they involve competition for elected representation.

CREATING LONG-TERM COALITIONS

As all of these studies demonstrate, group commonality and shared interests can serve as a basis for coalitions. But are shared values enough to hold groups together, especially when they are each fighting for power and a piece of the political pie? Kaufman (2003) addresses this question by arguing that the more Hispanics view their social, economic, and political opportunities as linked to the status of other minorities in the United States, the more likely it becomes that they will participate in minority-led political coalitions. Kaufman's work differs from other studies on coalition politics, since she examines the factors that contribute to durable—not temporary—coalitions and electoral alliances. The commitments that Blacks and Hispanics make toward one another in such alliances need to incorporate both symbolic and pragmatic components; Blacks and Hispanics are unlikely to engage in sustainable political coalitions if their perceptions of group commonality are low. Kaufman's argument is largely influenced by work on Black politics and the concept of "linked fate" (Dawson 1994), wherein Blacks' history of slavery, segregation, and discrimination created a powerful collective or group identity that has been expressed in their political behavior. This sense of linked fate has the ability to cut across class and social differences. Basing her argument on similar reasoning, Kaufman concludes that the more that racial and ethnic minorities in the United States share the concept of linked fate, the more likely they will be able to develop and maintain enduring political coalitions.

In testing this argument, Kaufman identifies four factors that influence the likelihood of creating a viable Hispanic–Black coalition: degree of Hispanic acculturation, level of pan-Hispanic affinity, amount of perceived discrimination against Hispanics, and perception of Hispanic racial identity. A more in-depth look at these four factors using 2006 survey data from the Pew Hispanic Center can help us to better understand the future prospects for minority-led coalitions.

Measuring the extent to which the first factor, acculturation, has taken place requires determining whether Hispanics follow the assimilation model or the conflict hypothesis model. The latter model predicts that as immigrants become more aware of the social inequalities and discrimination that exist in the United States, and as they spend more time in the United States, they will become more likely to resist adopting the values and beliefs of the larger society.

The classic assimilation model, by contrast, predicts that with time, immigrants will begin to behave in accordance with American culture and society so that they "blend in," thereby weakening their ties to their native languages and cultures. As discussed in chapter 1, and as other studies have found (e.g., Shaw et al. 2000), Hispanics believe in the importance of adopting the core values and culture of American society: 72.2 percent of Hispanics think that it is either very important or somewhat important for Hispanics to change in order to blend into larger society. Moreover, recall that most Hispanics support the need to speak English, vote in U.S. elections, believe in the U.S. Constitution, and become citizens in order to be part of American society. Also, first- and second-generation Hispanics are more likely to believe in the importance of future generations of Hispanics' speaking Spanish than are third-generation Hispanics (73.4 percent versus 54.9 percent); thus, the importance of preserving Hispanic cultural ties appears to decline the longer Hispanics remain in the United States. These recent surveys indicate that Hispanics seem eager to acculturate into American society, suggesting that it is unlikely that Hispanics will perceive themselves as sharing a fate with Blacks as an "outsider" or minority group.

The second factor identified by Kaufman pertains to pan-Hispanic affinity, meaning the extent to which Hispanics think of themselves in a pan-ethnic manner as opposed to identifying with their country of origin. As we saw in chapter 1, survey data from the Hispanic National Political Survey in 1992 suggests that a strong pan-Hispanic ethnic identity ceases to exist (de la Garza and DeSipio 1992). And as data from the 2006 Pew Survey indicate, presented in table 6.1, these attitudes have not changed much over the past decade. Table 6.1 is based on two questions pertaining to Hispanic commonality and pan-ethnic affinity. Hispanics were asked whether they think that "Hispanics/Latinos from different countries today share one Hispanic/Latino culture" or all "have separate and distinct cultures." Hispanics were also asked whether they felt that "Hispanics/Latinos from different countries today are working together to achieve common political goals" or "are not working together politically." Regardless of how Hispanics racially defined themselves, an overwhelming majority (more than 70 percent) viewed Hispanics as possessing separate and distinct cultures, as opposed to sharing one "Hispanic" or "Latino" culture. But note that a majority of Hispanics felt that they were working in a collective and cohesive fashion in order to achieve common political goals. This bodes well for the prospects of coalition, given Kaufman's assertion that a strong Hispanic pan-ethnic identity is needed in order for Hispanics to coalesce with other racial/ethnic groups in the United States.

One way in which this pan-ethnic identity might develop in the future is through the media, should the mass media in the

TABLE 6.1
Hispanic Opinions on Pan-ethnic Indicators

	Racial category			
	Anglo	Black	Hispanic	Other
Hispanics/Latinos from different countries today...				
Share one Hispanic/Latino culture	20.6	22.0	22.2	21.3
Have separate and distinct cultures	77.1	75.2	75.0	75.8
Hispanics from different countries today...				
Are working together to achieve common political goals	51.7	61.5	58.6	58.4
Are not working together politically	39.1	30.3	32.8	31.9
N	746	109	756	310

Source: Pew Hispanic Center, 2006 Hispanic Immigration Study.
Note: Row entries are column percentages.

United States continue to target and advertise to Hispanics as a single homogeneous group. Political institutions and organizations may also help encourage the development of this pan-ethnic identity if they believe that the use of pan-ethnic identity helps them to achieve their political goals.

Another indicator of ethnic commonality is the perception of discrimination and shared outsider status of racial and ethnic minorities. High levels of perceived discrimination by Hispanics and Blacks should increase their feelings of shared fate and group commonality. The Pew Hispanic 2006 National Survey of Latinos can once again provide us with some insights into Hispanics' experiences with discrimination. Table 6.2 presents the answers to several different questions pertaining to discrimination. When asked about discrimination in general, 61.7 percent of Hispanics replied that they consider it to be a major problem, 21.7 percent think it is a minor problem, and 13.8 percent feel that discrimination is not a problem at all. Thus, most Hispanics perceive discrimination to be a significant issue in their daily lives and one that could potentially increase feelings of group commonality with Blacks. And perhaps in light of the immigration reforms that have gained national attention in recent years, a majority of Hispanics (51.4 percent) feels that discrimination against Hispanics in the

TABLE 6.2
Hispanic Opinions on Discrimination

	Percent
General attitudes	
Discrimination against Hispanics. . .	
Major problem	61.7
Minor problem	21.7
Not a problem	13.8
Don't know	2.2
Discrimination against Hispanics in the past few years has become. . .	
More common	51.4
Less common	16.6
Stayed about the same	29.5
N	2,000
Causes of discrimination	
Income and education major/minor cause of discrimination	
Major	67.9
Minor	18.9
Not a cause	10.7
Skin color major/minor cause of discrimination	
Major	47.1
Minor	25.3
Not a cause	25.8
Language major/minor cause of discrimination	
Major	71.6
Minor	18.8
Not a cause	8.9
Immigration status major/minor cause of discrimination	
Major	72.0
Minor	15.7
Not a cause	8.8
N	1,666

Source: Pew Hispanic Center, 2006 Hispanic Immigration Study.

past several years has become more common; the remaining 29.5 percent believe discrimination to have remained about the same, and 16.6 percent feel that discrimination against Hispanics has decreased.

Hispanics were also asked to share their opinions on what they believe to be the major causes of discrimination. Respondents were asked to categorize each of four different causes of discrimination as major causes, minor causes, or not a cause of discrimination: income and education, skin color, language, and immigration status. The results show that language and immigration status are the two factors that Hispanics view as the main causes of discrimination: 71.6 percent of Hispanics see language as a major cause of discrimination, while an almost equal percentage, 72 percent, view their immigration status as a main cause of discrimination. A slightly lower percentage of Hispanics, 67.9 percent, feel that their income and educational status is a cause of discrimination. These factors are clearly linked to Hispanics' position as immigrants in the United States, compounded by stereotypes that most Hispanics living in the United States are here without legal status and that they are unwilling to learn English (García Bedolla 2005). The fact that English-language proficiency, educational background, and legal status are linked to economic and job opportunities perhaps explains why only 47.1 percent of Hispanics feel that skin color is a major cause of discrimination.

How Hispanics identify themselves racially is the final factor Kaufman identifies as important to minority-led coalitions. The expectation is that Hispanics who consider themselves Hispanic/ Latino should be more likely to identify with Blacks than Hispanics who identify themselves as Anglo. The logic behind Kaufman's argument is that Hispanics who identify themselves as Hispanic, as opposed to Anglo, may possess a higher degree of minority group consciousness. In the 2006 Pew Survey, 37.3 percent of Hispanics responded that they considered themselves racially to be Anglo, while an almost equal percentage, 37.8 percent, identified racially as Hispanic or Latino. Five and a half percent of Hispanics surveyed considered themselves as Black/ African American, 15.5 percent some other race, and 0.5 percent as Asian. Based on this indicator, there may not be very strong racial group consciousness among Hispanics, since almost equal percentages see themselves as being Anglo, as who consider themselves to be Hispanic or Latino.

Kaufman's own analysis finds that pan-Hispanic affinity, Hispanics' attitudes toward acculturation, racial identification, and ethnicity, predict that Hispanics should share group interests with Blacks. For Kaufman, a strong pan-Hispanic identity is the factor that best explains Hispanic affinity toward Blacks. Subgroup differences also influenced the extent to which Hispanics identified with Blacks: Cubans, Puerto Ricans, Dominicans, and Salvadorans were all more likely to identify with Blacks than were Mexican Americans. However, Kaufman's analysis revealed that the demographic, political, and perceived discrimination variables had no impact on Hispanic–Black relations. These findings suggest that Hispanic leaders need to emphasize a pan-ethnic identity if they wish to build a coalition with Blacks. But this goal may be difficult to achieve in practice, given the diversity and heterogeneity of the Hispanic electorate.

It is also important to consider the social and geographical context in which minority-led coalitions form. We turn to research on group conflict and group interest for leverage on this topic. They are both broad contextual theories identifying the macro-contextual factors under which group conflict is more likely to occur in city politics. Previous researchers have examined the effect of group conflict on voting behavior at the local level (Bobo and Hutchings 1996). The one contextual factor that is central to this theory is perceived group conflict, since it can directly impact voting behavior and attitudes (Kaufman 2003). Conflict can be defined as resentment emerging between minority groups based on perceived tension; the expectation is that minority group members will be more cognizant of interracial competition than will be the members of dominant groups.

Group conflict theory predicts that perceived competition among groups generates hostilities, thereby activating group identities and making them salient. As such, the likelihood of electing a minority candidate into office diminishes when tensions run high. This is because perceived competition among groups results in group-centered voting behavior rather than the development of minority coalitions. Thus, high levels of group conflict may lead to "group distinctive" voting. On the other hand, in situations in which little group tension exists, the theory expects partisan loyalties to motivate electoral choices, thereby improving the chances that a minority candidate will be elected. Kaufman tests these predictions on a series of mayoral elections in New York and Los Angeles spanning a thirty-five-year period. Overall, she finds support for the theory of group conflict. In 1973, for instance, when levels of racial group conflict were relatively low, minorities worked with one another to elect the first Black mayor of Los Angeles, Tom Bradley. In contrast, the 1992 mayoral election was held shortly following the Los Angeles riots, an event that generated a great deal of racial tension among minority groups. Thus, Kaufman attributes to group-centered voting behavior the loss of the minority candidate, Mike Woo, to his Anglo contender, Richard Riordan.

GROUP PERCEPTIONS AND ATTITUDES

So far, we have discussed the factors that contribute to the creation of long-term coalitions of racial and ethnic minorities in the United States. However, it is unclear how minority groups perceive one another and the extent to which they feel that they have anything in common. Having information about such attitudes is key to determining whether minorities are likely to coalesce both inside and outside the political arena. We turn to a unique survey conducted in 2005 to address these questions. The Intergroup Relations Survey, which was sponsored by the National Conference for Community and Justice (NCCJ), consists of the responses of a nationally representative sample of U.S. adults to a series of questions ascertaining their opinions on racial group relations.[4] We also present information from the 2006 LNS, because it includes several questions pertaining to perceptions of commonality with other racial and ethnic groups as well as perceptions of Hispanic competition with Blacks. The information from the NCCJ provides us with the opportunity to compare the opinions and attitudes of Anglos, Asian Americans, Blacks, and Hispanics, while the LNS offers us a more in-depth understanding of the Hispanic attitudes toward the current state of intergroup

[4]The interviews were conducted in Spanish and English by Princeton Data Source, LLC, from January 13 through March 30, 2005. The margin of error is +/−3.1 percent.

relations. Table 6.3 presents racial and ethnic group perceptions of closeness to other minorities in the United States. Respondents were asked to evaluate how close they feel toward the following groups: Anglos, Asian Americans, Blacks, Hispanics, and immigrants. Their responses ranged from "very close" to "close" to "neutral" to "far" to "very far" and finally to "do not know enough about group to say." We analyze these responses by a respondent's self-reported race/ethnicity.

The data presented in table 6.3 offer a number of important insights. First, focusing just on racial and ethnic group comparisons, we see that Anglos, Blacks, and Hispanics all feel most distant to Asian Americans. While it is notable that all three groups share this perception, it is not immediately obvious why this is so. Perhaps the idea that Asian Americans are viewed as "perpetual foreigners" may help to explain the attitudes expressed by Blacks, Hispanics, and Anglos (Wu 2002). In terms of the group they feel closest to, Anglos feel closest to Hispanics (57.5 percent), while Blacks, Hispanics, and Asian Americans all feel closest to Anglos (56.3, 53.7, and 58.9 percent, respectively).

Thus, it appears that none of the three ethnic or racial groups feels close to any other ethnic/racial group; instead, the members of all three groups believe they have more in common with Anglos. The expectation that racial and ethnic minorities in the United States may have a greater sense of rapport with one another as a result of their shared status as minorities is not borne out in the responses provided to this survey question. The results also suggest that future prospects for a purely minority-led coalition, especially one that would include Asians, may be unlikely. These findings also suggest, however, that Asians, Blacks, and Hispanics are willing to form coalitions with Anglos, the most dominant and established racial group in politics.

Survey respondents were also asked to evaluate their relationship with immigrants. Given the immigrant background of a large percentage of Hispanics and Asian Americans, it is not surprising that they feel much closer to immigrants than do Anglos and Blacks. In fact, 64.4 percent of Hispanics feel either very close or close to immigrants, and 59.4 percent of Asian Americans feel very close or close to immigrants. As a point of comparison, 46 percent of Anglos feel close to immigrants, while a smaller percentage of Blacks, 31.6 percent, responded in this manner.

TABLE 6.3
Ethnic/Racial Group Perceptions of Closeness

How close do you feel to the following groups. . .	Anglo respondents	Asian respondents	Black respondents	Hispanic respondents
Anglos				
Very close	—	13.5	12.0	12.4
Close	—	45.4	44.3	41.3
Neutral	—	35.8	34.4	37.1
Far	—	1.9	3.6	5.7
Very far	—	1.0	2.4	1.6
DK enough about group to say	—	2.4	2.8	1.8
Asians				
Very close	5.6	—	5.7	4.4
Close	22.7	—	20.5	21.9
Neutral	39.2	—	33.2	31.0
Far	9.4	—	9.2	17.3
Very far	3.6	—	5.3	6.0
DK enough about group to say	18.2	—	25.8	17.1
Blacks				
Very close	11.0	9.2	—	11.0
Close	42.7	27.5	—	37.5
Neutral	36.6	45.4	—	33.7
Far	5.0	7.7	—	10.6
Very far	1.5	2.4	—	3.8
DK enough about group to say	2.5	7.7	—	3.3
Hispanics				
Very close	21.9	8.7	14.6	—
Close	35.6	27.5	35.7	—
Neutral	30.2	44.9	28.4	—
Far	4.1	9.2	4.5	—
Very far	1.2	1.9	2.7	—
DK enough about group to say	6.5	7.7	14.1	—
Immigrants				
Very close	13.1	17.4	8.5	21.4
Close	32.9	42.0	23.1	43.0
Neutral	32.0	27.5	33.0	26.7
Far	5.8	3.4	7.9	3.0
Very far	4.2	2.4	4.7	1.6
DK enough about group to say	11.4	6.8	21.7	4.1
N	1297	207	718	630

Source: 2005 Intergroup Relations Survey.
Note: Cell entries are column percentages; DK = "Don't know."

Table 6.4 presents respondents' opinions about the existence of discrimination against their own racial or ethnic group as well as against other groups. With respect to Anglos, they feel that immigrants face the greatest amount of discrimination (27.4 percent), followed by Hispanics (20.6 percent), Blacks (11 percent), themselves (7.1 percent), and, lastly, Asian Americans (6.3 percent). Moreover, Anglos view themselves as suffering the least amount of discrimination (32.3 percent), followed by Asian Americans, Hispanics, and Blacks. Similar to Anglos, Asian Americans also feel that immigrants encounter the most discrimination, but they rate discrimination against themselves more highly than against Hispanics. Interestingly, Asian Americans perceive discrimination toward Blacks to be less common than discrimination against their own group and against Anglos. The majority of Asian Americans also feel that Anglos, relative to the other groups, suffer the least from discrimination; this view mirrors Anglos' views, except that Anglos do not perceive that there is much discrimination against Asian Americans.

Blacks' opinions on group discrimination differ markedly from the views held by Anglos and Asian Americans. Black survey respondents feel that their racial group suffers the most from discrimination: 54.7 percent of them hold this view. Consistent with Anglo and Asian American attitudes, relative to other groups, Blacks feel that Anglos face the least amount of discrimination.

Our final point of comparison turns to the opinions held by Hispanics. While 49.1 percent think that immigrants face the greatest amounts of discrimination, 35.9 percent of Hispanic survey respondents feel that it is Hispanics who suffer the most from discrimination. A larger percentage of Hispanics also view Blacks as facing more discrimination than Asian Americans and Anglos. And, consistent with the trends thus far, Hispanics perceive Anglos to be the group least discriminated against.

These survey responses suggest that Anglos, Asian Americans, Blacks, and Hispanics generally agree that Anglos are the group whose members suffer the least discrimination. And while Anglos, Asian Americans, and Hispanics all agree that immigrants experience the most discrimination, Blacks see the members of their own group as being the target of discrimination more so than any other racial or ethnic group. Recall that discrimination is one factor that influences the prospects of developing enduring

TABLE 6.4
Ethnic/Racial Group Perceptions of Discrimination toward
Other Ethnic/Racial Groups

How much discrimination is there against. . .	Anglo respondents	Asian respondents	Black respondents	Hispanic respondents
Anglos				
A great deal	7.1	1.9	7.9	5.4
Some	35.8	20.3	35.0	23.5
Only a little	21.2	18.8	20.8	18.9
None at all	32.3	54.6	30.8	46.0
Don't know	3.6	4.4	5.6	6.2
Asians				
A great deal	6.3	10.1	12.4	10.6
Some	43.6	47.3	43.5	28.7
Only a little	18.6	28.0	16.2	17.0
None at all	16.8	11.6	11.0	20.8
Don't know	14.7	2.9	17.0	22.9
Blacks				
A great deal	11.0	9.2	54.7	28.1
Some	42.7	27.5	33.8	35.4
Only a little	36.6	45.4	5.6	15.6
None at all	5.0	7.7	4.2	14.1
Don't know	1.5	2.4	1.7	6.8
Hispanics				
A great deal	20.6	10.1	28.7	35.9
Some	49.2	40.1	44.2	36.8
Only a little	15.9	24.2	11.0	13.8
None at all	10.7	15.9	7.9	11.3
Don't know	3.6	9.7	8.2	2.2
Immigrants				
A great deal	27.4	18.4	31.8	49.1
Some	46.4	48.8	42.2	28.6
Only a little	13.4	18.4	11.0	9.8
None at all	7.7	8.7	6.8	7.8
Don't know	5.1	5.8	8.2	4.5
N	1297	207	718	630

Source: 2005 Intergroup Relations Survey.
Note: Cell entries are column percentages.

and stable minority coalitions. Given that the two largest immigrant groups in the United States, Hispanics and Asian Americans, both believe that immigrants suffer more discrimination than any other group, this shared attitude may be grounds for cooperation and commonality, particularly on the issue of immigration reform.

The final set of questions that we examine, presented in Table 6.5, focuses on more general attitudes toward group relations. Here, survey respondents were asked whether they "generally get along with" other racial and ethnic groups. Again, we analyze survey responses based on the respondent's ethnic or racial identity. Across all four groups, the majority of respondents say that they generally get along with the group in question; however, differences do exist by racial/ethnic group. Of the three ethnic or racial groups, Anglos feel that they get along the most with Asian Americans (78 percent), followed by Hispanics (71.9 percent) and Blacks (71.6 percent). This runs somewhat at odds with Anglos' responses that they feel the least close to Asian Americans. It may be the case that Anglos get along better with Asian Americans in the workplace or other situations but do not feel close to them in terms of a shared culture. This would be consistent with Wu's (2002) characterization of Asian Americans as perpetual foreigners, so despite the fact that many individuals of Asian descent have lived in the United States for five or more generations, they may always be perceived of as being foreign or exotic, particularly as it relates to culture.

Asian Americans' own views on group closeness are consistent with their attitudes toward group relations. They believe that they get along with Anglos to a much a greater extent than they do with Hispanics or Blacks (91.5 percent versus 73.4 percent and 63.3 percent, respectively). Moreover, most Asian Americans feel that they are less likely to get along with Blacks than with Hispanics or Anglos. These attitudes may have been influenced by Black–Korean tensions in New York (Kim 2000) and Los Angeles (Song 2005) or by the media's portrayals of the friction that has occurred between these two groups.

Blacks' views on group relations differ from their attitudes on group closeness. A larger percentage of Blacks feel that they get along with Hispanics (76.3 percent) than with Asian Americans (58.4 percent) and Anglos (59.2 percent). The reason for this may

TABLE 6.5
Ethnic/Racial Group Perceptions of Group Relations

Do you think you generally get along with...	Anglo respondents	Asian respondents	Black respondents	Hispanic respondents
Anglos				
Get along	—	91.5	59.2	67.3
Do not get along	—	4.0	36.1	29.5
Don't know	—	4.5	4.7	3.2
Asians				
Get along	78.0	—	58.4	53.0
Do not get along	11.4	—	26.8	27.0
Don't know	10.6	—	14.8	20.0
Blacks				
Get along	71.6	63.3	—	60.0
Do not get along	25.1	30.7	—	32.7
Only a little	3.3	6.0	—	7.3
Hispanics				
Get along	71.9	73.4	76.3	—
Do not get along	22.3	19.6	16.7	—
Don't know	5.7	7.0	7.0	—
N	1297	199	676	630

Source: 2005 Intergroup Relations Survey.
Note: Cell entries are column percentages.

be due to the shared socioeconomic characteristics and residential patterns of Hispanics and Blacks. Residentially, many Blacks and Hispanics are concentrated in urban areas; from a socioeconomic perspective, Hispanics and Blacks are also clustered in similar industries (Jennings 1992). All of these interactions could perhaps positively influence Blacks' views of Hispanics. Given that some studies point to the possibility of increasing levels of competition and conflict between these two groups (see Vaca 2004), it is interesting that survey data like these indicate that the friction between Blacks and Hispanics may not be as problematic as some argue.

Finally, we see that Hispanic respondents' views on group relations are similar to their attitudes on group closeness. Sixty-seven percent of Hispanics feel that they get along with Anglos, followed by Blacks (60 percent) and Asian Americans (53 percent). Recall that the majority of Hispanic respondents also felt closest to Anglos (12.4 percent), followed closely by Blacks (11 percent). Unfortunately, while more Blacks say that they get along with Hispanics than with Anglos and Asian Americans, Hispanics feel slightly closer to Anglos. Moreover, a larger percentage of Hispanics, 32.7 percent, say they do not get along with Blacks than say the same about Anglos (29.5 percent) or Asian Americans (27 percent). Thus, a rather conflicted scenario emerges with respect to Hispanic–Black relations. While Blacks perceive they get along better with Hispanics than with Asian Americans, Hispanics believe that they are less likely to get along with Blacks than with other racial groups. Based on these survey results, the notion of creating a viable and enduring Hispanic–Black coalition may be a real challenge. But once again, it is clear that Anglos have the advantage when it comes to forming coalitions, since both Asian Americans and Hispanics not only perceive themselves to be closest to them but also feel that they get along best with them.

As a point of comparison, table 6.6 presents the data from the 2006 Latino National Survey (LNS) on racial and ethnic group commonality. While the questions are somewhat similar to those in the NCCJ, group commonality questions in the LNS are more specific; one question asks Hispanics the extent to which they perceive group commonality based on the socioeconomic situation of the group, while the other focuses on group commonality based on the group's political situation. Thus, these questions offer a more detailed and in-depth understanding of Hispanics' views toward other racial/ethnic groups. The LNS, similar to the Intergroup Relations Survey, asked Hispanics to evaluate their relations with Blacks, Anglos, and Asian Americans.

Hispanic opinions on intergroup relations from the LNS are remarkably similar to those from the Intergroup Relations Survey. Again, we see that Hispanics perceive the least amount of commonality with Asian Americans, in terms of both their socioeconomic and their political situation. Note that 28.3 percent of Hispanics believe that they have nothing in common with Asian Americans from a socioeconomic standpoint, relative to the 15.5 percent of Hispanics who feel this way toward Anglos and 15.1

TABLE 6.6
Hispanic Perceptions of Commonality with
Racial /Ethnic Groups in the U.S.

Racial/ethnic group	Amount of commonality based on socioeconomic situation	Amount of commonality based on political situation
Anglos		
Nothing	15.5	15.7
Little	26.7	29.6
Some	30.4	28.4
A lot	17.8	15.2
Don't know/no answer	9.6	11.1
N	8,634	8,634
Asians		
Nothing	28.3	27.2
Little	25.7	26.3
Some	21.0	21.9
A lot	10.2	9.1
Don't know/no answer	14.7	15.5
N	3,415	3,415
Blacks		
Nothing	15.1	13.4
Little	21.4	25.5
Some	31.6	31.4
A lot	20.6	17.6
Don't know/no answer	11.3	12.2
N	8,634	8,634

Source: Latino National Survey of 2006.
Note: Cell entries are column percentages.

percent toward Blacks. Likewise, 27.2 percent of Hispanics feel that they share no common political ground with Asian Americans; only 15.7 percent of Hispanics feel this same way toward Anglos and 13.4 percent toward Blacks.

But in a result that differs from Hispanic opinions in the Intergroup Relations Survey, Hispanics in the LNS perceive the greatest amount of commonality with Blacks, followed by Anglos (however, these differences are relatively small). Approximately 20 percent of Hispanic respondents perceived their socioeconomic circumstances to be very similar to Blacks, relative to 17.8 percent of Hispanics who held this same view toward Anglos. In a similar fashion, slightly more Hispanics view their political situation as similar to that of Blacks, 17.6 percent, than they do to Anglos, 15.2 percent. Since the differences between these responses are rather small, it is safe to conclude that Hispanics perceive they have the greatest commonality with Anglos and Blacks, and the least commonality with Asian Americans.

Finally, the 2006 LNS provides some much-needed insight into the existence of competition and tension between Hispanics and Blacks, particularly in light of the media's punditry during the 2008 presidential election (see Nagourney and Steinhauer 2008 for an example). The LNS asked Hispanics to evaluate the degree of competition that exists between Hispanics and Blacks in getting jobs, getting government jobs (city or state), accessing quality education and schools, and electing representatives to office. Table 6.7 presents Hispanics' responses to these questions.

Hispanic opinions on the existence of competition with Blacks indicate that they generally perceive little or no economic conflict. For example, the majority of Hispanics, 52.4 percent, feel that no competition exists with Blacks in finding a job. A plurality of Hispanics, 40.6 percent, perceives that no competition exists in attaining government employment. The final socioeconomic question pertains to education and schooling; we see once again that a plurality of Hispanics sees no competition with Blacks in this area. Turning to the political arena, 35.6 percent of Hispanics view strong competition to exist with Blacks in electing Hispanic representatives into office. At the same time, however, an almost equal percentage of Hispanics, 34.9 percent, feel that competition with Blacks to elect Hispanics into office is nonexistent.

These findings paint a rather mixed picture of Hispanic relations with Blacks. While it certainly appears that Hispanics do not perceive any sort of competition with Blacks in terms of jobs or educational access, Hispanics appear to be conflicted when it comes to Hispanic–Black competition in the political arena. While one-third of the respondents from the LNS believe that a strong degree of competition exists between themselves and Blacks, another one-third of the respondents perceive no competition at all.

TABLE 6.7
Hispanic Perceptions of Competition with Blacks

	Degree of competition that exists with blacks in...
Getting jobs	
None	52.4
Weak	21.0
Strong	26.6
Getting government jobs (city or state)	
None	40.6
Weak	25.8
Strong	33.6
Electing representatives into office	
None	34.9
Weak	29.5
Strong	35.6
Access to education and quality schools	
None	46.9
Weak	24.3
Strong	28.8
N	8,634

Source: Latino National Survey of 2006.
Note: Cell entries are column percentages.

Of course, these views explain only one side of the story, since these questions were only posed to Hispanics. Nonetheless, these findings provide us with several key insights regarding the contexts in which Hispanics sense the potential for conflict with Blacks and when they do not.

CONCLUSION

The primary goal of this chapter was to explore the current state of intergroup relations in the United States and whether the possibility of durable and long-lasting minority coalitions is realistic. In general, minority groups feel closer to Anglos than to other minorities; this bodes well for the creation of Anglo–minority co-alitions, but the prospects for the development of minority-only coalitions appear to be less promising. In both of the surveys that we analyzed, Hispanics perceive that they have the least amount in common with Asian Americans. This means that in cities with a similar demographic composition to that of Monterey Park, California, the likelihood of forming a durable Hispanic–Asian coalition may be somewhat of a challenge.

On the other hand, Asian Americans and Hispanics share the belief that immigrants suffer the most from discrimination; this commonality could potentially form the basis for a coalition be-tween them. We also found that Anglos and Hispanics report getting along best with Asian Americans, while a larger percent-age of Blacks feel that they get along with Hispanics than with Anglos or Asian Americans. Moreover, based on a question from the LNS, more than one-third of Hispanics believe that their like-lihood of doing well depends on Blacks doing well. This gives us some sense that Hispanics perceive some sort of "linked fate" with other minority groups, which was one of the key factors in the creation of an enduring minority coalition. As previous re-search has pointed out, the dynamics of intergroup relations are nuanced and cannot be easily categorized as an Anglo/non-Anglo dichotomy. Given this reality, the notion that all minority groups are likely to work together in the near future or that Hispanics and Blacks or Hispanics and Asians will naturally coalesce may also need to be reassessed.

The Complexity of Studying
Hispanic Political Behavior

BY NOW, READERS should have some sense for the complexities of Hispanic political behavior in the United States, as well as some of the complexities involved in the study of Hispanic political behavior. We have provided in the preceding chapters a portrait that documents the demographic changes in the Hispanic population in the United States, as well as Hispanic participation in politics, voting behavior in national elections, views on important political issues, perspectives on other minority groups, and political values.

Along the way, we have also looked at some of the important nuances of Hispanic political behavior, with repeated emphasis on the simple observation that Hispanics in the United States are not a single, monolithic electorate. Instead, there are many fault lines that need to be examined to understand Hispanic political behavior and many attributes of Hispanics that make them a distinct but important component of the national electorate. As we have repeatedly seen, these include national origin, generational status, and language use. Such attributes are part of what make for a distinct Hispanic, or Latino, political identity in the United States, but they are also characteristics that need to be included in any analysis of Hispanic political behavior, because they explain important differences within this community in attitudes, opinions, and behavior.

We are aware that our analysis in this book is by necessity cursory: we have attempted here to give a broad overview of Hispanic political behavior, and the research reported in these pages is intended to give the reader some perspective on how Hispanics view the political world and how their political behavior differs from that of Anglos and members of other minority groups. Each of the separate subjects that we have considered in the preceding chapters could easily be the subject of book-length treatments—a research agenda that we wholeheartedly endorse!

While recent decades have seen a dramatic increase in the amount of attention that the research community has showered on Hispanics and Latinos in the United States, much still needs to be understood about the political behavior of Hispanics.

What Have We Learned?

Our study has covered an array of aspects related to Hispanic political behavior, and we have tried to situate our analysis within both theoretically driven and comparative perspectives. Our first chapter concentrated on the notion of Hispanic political identity. There we argued that because of a variety of factors, Hispanic political identity is constantly changing and highly fluid. And our data analysis supported this argument, in particular as we focused on how the role of shared ethnic identity and the importance of maintaining Spanish as a "mother tongue" become less important by the third generation that an individual of Hispanic descent has been in the United States.

Chapter 2 in our study examined the public opinion and partisanship of Hispanics, exploring the attitudes of Hispanics and non-Hispanics across a variety of general issues, but also focusing on issues that might be of specific concern to the Hispanic community, like immigration and bilingual education. We also examined the factors that contribute to the acquisition of partisanship among Hispanics. While a detailed analysis of the determinants of Hispanic public opinion and partisanship is well beyond the scope of our present work, we found that Hispanic public opinion and partisanship differs from non-Hispanic opinions across many of the issues we studied. Some of these differences likely arise from variations in political knowledge, predispositions and values; but some of these differences may also arise because some of these issues are of immediate concern to Hispanics, such as immigration. We also saw that on some issues, like jobs, education, and the economy, Anglos, Blacks, and Hispanics have much in common. In terms of how Hispanics acquire their partisanship, we found that while traditional predictors such as ideology and demographics are important, other factors that are unique to Hispanics, such as their ethnicity and generational status, also influenced whether they choose to identify with either of the two major political parties or as an independent.

Chapter 3 turned to the question of Hispanic voter participation. We examined Hispanic political participation through a number of different lenses, beginning first by looking at their participation in presidential elections, where we showed that Hispanic turnout lags that of both Blacks and Anglos. But the other lens we used to study Hispanic political participation looked beyond the ballot box, where we showed that Hispanics are highly involved in nonpolitical activities in their communities, as well as being active in certain types of campaign activities. We also studied the 2006 immigration demonstrations, and while we cannot at this point say what their long-term implications may be for Hispanic political mobilization, it is clear that those demonstrations and protests show that there are conditions under which Hispanics can be mobilized to express their opposition to certain types of public policies.

Our fourth chapter turned to a poorly studied aspect of Hispanic political behavior: political knowledge and interest in politics. Here we found that Hispanic political knowledge lags that of Anglos, which we argued was a disturbing finding. Political knowledge is seen as an important foundation for many other aspects of political behavior, in particular, a voter's ability to evaluate candidates and the campaign information they provide. To some extent, the differences in political knowledge between Hispanics and Anglos might be due to differences in political socialization and civic education, but as Abrajano (2010) has argued, they are also rooted in how candidates approach the Hispanic electorate.

In chapter 5, we shifted our attention to how Hispanics vote in presidential and midterm federal elections. We focus on presidential and midterm election voting for a number of reasons, one being that voting in federal elections is considered among the more important political choices Americans are asked to make. Moreover, because voter choice in federal elections has been widely studied, especially presidential election vote choice for Anglos, we were able to draw on this wealth of existing research. We showed that generally speaking, Hispanic voters cast ballots in federal elections much like Anglo and Black voters do: according to partisanship and political ideology, and their evaluations of the state of the national economy and their own pocketbooks. Within this general portrait, we found subtle differences in the factors that might matter more or less in Hispanic voting behavior relative to Anglos and Blacks, but overall we conclude that the major theories of voter decision making apply to Hispanics.

Chapter 6 brought to the fore our comparative focus, since in this chapter we studied intergroup relations. Here, as we studied this complex question, we found two different patterns of intergroup perceptions. On the one hand, minority groups generally feel closer to Anglos than to other minorities. This implies that the preconditions for possible political cooperation between Anglos and minorities exist. But on the other hand, we also found that perceptions of intergroup relations are quite complex and are heavily dependent on which pairing of minority groups is under analysis. This implies that developing political cooperation between minority groups is neither easy nor inevitable.

New Directions in the Study of Hispanic Political Behavior

We began this book by discussing some of the most commonly held beliefs or "conventional wisdoms" regarding Hispanic political behavior in the United States. Our goal throughout this book was to explore the validity of these beliefs through various data and information sources. Well before we began to write this book, both of us had been studying Hispanic political behavior for some time in a series of collaborative projects and also in our own independent work. Throughout our research, we have found that our work has been plagued by what we see as two central problems with academic research on Hispanic political behavior: a lack of theory and a lack of quality data.

When it comes to theory, our own work has raised what we see as a core dilemma for those who might want to develop coherent theoretical models for studying Hispanic political behavior. On the one hand, there is much that indicates that the behavioral theories that have been developed going back to the 1940s have much going for them when applied to study Hispanic political behavior. We know, for example, that the models developed by Campbell, Converse, Miller, and Stokes about partisanship and its basic role in explaining political behavior can help and have helped us understand the partisanship of Hispanics and how partisanship might affect key political behavior like voting in national elections. So there is much to be said for the general application of existing political theory toward the study of Hispanic political behavior, and we urge future researchers to use existing behavioral theories as they seek to study Hispanics.

But on the other hand, we also know that there is much that differentiates Hispanics from Anglos, African Americans, Asian Americans, and other subpopulations of the electorate. These factors that drive Hispanic or Latino distinctiveness also need better theoretical elaboration; in particular, a key research question is determining when the attributes that make Hispanics distinct from the rest of the electorate are relevant for political attitudes or behaviors and when these attributes are irrelevant. In some situations, we suspect that the determining factors will be social or economic; for example, as the social and economic experiences of many Hispanics are quite distinct from others in the eligible electorate, it is likely that such differences will play themselves out in how Hispanics acquire basic political values and predispositions—as well as how political values and predispositions themselves become reflected in political behavior. We also expect that the determining factors in some situations will be inherently political: for example, we believe that the political mobilizations that have accompanied the issue of illegal immigration, both in the early 1990s in California and throughout the nation in 2006 and 2007, have been and will likely continue to be important determinants of Hispanic political behavior.

In addition to understanding when Hispanic distinctiveness matters relative to other groups in the electorate, we also need theoretical development to better understand when and how intragroup differences may also affect the attitudes and behaviors of Hispanics. Just as we suspect that variations in the use of Spanish or English news media, in national origin, and in generational status might have nonpolitical triggers, we also anticipate that they will have political triggers. For example, while it may very well be that the sources of national origin differences in partisan affiliations have a political origin (e.g., Cubans' lasting support for Republicans because of the Republican Party's harder line

against Castro's Cuba), such differences may also arise from social or economic factors. At this point, there simply is not a great
body of theory that scholars can draw upon to understand when
differences within the Hispanic population should matter—not
to mention *which* population differences might matter.

Compounding the problem is the lack of quality data about
Hispanic political behavior. The release of the first Latino National Political Survey (LNPS) in 1989 sparked an early round of
important research on Hispanic political behavior, and the release of the successor to the LNPS, the Latino National Survey of
2006, is already beginning to spark further research. The datasets
released by the Pew Hispanic Center and by Annenberg have allowed for some studies of Hispanic political behavior, but these
data collection efforts, while productive, have been limited by
their size and scope, by their infrequency and inconsistency, and
by the lack of methodological research on the best ways to collect
data on Hispanics and Latinos.

The existing studies of Hispanics, particularly survey-based
studies, have typically been of very limited size and scope. Pars-
ing these problems can be done in a number of different ways,
but typically survey studies of Hispanics involve either relatively
large samples but limited numbers of variables or large numbers
of variables but a small sample size. As of 2008, no survey study
of Hispanics has yet been released that includes both a large
sample of both Hispanics and non-Hispanics and a large array of
variables for study. To be able to analyze the important differences within the Hispanic population as well as between Hispanics and other racial/ethnic groups, we need large samples of
each group; to begin to adequately analyze the complexity of
Hispanic attitudes and behaviors, we need lots of variables.

Moreover, survey studies of Hispanics that are made available
for public research are conducted very infrequently and incon-
sistently. Nearly two decades separate the LNPS from the more
recent, academically led, 2006 LNS. In nearly all of the Pew Hispanic Center surveys, the set of questions posed to respondents
fluctuates considerably across surveys, making it very difficult to
develop a consistent database with which to study cross-sectional
changes in Hispanic political attitudes or behavior.

There is also a dearth of research on the basic methodology of
studying Hispanic political behavior, especially on the survey

methodologies associated with collecting samples of Hispanics. Are traditional random-digit dialing (RDD) telephone methods appropriate for collecting samples of Hispanics, or are they too expensive? Should RDD methods be augmented by focusing mainly on telephone exchanges with higher-density Hispanic populations? Are list-based methods sufficient? What about Internet-based, or automated telephone, sampling? Or is some combination of these methods the best approach for balancing accuracy and cost?

Once a sampling strategy has been developed, there are then a myriad of additional methodological questions regarding survey studies of Hispanic political behavior that have attracted little or no academic research. What differences exist between Hispanic survey respondents who complete an interview in English and those who complete it in Spanish, and what effort should be made to provide interviews in Spanish? How should questions be worded for Hispanic respondents? Should nuances of context or culture be taken into account in question wording and ordering? And once data have been collected, how does one generate sampling weights so that the sample frequencies match back to the population, given that in most situations we do not know the size of Hispanic populations (especially of the voting population) with certainty? These are just some of the many methodological issues that will need to be addressed if we wish to take the study of Hispanic political behavior seriously.

Looking to the Future

Our suspicion, and one of our motivations for writing this book, is that we are on the brink of a revolution in the study of Hispanic political behavior in the United States. The push for a better understanding of Hispanic political opinions and behaviors arises from Hispanics' increased prominence in American politics, as well as the continued population growth of Hispanics in communities throughout the nation. The push also comes from scholars, who are armed with new methodological tools, better data, and new questions to ask about political behavior in the United States.

The two themes regarding contemporary scholarship—and research in the near future—on Hispanic political behavior that we stress in this book are the need to be comparative in our study of Hispanics and the need to study the heterogeneity within the Hispanic community. As we have done repeatedly in this book (and in our other work on Hispanics), we believe that it is imperative to compare Hispanics to Anglos, African Americans, and Asian Americans. These comparisons allow us to better understand the distinctiveness of Hispanics as well as their similarities. There are long-standing research literatures regarding Anglo political behavior, and there is a strong and growing body of research on African American political behavior. Scholars examining Hispanic political behavior will learn much by comparing Hispanics with other racial and ethnic groups.

The distinctiveness within the Hispanic community will be a vein that scholars will mine for many years to come. At this point, we simply do not know enough about how the various fault lines in the Hispanic community, including differences in language use, generational status, national origin, and religious affiliation, create similar schisms in political opinions, values, and behavior. This is not to say that research has not been done on these potential sources of heterogeneity, but more research is clearly needed about how these many differences in the Hispanic community can have political consequences.

We say they "can" have political consequences because it is also by no means inevitable that differences within the Hispanic community, or for that matter between Hispanics and members of other racial and ethnic groups, will necessarily become politicized. As one of us has argued in other work, it is the case that political campaigns target subgroups like Hispanics with certain types of messages and imagery; it is also the case that groups within the Hispanic electorate itself are sometimes subjected to certain specific political communications. Why campaigns and candidates choose to engage in such strategies is something that other scholars will need to consider, as well as the related question of the effects that such "micro-targeting" strategies might have.

How candidates, politicians, and political parties choose to communicate to Hispanics, moreover, carries with it several normative implications. If political campaigns continue to appeal to Hispanics with an emphasis on symbolic and cultural messages, Hispanics may have trouble improving their levels of political knowledge and interest, since these types of messages contain little information about a candidate's policy positions. Moreover, if politicians and political parties persist in carrying out their get-out-the-vote efforts by only targeting "likely voters" or mobilizing individuals through nonpersonal means, they may be missing out on the opportunity to reach out to millions of new voters. And finally, if political parties do not seize the opportunity to play a similar role as they did in the early 1900s, by serving to incorporate and socialize America's most recent newcomers to the U.S. political system, the Hispanic electorate's interest and activity in politics may become even lower than those of Anglos and Blacks. While numerous civic institutions have stepped into this role (Wong 2006), they also face a tough dilemma in deciding whether to devote their limited resources to naturalization and citizenship drives or on registration and mobilization efforts.

It is critical for Hispanics to become more involved in American politics for several reasons. First, increased political participation among the nation's largest immigrant group indicates that the democratic traditions that we hold so dear, such as equal opportunity, are being practiced and upheld. In addition, while the Hispanic share of the U.S. population continues to grow, the proportion of Hispanic officials elected to local, state, and federal positions still does not correspond to their total population size, and their rates of registration and turnout remain lower than that of non-Hispanics. If Hispanics are not primarily the ones making decisions about their political well-being, then those elected to serve Hispanic communities may have little incentive to respond to their policy concerns and interests.

* Postscript *

HISPANICS AND THE 2008 ELECTION

T HE 2008 PRESIDENTIAL ELECTION was a landmark event
for numerous reasons. The Democratic primaries saw Bill Richardson competing for the nation's highest elected office, making
him the first viable Hispanic candidate to do so. As a Hispanic, the
current governor of New Mexico, former United Nations ambas-
sador, and secretary of energy in the Clinton administration, Richardson was considered early in the Democratic primary process to
be a formidable candidate. However, other historic candidacies in
the Democratic Party—those of Senators Hillary Clinton and Barack
Obama—quickly overshadowed Richardson, and he placed fourth
in both Iowa and New Hampshire. Richardson withdrew from the
race early on in the primaries (January 9, 2008), but did provide
Obama with a critical early endorsement that might have helped
Obama solidify Hispanic support in some of the later Democratic
primaries, and of course, later in the general election.

The Republicans also continued their courtship of the Hispanic
vote in 2008. With the eventual nomination of Senator John Mc-
Cain as their nominee, a candidate who had successfully campaigned in the past for Hispanic votes in his home state of Arizona—and who had at one point championed significant federal
immigration reform—it was possible that the Republicans could
repeat the success that they had in 2004 with Hispanic voters.
McCain, who also appealed to history by selecting a female vice
presidential candidate, then Alaska governor Sarah Palin, worked
hard to appeal to Hispanics in the general election, though in the
end the Republicans fell short of the high-water mark they hit in
2004 with the Hispanic electorate.

Thus, as in past elections, the Hispanic electorate received a
considerable amount of attention from the two major party candidates, the political parties, as well as the media. Perhaps most
memorable about this presidential election as it relates to Hispanics is that they were in the spotlight very early on in the process. The changes in the presidential primary schedule, which
resulted in a longer campaign season, partially explain why Hispanics were the center of attention in many of the primary races.
In particular, the Democrats allowed Nevada to hold their party

caucuses on January 19, in part to get their candidates to campaign in a southwestern state with a significant Hispanic population. And according to Barreto et al. (2008) as well as many media reports, Hispanics' overwhelming support for Clinton helped her stay in the race as long as she did.[1]

Hispanics in this election were considered pivotal for many of the same reasons we discussed throughout this book (e.g., group size, geographic concentration, swing voter potential), but one of the more important reasons for the attention on Hispanics in 2008 was their concentration in key battleground states and their potential to be the deciding factor in them. The battleground states in the 2008 election—New Mexico, Colorado, Florida, and Nevada—all contained sizeable Hispanic populations. Hundreds of print and broadcast stories focused on the Hispanic electorate, highlighting their important role as a swing vote in the above-mentioned states. In Nevada, for example, Hispanics made up 24 percent of the state's population and 12 percent of eligible voters. The state party as well as the Culinary Union, which has over sixty thousand members, volunteered their efforts to assist Hispanics in the citizenship process and register them to vote.[2] Hispanics were also viewed as crucial on Super Tuesday (during which twenty-two states had their primaries) because it included the primaries held in California, New Jersey, and Pennsylvania. Clinton won Nevada, 51 to 45 percent, with 64 percent of Hispanics casting their ballots in her favor. In fact, Clinton won the support of the majority of Hispanics in Arizona, California, New Jersey, New Mexico, and Texas. Only in Illinois did Obama garner a larger share of the Hispanic vote than did Clinton, though by a very small margin (50 percent versus 49 percent). In all the available polls taken during the primaries, Clinton's support among Hispanics averaged 58 percent, while Obama's average support from Hispanics was 34 percent.[3]

[1]Hispanic support for Clinton in the primaries was attributed to her strong name recognition within the Hispanic community, along with her early efforts to seek out endorsements from prominent Latino officials and community leaders. For more discussion on this subject matter, see Barreto et al. (2008).

[2]Nedra Pickler, "Obama Wins Support of Powerful Nevada Union," Associated Press State and Local Wire, January 9, 2008.

[3]These estimates are based on polls conducted by Gallup, CBS/NYT, Democracy Corps, Economist/YouGovPolimetrix, Field, Fox News/Rasmussen, GWU/Tarrance Group, Harris, USA Today, IPSOS, Pew, Mason Dixon, Public Policy Polling, QuinnipiacU/WSJ/WP, Suffolk University, and Survey USA.

Some reports by the media, as well as a statement made by Clinton consultant Sergio Bindixen, attributed Hispanic support for Clinton as rooted in an unwillingness to support a Black candidate. As our analysis in chapter 6 demonstrated, more than 60 percent of Hispanics from the 2006 Latino National Survey perceived little to no competition with Blacks in electing co-ethnics into office. Instead, just under a majority of Hispanics in this survey felt that Blacks and Hispanics have either some or a great deal of commonality with Blacks in the political arena. Moreover, in the 1983 Chicago mayoral election, Harold Washington won the support of 75 percent of the Hispanic vote in the general election (Betancur and Gills 2000b).

The more likely story, then, is that Clinton's support among Hispanics can be attributed to her strong name recognition as first lady and senator of New York; during Bill Clinton's presidency, Hispanics supported him in large numbers (see chapter 5). In addition, Hillary Clinton was wise to seek the endorsements of prominent Hispanic elected officials at the onset of the campaign; she also developed a highly effective Hispanic outreach campaign. Thus, Clinton's success with Hispanics may have more to do with their familiarity with her, as opposed to any type of racial animosity. Based on the exit poll estimates from the general election, it is clear that Hispanics had no qualms about supporting a Black candidate.

CAMPAIGNING TO HISPANICS IN 2008

Similar to previous presidential races, the primary mode of communication used by the candidates to reach out to Hispanics was televised political ads. As we write this postscript, and using the best information when this book goes to press, we estimate that candidates in the Democratic presidential primaries and caucuses spent more than $4 million on televised Spanish-language ads, which was more than the total spent on primary advertising in the past two presidential primaries combined (Segal 2008).[4] Univision Communications (the largest Spanish-language media outlet in the United States) estimated that it would sell $37 million

[4]Mitt Romney and Rudy Giuliani also advertised in Spanish during the Republican primaries.

in political advertising in 2008.[5] As further recognition of the importance of the Hispanic electorate, the Democratic debates that took place in Miami, Florida, on September 9, 2007, marked the first ever nationally televised bilingual debate.[6] Democratic contenders' official campaign websites were also available in Spanish, but among Republicans, Mitt Romney was the lone candidate to translate his website into Spanish. Only in the general election did the Republican candidate, John McCain, launch a Spanish-language version of his website, which was announced on Cinco de Mayo (fifth of May).

The top two contenders for the Democratic nomination, Senators Hillary Clinton and Barack Obama, began their Spanish advertising campaigns on Super Tuesday in the states of Arizona, California, Connecticut, and New York. As the primary season intensified, a considerable number of Spanish language ad buys were made in Texas and Puerto Rico. During the primary season, Obama produced three Spanish-language ads: "Como Padre" (Like a Father), "Hope," and "Gutierrez." The messages in these ads focused on Obama's role as a father, efforts to improve health insurance, economic assistance to attend universities, and new laws so that families could keep their homes. The "Gutierrez" commercial featured Congressman Luis Gutierrez (D-IL), who spoke of his involvement with Obama as a community activist in Chicago, as well as his participation in the immigration rallies that took place in May 2006. He also discussed Obama's commitment to immigration reform. In a general election ad entitled "El Sueño Americano" (American Dream), Obama spoke Spanish throughout the ad, with the content discussing his commitment to providing quality education, so that families could fulfill the American Dream. Another ad, called "Opportunidad" (Opportunity), aired in Nevada and also focused on education. Here, Obama explained his plan to offer college students a $4,000 tuition credit in exchange for community service. Obama also released a Spanish-language radio ad in the general election that portrayed him as a person who shares many of the same experiences as the Hispanic electorate (e.g., "raised by his mother with the support of

[5]Daniel Roth, "Politics Pays Off for Spanish TV," McClatchy Newspapers, October 27, 2008.

[6]The debate was sponsored by Univision, and questions and answers were simultaneously translated from English to Spanish.

his grandparents"). In the final weeks of the general election, Obama aired a thirty-minute "infomercial" on the major networks, Black Entertainment Television (BET), and Univision.[7]

McCain began his Spanish-language campaign in the general election and used both radio and televised political ads. His Spanish-language ad, entitled "624787," aired in New Mexico and was primarily a biographical spot that discussed McCain's experience in the armed services and his time spent as a prisoner of war; this ad also touched upon the need to end partisan divisions. Moreover, the McCain campaign produced a negative Spanish-language ad, in which he accused Obama and the Democrats for defeating immigration reform efforts that included a guest worker program with a pathway to citizenship, and increased security of the nation's borders.[8] As of November 2008, McCain and the Republican National Committee produced seven Spanish-language radio ads.[9] These political spots focused on McCain's background, Hispanic involvement in the armed forces, and immigration, as well as the Colombia Free Trade Agreement. One of these radio ads featured Frank Gamboa, a Hispanic who was McCain's roommate at the U.S. Naval Academy. In the ad, Gamboa attacks Obama for only recently recognizing the importance of the Hispanic electorate. McCain's Spanish-language advertising efforts were primarily aimed at Hispanics in the battleground states of Nevada, New Mexico, and Colorado.

These political spots demonstrate that both Obama and McCain strayed very little from the Spanish-language political ads developed by previous presidential candidates (Abrajano 2010). McCain's Spanish-language ads mostly emphasized his service in the armed forces as a way to connect with the many Hispanics who serve in the nation's military. Along with his position on immigration, Obama fostered a connection with Hispanics by emphasizing the immigrant experience. Both candidates also featured endorsements from prominent Hispanics in their commercials. But as an editorial statement from the *San Diego Union*

---

[7]In Univision, the commercial was aired in English with Spanish subtitles.

[8]This ad is entitled "Which Side Are They On?" and was aired on September 12, 2008.

[9]These ads are: "Recipe," "Estas Listo Para Obama?" (Are You Ready for Obama?), "Cuba Prisoners," "Colombia Free Trade," "God's Children, Values," and "Commitment vs. Rhetoric."

Tribune explained, "To win votes, the candidates in both parties have to find ways to communicate with Hispanic voters in ways that are substantive and respectful.... Hispanics care about the same issues as other Americans."[10] This sentiment echoes the conclusions that we reached in our chapter on political knowledge when we stressed the importance of communicating substantive and informative policy messages to Hispanics as one way to boost their knowledge of American politics.

In this presidential campaign, one unique trend emerged in terms of Hispanic outreach efforts—the increased use of negative advertising. One of McCain's attack ads, "Fraudulent," accuses Obama and the Democrats for killing the immigration reform bill proposed in 2006.[11] It also contained a visual image of Joseph Biden, Obama's running mate, quoted as saying that "Mexico is dysfunctional." McCain's other negative ad, "Riesgo" (Risk), focused on taxes and stated that Obama would raise taxes, especially for those with small businesses. Many of the statements in the "Fraudulent" ad were false, since Obama voted in favor of immigration reform; in fact, he supported the plan that would offer a pathway to citizenship, one provision that McCain did not support.

Obama's negative ads, "Dos Caras" (Two Faces) and "No Hay Mayor Obligacion" (No Greater Obligation), were broadcast in the four battleground states of Florida, New Mexico, Nevada, and Colorado. In the "Dos Caras" ad, McCain and the Republicans were portrayed as being intolerant toward Hispanics. Moreover, McCain is linked to conservative commentator Rush Limbaugh's views on Mexicans; the ad featured the following quote by Limbaugh, "Mexicans are stupid and unauthorized." In reality, these statements were false, because Limbaugh and McCain were never allies on the immigration issue; in fact, Limbaugh has criticized McCain for his position on immigration. Obama's other attack ad capitalized on McCain's statement that "the fundamentals of the economy are strong," despite the mortgage crisis and economic downturn that had happened in recent months.

[10]Editorial, *San Diego Union Tribune*, January 18, 2008.
[11]These two attack ads—"Riesgo" (Risk) and "Fraudulent" (Fraudulent)—were aired in September 2008.

The presidential contenders also addressed the nation's Hispanic political leaders at several conferences: the National Association for Hispanic Elected Officials (NALEO), the League of United Latin American Citizens (LULAC), and the National Council of La Raza (NCLR). In the speeches made to these groups, Obama promised to make immigration reform one of his main priorities during his first year in office; he also reaffirmed his commitment to health care, education, and the mortgage crisis. Further, Obama introduced his small business plan to these groups—one that would provide a tax credit to employers who offer health insurance to their employees. McCain's speeches focused on the need to create more jobs, by way of providing economic incentives to small businesses, as well as a health care plan that would provide households with a $5,000 tax credit in order to make their own health care decisions. Just days before the election (November 1), both candidates also made appearances on *Sabado Gigante*, Univision's longest-running program.

Once again, this presidential election highlighted the important role that Hispanics play in our nation's political fabric. As we discuss in more detail later, Hispanics' strong support for Obama essentially erased the gains made by Bush in 2004, but many questions remain unanswered about Hispanic political behavior in 2008.

Hispanic Vote Choice in the
2008 Presidential Election

In the end, Hispanic voters strongly supported Democratic senators Barack Obama and Joe Biden over Republican senator John McCain and Governor Sarah Palin by a margin of more than 2 to 1. Nationally, the National Election Pool (NEP) estimates two-thirds of Hispanics, 66 percent, voting in favor of Obama/Biden, and 32 percent supporting McCain/Palin. Obama's share of the Hispanic electorate comes only second to the percentage of votes Bill Clinton received from Hispanics back in 1996 (71.7 percent).[12]

[12]In general election polling, Hispanics favored Obama to McCain by a considerable margin. On average, 57 percent of Hispanics supported Obama, compared to 32 percent in favor of McCain.

Estimates from the NALEO Educational Fund indicate that in Virginia, where the margin of victory was estimated at 120,000, approximately 67,000 Hispanics voted for Obama. And in Florida, where the margin of victory was estimated at 178,745, the NALEO Educational Fund's analysis estimates that more than half a million Hispanics voted for Obama.[13] His success among Hispanics in Florida, who have traditionally supported the Republican candidate, was particularly remarkable; Obama captured 57 percent of the Hispanic vote in that state.[14] Based on these early estimates, it appears that Hispanics played a crucial role in turning these states from red to blue.

Initial indications are that political participation in the 2008 presidential election by both Hispanic and Black voters might have been higher than in the 2004 presidential election. Earlier in our work, we presented CPS data (figure 3.2) that estimated Black voters making up 11 percent of the electorate in 2004, while Hispanic voters made up 6 percent of the 2004 electorate. While directly comparable data are not yet available for analysis as we write this postscript, the 2008 NEP estimates that 9 percent of the electorate was Hispanic and 13 percent was Black. Furthermore, independent turnout analysis by the William C. Velasquez Institute (WCVI) estimated that Hispanic voters made up 7 percent of the electorate.[15] Whether this increase in Hispanic turnout can be attributed to the 2006 immigration marches and protests remains to be studied in more detail.

In figure P.1 we provide data from the media consortium exit poll (the NEP), presenting candidate support by voters from the various racial and ethnic groups in the 2008 election. We see first that Black voters overwhelmingly indicated to exit pollsters that they supported Obama (95 percent). We see a strong preference for Obama coming from both Hispanic voters (67 percent) and Asian voters (62 percent). It was only among Anglos where the majority did not cast their ballots in favor of Obama (43 percent).

[13]"Unprecedented Latino Voter Turnout Plays Critical Role in Early Outcome of the Presidential Election," NALEO Educational Fund news release, November 4, 2008, http://www.naleo.org/pr11-04-08b.html.

[14]In 2004, George W. Bush received 56 percent of the Latino vote in Florida.

[15]Antonio Gonzalez and Steven Ochoa, "The Latino Vote in 2008: Trends and Characteristics," William C. Velasquez Institute, http://www.wcvi.org.

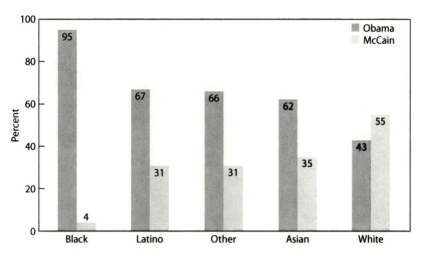

FIGURE P.1: 2008 presidential vote choice, by racial/ethnic group

Thus, it is clear that Hispanic voters strongly supported the Democratic presidential candidate in 2008, given that McCain's Hispanic vote share (31 percent in the NEP data) was significantly lower than the consensus estimate of Bush's Hispanic support in 2004 (40 percent). These outcomes are consistent with the historical voting patterns of racial and ethnic minorities analyzed in chapter 5; Black support for the democratic candidate continued to exceed the 80 percent threshold, while Hispanic and Asian support reached 60 percent or more.

In what could be considered a reflection of the great interest in Hispanic political behavior during the 2008 general election, many polls were conducted regarding the preferences and opinions of Hispanics. In figure P.2 we plot the Obama and McCain vote shares among Hispanic voters, from all of the polls we could find of Hispanic voters collected after June 2008. In this graph we also plot lines that give readers a sense of the overall trends over time. It is interesting to note that as early as June 2008, Obama had a substantial lead over McCain, with approximately a 25 percent gap separating the Democrat and Republican in the early summer of 2008. This gap was relatively stable, with some slight tightening through the convention period; but after the financial crisis hit Wall Street and Main Street in mid-September 2008,

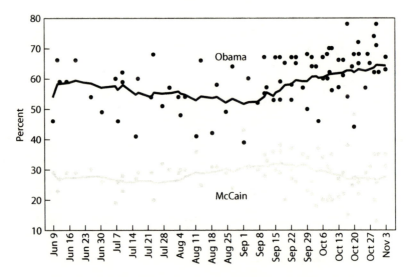

FIGURE P.2: Public opinion on presidential vote intent,
June–November 2008

Obama's lead among Hispanics increased steadily until election day, mirroring a pattern seen in most national polls of the entire electorate.

The NEP also provided data on Hispanic vote shares for both presidential candidates by state, and we present that data in figure P.3. While not all states with significant Hispanic populations are represented in this graph, some interesting information can still be gleaned from these data. In figure P.3 we array the states by the size of the Obama–McCain margin, beginning with Arizona, where the gap was relatively small, and ending with New Jersey, where the gap was sizeable. We also provide in figure P.3 the estimated Hispanic share of the electorate in each state (in parentheses next to each state's label on the horizontal axis).

As shown in figure P.3, the two states in which the Obama–McCain gap was the smallest were Arizona and Florida—where Hispanics made up 16 percent and 14 percent of each state's electorate, respectively. That the gaps were relatively small in these two states is not surprising, as Arizona is McCain's home state, and Florida is home to many Republican-leaning Hispanic voters. But it is also important to note that in both of these states, the exit polls show that the gap favored Obama, and thus Obama won

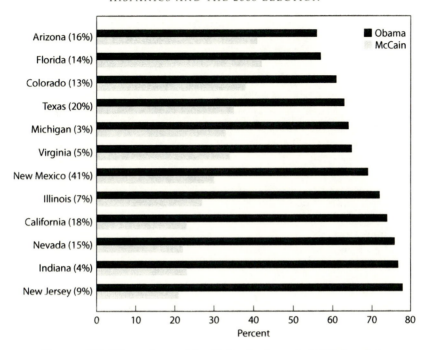

FIGURE P.3: Hispanic presidential vote share in 2008, by state

these two states where one might have expected McCain to run well among Hispanics. Also, the state-by-state analysis reveals that Hispanic voters made up relatively large components of the electorate in important Rocky Mountain and southwestern states, including Colorado (13 percent), Nevada (15 percent), and New Mexico (41 percent). In each of these states, Obama decisively beat McCain among Hispanic voters in the 2008 presidential election, with a margin of victory among Hispanic voters of 23 percent in Colorado, 39 percent in New Mexico, and 54 percent in Nevada.

So how did Obama manage to do so well among Hispanic voters, especially in the Rocky Mountain and southwestern states? At this point, this is an open (and important) research question and one that we cannot answer with the data now available. But we can look at some of the available data and see what might have driven Hispanic voters to strongly support Obama in the 2008 presidential election.

In table P.1 we provide some additional information from the national exit polls; here we give responses to a "most important

TABLE P.1
Voters' Opinions on the Most Important Issues Facing the Country

	Obama	McCain
Full sample		
Energy policy (7%)	50%	46%
The war in Iraq (10%)	59%	39%
The economy (63%)	53%	44%
Terrorism (9%)	13%	86%
Health care (9%)	73%	26%
Hispanics (N = 683)		
Energy policy (8%)	—	—
The war in Iraq (10%)	78%	20%
The economy (61%)	63%	36%
Terrorism (9%)	32%	68%
Health care (9%)	71%	29%
Whites (N = 6,142)		
Energy policy (7%)	43%	54%
The war in Iraq (9%)	50%	48%
The economy (63%)	45%	53%
Terrorism (10%)	10%	90%
Health care (8%)	64%	34%
Blacks (N = 1,198)		
Energy policy (6%)	98%	—
The war in Iraq (12%)	88%	11%
The economy (62%)	98%	2%
Terrorism (2%)	—	—
Health care (16%)	99%	1%

Source: 2008 National Election Pool Survey.

Note: Entries in parentheses in the first column are the percentage of voters who identified that particular issue as the most important one facing the country. Entries in columns 2 and 3 are responses to the same question, but broken down by vote choice.

issue" question presented to voters in the national exit poll. We start in table P.1 by discussing the results for the full sample, based on one's vote choice. Here we see that 63 percent of all voters considered the economy as the most important issue facing the country. And among this group, the voters supported Obama by a 9-point margin (53 percent to 44 percent). The remaining four issues were a much lower priority to voters in the 2008 presidential election. Only 10 percent cited the Iraq War as the most important issue (with Obama managing a 20-point lead among those voters), while terrorism and health care tied in importance, with each being identified by 9 percent of the electorate as most important. It is worthwhile to note here that among the 9 percent in the electorate who saw terrorism as the most important issue, McCain had a 73-point lead, while among the 9 percent who saw health care as most important, Obama had a strong 47-point lead. Recall that in our analysis of the determinants of party identification (see chapter 2), Hispanics who supported government-sponsored health insurance were less likely to identify as a Republican than as a Democrat or independent. Thus, it should come as no surprise that Hispanics who viewed health care as the important issue preferred Obama to McCain by such a wide margin.

Remarkably, when we look at the exit poll data on the most important issue and vote choice stratified by race and ethnicity, we see that there was much agreement about the most important issue in this election: 63 percent of white voters, 62 percent of Black voters, and 61 percent of Hispanic voters considered the economy as the most important issue facing the country. But the issue of the economy broke differently across racial and ethnic groups: among Hispanics and Blacks who saw the economy as the most important issue, Obama was the clear favorite, but among whites who rated the economy as the most important issue, McCain had an 8-point lead. A much lower percentage of white and Hispanic voters saw the Iraq War and terrorism as important issues (9 or 10 percent of each group's voters). White voters who saw terrorism as important issue strongly supported McCain (by an 80-point margin), while Hispanics who felt terrorism was the priority supported McCain by a lower margin (36 percentage points). White voters who saw the Iraq War as most important favored Obama by a slim 2-percentage-point margin, while Hispanics who saw the Iraq War as the most important issue facing the country gave Obama a much stronger lead, 58 percentage points (Blacks perceiving the Iraq War as important strongly supported Obama, 88 percent to McCain's 11 percent).

We now have some initial evidence that indicates why Obama performed so well among Hispanics in 2008. It may have also been the case that Obama was able to win back some of the Hispanic votes that went to Bush in 2004. Recall that Hispanic voters were attracted to Bush in 2004 because of his stance on moral values and his national security message, despite Hispanics' concerns about the economy and other issues like health care and education that might have favored Kerry's candidacy (Abrajano, Alvarez, and Nagler 2008). While we do not yet have access to the sort of data that we used in our study of the 2004 presidential election, the data presented in table P.1 demonstrate that Hispanics who were overwhelmingly concerned about the economy supported Obama by a reasonable margin. Moreover, Obama's campaign seemed to have minimized concerns about terrorism and national security among Hispanics, and they were able to completely remove the issue of moral values issues from the table.

Looking Ahead to 2010 and Beyond

The 2008 presidential election was historic in many ways, and our examination of some initial data indicates that the Hispanic vote played an important role in the Obama victory. It is much too early to determine whether the 2008 election signals a large-scale political shift in the United States, and it is not clear that Obama and the Democratic Party will manage to consolidate their gains in 2010 and beyond. As we write this postscript, with Obama in the first one hundred days of his presidency, it is clear that his administration—and the ruling Democratic Party—face political, economic, and foreign policy challenges that might themselves be of historic importance.

How Hispanic voters react in the future will continue to be a question of the issues at hand in any particular future election, as well as how the parties and candidates vie for the Hispanic vote. Hispanic voters did support Obama strongly in 2008, but it is always worth remembering that Kerry did not fare as well in 2004 among Hispanic voters, which to us is a strong reminder that no political party in the United States can take the Hispanic vote for granted. As the loyalty of Hispanic voters has yet to be captured by either the Democrats or Republicans, each presidential year provides both parties with an opportunity to capture the largest racial and ethnic minority group in our nation.

* Appendix *

RESEARCH DESIGN AND ORGANIZATION

IN THIS BOOK, we draw upon data mainly from six sources, though occasionally we examine other data sources: the American National Election Survey (NES), the National Annenberg Election Survey (NAES), the U.S. Census Bureau's Current Population Survey (CPS), exit polls from the news media of the national general elections from 1992 through 2006, the Latino National Survey (LNS) of 2006 (Fraga et al. 2006), and several nationwide surveys conducted by the Pew Hispanic Center. The first three surveys are the preeminent sources for individual-level data on American political behavior, because they asked respondents a wide array of questions as well as a series of in-depth questions relating to politics. Unfortunately, the NES interviews only a very small percentage of Hispanics in their surveys; the sample of Hispanics in every NES survey from 1964 through 2004 has never exceeded one hundred.[1] The NAES interviewed a larger number of Hispanics but in 2000 made no distinctions by Hispanic subgroup and, in both 2000 and 2004, no distinctions by Hispanics' generational status. Given that subgroup and generational status are two key attributes that explain Hispanic political behavior, we need to analyze data that include answers to these questions, as well as to more specific ones pertaining to Hispanic identity and culture. As such, we supplement the NAES with data from the Pew Hispanic Center, the leading resource for political information on Hispanics. The surveys conducted by Pew draw on a nationally representative sample of Hispanics, are offered in both Spanish and English, include questions pertaining to both ethnicity and generational status, and consistently interview a sizeable number of individuals ($N > 1,000$). We use the media exit poll data in our chapter on Hispanic vote choice, because exit polls provide large samples of actual voters as they leave the polling place on election day. Exit polls have their drawbacks: most importantly, they are not probability samples of the sort used in most academic research, and they typically

[1]In addition, the NES conducts their interviews in English only, creating another form of selection bias in the data.

employ very short and simple survey questionnaires. Nonetheless, they provide an amazing wealth of data about how Hispanics vote in national general elections and how their preferences and voting behavior compare to those of other racial and ethnic groups. The CPS data, finally, are used primarily to discuss Hispanic participation in recent presidential elections: the CPS Voter Supplement (for which research is conducted in November of each federal election year) contains interviews with tens of thousands of registered voters, including a relatively large and representative sample of Hispanic registered voters. Since the Census Bureau does not include many survey questions we view as important given our academic interests, however—such as the partisanship of registered voters—the CPS data are limited in their utility for our purposes.

We also take advantage of the recently released 2006 Latino National Survey. This survey was a collaborative effort among some of the nation's preeminent scholars of Hispanic politics—Luis Fraga, John A. Garcia, Rodney Hero, Michael Jones-Correa, Valerie Martinez-Ebers, and Gary Segura. The LNS was in the field from November 17, 2005, to August 14, 2006, and represents approximately 87.5 percent of the Hispanic population in the United States. The LNS offers scholars an unprecedented opportunity to understand the Hispanic population like never before, as the survey interviewed more than 8,600 Hispanics with 165 survey response items pertaining to their political, social, and cultural attitudes.

* References *

Abrajano, Marisa. 2010. *Campaigning to the New American Electorate: Advertising to Latino Voters*. Palo Alto, CA: Stanford University Press.

Abrajano, Marisa, and R. Michael Alvarez. Forthcoming. "Why Are Latinos More Politically Trusting than Other Americans?" *American Politics Research*.

Abrajano, Marisa A. 2005. "Who Evaluates a Presidential Candidate by Using Non-Policy Campaign Messages?" *Political Research Quarterly* 58:55–67.

Abrajano, Marisa, R. Michael Alvarez, and Jonathan Nagler. 2005. "Race Based vs. Issue Voting: A Natural Experiment." *Political Research Quarterly* 58:203–18.

Abrajano, Marisa, R. Michael Alvarez, and Jonathan Nagler. 2008. "The 2004 Hispanic Vote: Insecurity and Moral Concerns." *Journal of Politics* 70(2): 368–82.

Abrajano, Marisa, and Simran Singh. 2009. "Examining the Link Between Issue Attitudes and News Source: The Case of Latinos and Immigration Reform." *Political Behavior* 31(1): 1–30.

Abramowitz, Alan I. 1995. "It's Abortion, Stupid: Policy Voting in the 1992 Presidential Election." *Journal of Politics* 57:176–86.

Abramson, John R., John H. Aldrich, and David Rohde. 2002. *Change and Continuity in the 2000 Elections*. Washington, DC: CQ Press.

Adams, James. 1999. "An Assessment of Voting Systems Under the Proximity and Directional Models of the Vote." *Public Choice* 98:131–51.

Aldrich, John. 1995. *Why Parties? The Origin and Transformation of Political Parties in America*. Chicago: University of Chicago Press.

Alvarez, R. Michael. 1997. *Information and Elections*. Ann Arbor: University of Michigan Press.

Alvarez, R. Michael, and Stephen Ansolabehere. 2002. "California Votes: The Promise of Election Day Registration." Demos, available at http://vote.caltech.edu/media/documents/california_votes.pdf.

Alvarez, R. Michael, Delia Bailey, and Jonathan Katz. 2007. "The Effect of Voter Identification Laws on Voter Turnout." Working paper, California Institute of Technology.

Alvarez, R. Michael, and John Brehm. 1995. "American Ambivalence Towards Abortion Policy: Development of a Heteroskedastic Probit Model of Competing Values." *American Journal of Political Science* 39: 1055–82.

Alvarez, R. Michael, and John Brehm. 2002. *Hard Choices, Easy Answers: Values, Information, and American Public Opinion*. Princeton, NJ: Princeton University Press.

Alvarez, R. Michael, and Lisa García Bedolla. 2003. "The Foundations of Hispanic Voter Partisanship: Evidence from the 2000 Election." *Journal of Politics* 65:31–49.

Alvarez, R. Michael, and Thad E. Hall. 2005. "The Next Big Election Challenge: Developing Electronic Data Transaction Standards for Election Administration." IBM Center for The Business of Government.

Alvarez, R. Michael, and Jonathan Nagler. 2007a. "Election Day Voter Registration in Iowa." Demos briefing paper, available at http://vote .caltech.edu/reports/iowa_edr_alv-nagler3-07.pdf.

Alvarez, R. Michael, and Jonathan Nagler. 2007b. "Same Day Voter Registration in North Carolina." Demos briefing paper, available at http://www.votingtechnologyproject.org/reports/AlvNagler_ EDR-NC_Demos.pdf.

Alvarez, R. Michael, Jonathan Nagler, and Catherine H. Wilson. 2004. "Making Voting Easier: Election Day Registration in New York." Demos, available at http://vote.caltech.edu/media/documents/EDRNY0404.pdf.

Bailey, Delia, and R. Michael Alvarez. 2007. "Modeling Latino Voter Turnout in the 2000 and 2004 Elections." Paper presented at the Annual Meeting of the American Political Science Association, Chicago, IL.

Baldassare, Mark. 2004. PPIC Statewide Survey: Special Survey on Californians and their Future. Public Policy Institute of California, www. ppic.org.

Bali, Valentina A., and R. Michael Alvarez. 2003. "Schools and Educational Outcomes: What Causes the `Race Gap' in Student Test Scores?" *Social Science Quarterly* 84(2): 485–507.

Bali, Valentina A., and R. Michael Alvarez. 2004. "The Race Gap in Student Achievement Test Scores: Longitudinal Evidence from a Racially Diverse School District." *Policy Studies Journal* 32(3): 393–415.

Barabas, Jason. 2002. "Another Look at the Measurement of Political Knowledge." *Political Analysis* 10(2): 209.

Barreto, Matt A., Luis R. Fraga, Sylvia Manzano, Valerie Martinez-Ebers and Gary M. Segura. 2008. "'Should They Dance with the One Who Brung 'Em?' Latinos and the 2008 Presidential Election." PS: Political Science and Politics. 41(4): 753-760.

Barreto, Matt. 2007. "Si Se Puede! Candidates and the Mobilization of Latino Voters." *American Political Science Review* 101(3): 425–41.

Barreto, Matt, Gary Segura, and Nathan Woods. 2004. "The Mobilizing Effect of Majority–Minority Districts on Latino Turnout." *American Political Science Review* 98:65–75.

Bartels, Larry M. 1986. "Uninformed Votes: Information Effects in Presidential Elections." *American Journal of Political Science* 40(1): 194–230.

Berinsky, Adam J. 2005. "The Perverse Consequences of Electoral Reform in the United States." *American Politics Research* 33:471–91.

Betancur, John J., and Douglas C. Gills. 2000a. "The Restructuring of Urban Relations: Recent Challenges and Dilemmas for African Americans and Latinos in U.S. Cities." In *The Collaborative City: Opportunities and Struggles for Blacks and Latinos in U.S. Cities*, ed. John J. Betancur and Douglas C. Gills. New York: Garland.

Betancur, John J., and Douglas C. Gills. 2000b. "The African American and Latino Coalition Experience in Chicago under Mayor Harold Washington." In *The Collaborative City: Opportunities and Struggles for Blacks and Latinos in U.S. Cities*, ed. John J. Betancur and Douglas C. Gills. New York: Garland.

Betts, Julian R., Andrew C. Zau, and Lorien A. Rice. 2003. "Determinants of Student Achievement: New Evidence from San Diego." Public Policy Institute of California.

Binder, Norman E., Jerry Polinard, and Robert Wrinkle. 1997. "Mexican American and Anglo Attitudes Toward Immigration Reform." *Social Science Quarterly* 78:324–37.

Bloemraad, Irene. 2006. *Becoming a Citizen: Incorporating Immigrants and Refugees in the United States and Canada*. Berkeley: University of California Press.

Bobo, Lawrence, and Vincent Hutchings. 1996. "Perceptions of Racial Group Competition: Extending Blumer's Theory of Group Position to a Multiracial Social Context." *American Sociological Review* 61(6): 951–72.

Bogardus, Emory S. 1928. *Immigration and Race Attitudes*. New York: D. C. Heath.

Branton, Regina P. 2007. "Latino Attitudes toward Various Areas of Public Policy." *Political Research Quarterly* 60(2): 293–303.

Brians, Craig L., and Bernard Grofman. 1999. "When Registration Barriers Fall, Why Votes? An Empirical Test of a Rational Choice Model." *Public Choice* 99(1–2): 161–76.

Brians, Craig L., and Bernard Grofman. 2001. "Election Day Registration's Effect on U.S. Voter Turnout." *Social Science Quarterly* 82(1): 170–83.

Browning, Rufus, Dale Rogers Marshall, and David H. Tabb. 1984. *Protest Is Not Enough: The Struggle of Blacks and Hispanics for Equality in Urban Politics*. Berkeley: University of California Press.

Burden, Barry C. 2000. "Voter Turnout and the National Election Studies." *Political Analysis* 8(4): 389–98.

Cain, Bruce, and D. Roderick Kiewiet. 1984. "Ethnicity and Electoral Choice: Mexican American Voting Behavior in the California 30th Congressional District." *Social Science Quarterly* 65:315–27.

Cain, Bruce E., D. Roderick Kiewiet, and Carole J. Uhlaner. 1991. "The Acquisition of Partisanship by Hispanics and Asian Americans." *American Journal of Political Science* 35:390–422.

Campbell, Angus, Philip Converse, Warren Miller, and Donald Stokes. 1964. *The American Voter*. New York: John Wiley and Sons.

Campbell, J. Gibson, and Emily Lennon. 1999. "Historical Census Statistics on the Foreign-Born Population of the United States: 1850–1990." Working Paper No. 29, Population Division.

Carmines, Edward, and James Stimson. 1980. "The Two Faces of Issue Voting." *American Political Science Review* 74:78–91.

Carmines, Edward, and James Stimson. 1990. *Issue Evolution: Race and Transformation of American Politics*. Princeton, NJ: Princeton University Press.

Chandra, Kanchan. 2004. *Why Ethnic Parties Succeed: Patronage and Ethnic Headcounts in India*. New York: Cambridge University Press.

Combs, Michael W., and Susan Welch. 1982. "Blacks, Whites, and Attitudes Toward Abortion." *Public Opinion Quarterly* 46:510–20.

Converse, Philip E. 1961. "The Nature of Belief Systems in Mass Publics." In *Ideology and Discontent*, ed. David Apter. Free Press: New York.

Dahl, Robert A. 1961. *Who Governs? Democracy and Power in an American City*. New Haven, CT: Yale University Press.

Dawson, Michael. 1994. *Behind the Mule: Race and Class in African-American Politics*. Princeton, NJ: Princeton University Press.

de la Garza, Rodolfo O., Marisa Abrajano, and Jeronimo Cortina. 2008. "Get Me to the Polls on Time: Hispanic Mobilization and Turnout in the 2000 Election." In *New Race Politics: Understanding Minority and Immigrant Politics*, ed. Jane Junn and Kerry Haynie. New York: Cambridge University Press.

de la Garza, Rodolfo O., Angelo Falcon, and F. Chris Garcia. 1996. "Will the Real Americans Please Stand Up: Anglo and Mexican-American Support of Core American Political Values." *American Journal of Political Science* 40:335–51.

de la Garza, Rodolfo O., and Luis DeSipio. 1992. *From Rhetoric to Reality: Hispanic Politics in the 1988 Elections*. Boulder, CO: Westview Press.

de la Garza, Rodolfo O., and Louis DeSipio. 1996. *Ethnic Ironies: Latino Politics in the 1992 Elections*. Boulder, CO: Westview Press.

de la Garza, Rodolfo O., and Louis DeSipio. 2000. *Awash in the Mainstream: Latino Politics in the 1996 Elections*. Boulder, CO: Rowman and Littlefield.

de la Garza, Rodolfo O., and Louis DeSipio. 2005. *Muted Voices: Latinos and the 2000 Elections*. Boulder, CO: Rowman and Littlefield.

del Pinal, Jorge, and Audrey Singer. 1997. Generations of Diversity: Latinos in the United States. *Population Bulletin* 52(3), Population Reference Bureau. http://www.prb.org/pubs/population_bulletin/bu52-3/fertility.htm.

Delli Carpini, Michael X., and Scott Keeter. 1993. "Measuring Political Knowledge: Putting First Things First." *American Journal of Political Science* 37(4): 1179–206.

Delli Carpini, Michael X., and Scott Keeter 1996. *What Americans Know About Politics and Why It Matters*. New Haven, CT: Yale University Press.

DeSipio, Louis. 1996. *Counting on the Hispanic Vote: Hispanics as a New Electorate*. Charlottesville: University Press of Virginia.

DeSipio, Louis. 2001. "Building America, One Person at a Time: Naturalization and the Political Behavior of the Naturalized in Contemporary American Politics." In *E Pluribus Unum? Contemporary and Historical Perspectives on Immigrant Political Incorporation*, ed. G. Gerstle and J. Mollenkopf. New York: Russell Sage Foundation.

Downs, Anthony. 1957. *An Economic Theory of Democracy*. New York: Harper and Brothers.

Dyer, James, Arnold Vedlitz, and Stephen Worchel. 1989. "Social Distance among Racial and Ethnic Groups in Texas: Some Demographic Correlates." *Social Science Quarterly* 70:607–16.

Easton, David, and Jack Dennis. 1969. *Children in the Political System: Origins of Political Legitimacy*. New York: McGraw-Hill.

Erie, Steve. 1988. *Rainbow's End: Irish-Americans and the Dilemmas of Urban Machine Politics, 1840–1985*. Berkeley: University of California Press.

Espiritu, Yen Le. 1992. *Asian American Panethnicity, Bridging Institutions and Identity*. Philadelphia, PA: Temple University Press.

Falcon, Angelo. 1989. "Puerto Ricans and the 1989 Mayoral Election in New York City." *Hispanic Journal of Behavioral Sciences* 11:245–58.

Fearon, James. 2006. "Ethnic Mobilization and Ethnic Violence." In *The Oxford Handbook of Political Economy*, ed. Barry Weingast and Donald Wittman. New York: Oxford University Press.

Fenster, Mark J. 1994. "The Impact of Allowing Day of Registration Voting on Turnout in U.S. Elections from 1960 to 1992." *American Politics Quarterly* 22(1): 74–87.

Fraga, Luis R., John A. Garcia, Rodney Hero, Michael Jones-Correa, Valerie Martinez-Ebers, and Gary M. Segura. LATINO NATIONAL SURVEY (LNS), 2006 [Computer file]. ICPSR20862-v1. Miami, FL: Geoscape International [producer], 2006. Ann Arbor, MI: Inter-university Consortium for Political and Social Research [distributor], 2008-05-27.

Fry, Richard. 2007. "The Changing Ethnic Composition of U.S. Public Schools." Pew Hispanic Center Report.

Garcia, F. Chris, and Rodolfo O. de la Garza. 1977. *The Chicano Political Experience: Three Perspectives*. North Scituate, MA: Duxbury Press.

Garcia, John A. 2003. *Latino Politics in America: Community, Culture and Interests*. New York: Rowman and Littlefield.

Garcia, Maria Cristina. 1996. *Havana USA: Cuban Exiles and Cuban Americans in South Florida, 1959–1994*. Berkeley: University of California Press.

García Bedolla, Lisa. 2003. "The Identity Paradox: Latino Language, Politics and Selective Dissociation." *Latino Studies* 1:264–83.

García Bedolla, Lisa. 2005. *Fluid Borders: Hispanic Power, Identity and Politics in Los Angeles*. Berkeley: University of California Press.

Gerber, Alan S., and Donald P. Green. 2000a. "The Effect of a Non-Partisan Get-Out-the-Vote Drive: An Experimental Study of Leafleting." *Journal of Politics* 62:846–57.

Gerber, Alan S., and Donald P. Green. 2000b. "The Effects of Canvassing, Telephone Calls, and Direct Mail on Voter Turnout: A Field Experiment." *American Political Science Review* 94:653–63.

Ginsburg, Faye D. 1989. *Contested Lives: The Abortion Debate in an American Community*. Berkeley: University of California Press.

Gordon, Milton. 1964. *Assimilation in American Life: The Role of Race, Religion, and National Origins*. New York: Oxford University Press.

Graves, Scott, and Jongho Lee. 2000. "Ethnic Underpinnings of Voting Preference: Latinos and the 1996 U.S. Senate Elections in Texas." *Social Science Quarterly* 81:226–36.

Green, Donald, and Bradley Palmquist. 1990. "Of Artifacts and Partisan Instability." *American Journal of Political Science* 34(3): 872–902.

Greenstein, Fred I. 1965. *Children and Politics*. New Haven, CT: Yale University Press.

Gutierrez, David G. 1995. *Walls and Mirrors: Mexican Americans, Mexican Immigrants and the Politics of Ethnicity*. Berkeley: University of California Press.

Guzman, Betsy. 2001. "The Hispanic Population, Census 2000 Brief." http://www.census.gov/prod/2001pubs/c2kbr01-3.pdf.

Guzman, Betsy, and Eileen Diaz McConnell. 2002. "The Hispanic Population: 1990–2000 Growth and Change." *Population Research and Policy Review* 21:109–28.

Hajnal, Zoltan, Elisabeth Gerber, and Hugh Louch. 2002. "Minorities and Direct Legislation: Evidence from California's Ballot Proposition Elections." *Journal of Politics* 64:154–77.

Hajnal, Zoltan L., and Taeku Lee. 2008. "Race, Immigration, and Political Independents in America." Unpublished manuscript.

Hall, Elaine J., and Myra Marx Ferree. 1986. "Race Differences in Abortion Attitudes." *Public Opinion Quarterly* 50:193–207.

Hero, Rodney. 1992. *Hispanics and the U.S. Political System*. Philadelphia, PA: Temple University Press.

Hero, Rodney, and Kathleen M. Beatty. 1989. "The Elections of Federico Pena as Mayor of Denver: Analysis and Implications." *Social Science Quarterly* 70: 300–310.

Hetherington, Mark. 2005. *Why Trust Matters: Declining Political Trust and the Demise of American Liberalism*. Princeton, NJ: Princeton University Press.

Highton, Benjamin. 1997. "Easy Registration and Voter Turnout." *Journal of Politics* 59(2): 565–75.

Highton, Benjamin, and Arthur L. Burris. 2002. "New Perspectives on Hispanic Voter Turnout in the United States." *American Politics Research* 30(3): 285–306.

Hill, Kevin A., and Dario Moreno. 2005. "Battleground Florida." In *Muted Voices: Hispanics and the 2000 Elections*, ed. Rodolfo O. de la Garza and Louis DeSipio. Lanham, MD: Rowman and Littlefield.

Hood, M. V. III, Irwin Morris, and Kurt Shirkley. 1997. "Quedete or Vete: Unraveling the Determinants of Hispanic Public Opinion toward Immigration." *Political Research Quarterly* 50:627–47.

Horowitz, Donald. 1985. *Ethnic Groups in Conflict*. Berkeley, CA: University of California Press.

Horton, John. 1995. *The Politics of Diversity: Immigration, Resistance and Change in Monterey Park, California*. Philadelphia, PA: Temple University Press.

Huntington, Samuel P. 2004. *Who Are We? The Challenges to America's Identity*. New York: Simon and Schuster.

Hyman, Herbert H. 1959. *Political Socialization*. Glencoe, IL: Free Press.

Jacobson, Gary. 2006. "Public Opinion and the War in Iraq." Paper presented at the Annual Meeting of the American Political Science Association, Marriott, Loews Philadelphia, and the Pennsylvania Convention Center, Philadelphia, PA, August 31.

Jennings, James, ed. 1992. *Race, Politics and Economic Development*. New York: Verso.

Jimenez, Tomas. 2007. "Weighing the Costs and Benefits of Mexican Immigration: The Mexican-American Perspective." *Social Sciences Quarterly* 88(3): 599–618.

Jost, Kenneth. 2004. *Issues in Race and Ethnicity*. 3rd ed. Washington, DC: CQ Press.

Kaufman, Karen. 2003. *The Urban Voter: Group Conflict and Mayoral Voting Behavior in American Cities*. Ann Arbor: University of Michigan Press.

Key, V. O., Jr. 1964. *Politics, Parties and Pressure Groups*. New York: Thomas Y. Crowell.

Kiewiet, D. Roderick. 1983. *Macroeconomics and Micropolitics: The Electoral Effects of Economic Issues*. Chicago: University of Chicago Press.

Kim, Claire. 2000. *Bitter Fruit: The Politics of Black-Korean Conflict in New York City*. New Haven, CT: Yale University Press.

Kinder, Donald R., and Lynn M. Sanders. 1990. "Mimicking Political Debate with Survey Questions: The Case of White Opinion on Affirmative Action for Blacks." *Social Cognition* 8:83–103.

King, James D., and Rodney A. Wambeam. 1995. "Impact of Election Day Registration on Voter Turnout: A Quasi-experimental Analysis." *Policy Studies Review* 14(3/4): 263–78.

Knack, Stephen. 2001. "Election-Day Registration: The Second Wave." *American Politics Quarterly* 29(1): 65–78.

Knack, Stephen, and James White. 2000. "Election-Day Registration and Turnout Inequality." *Political Behavior* 22(1): 29–44.

Kotlowitz, Alex. 2007. "All Immigration Politics Is Local." *New York Times Magazine*, August 5.

Kozol, Jonathan. 2005. *Shame of the Nation: The Restoration of Apartheid Schooling in America*. New York: Crown Publishers.

Krosnick, Jon A. 1990. "Expertise and Political Psychology." *Social Cognition* 8: 1–8.

Lai, James S. 1999. "Racially Polarized Voting and its Effects on the Formation of a Viable Latino-Asian Pacific Coalition." *1998–1999 National Asian Pacific American Political Almanac*. Berkeley: University of California Press.

Larsen, Luke J. 2004. "The Foreign-Born Population in the United States: 2003, Population Characteristics." http://www.census.gov/prod/2004 pubs/p20-551.pdf.

Layman, Geoffrey. 2001. *The Great Divide: Religious and Cultural Conflict in American Party Politics*. New York: Columbia University Press.

Layman, Geoffrey C., and Edward G. Carmines. 1997. "Cultural Conflict in American Politics: Religious Traditionalism, Postmaterialism, and U.S. Political Behavior." *Journal of Politics* 59:751–77.

Layman, Geoffrey C., and John C. Green. 2005. "Wars and Rumours of Wars: The Contexts of Cultural Conflict in American Political Behavior." *British Journal of Political Science* 36:61–89.

Lazarsfeld, Paul, Bernard Berelson, and Hazel Gaudet. 1944. *The People's Choice: How a Voter Makes Up His Mind in a Presidential Campaign*. New York: Duell, Sloan and Pearce.

Leal, David. 2002. "Political Participation by Latino Non-Citizens in the United States." *British Journal of Political Science* 32:353–70.

Leal, David L., Matt Barreto, Jongho Lee, and Rodolfo O. de la Garza. 2005. "The Latino Vote in the 2004 Election." *PS: Political Science & Politics* 38:41–49.

Leege, David C., Kenneth D. Wald, Brian S. Krueger, and Paul D. Mueller. 2002. *The Politics of Cultural Differences: Social Change and Voter*

Mobilization Strategies in the post-New Deal Period. Princeton, NJ: Princeton University Press.

Leighley, Jan E. 2001. *Strength in Numbers? The Political Mobilization of Racial and Ethnic Minorities.* Princeton, NJ: Princeton University Press.

Leighley, Jan E., and Jonathan Nagler. 1992. "Individual and Systemic Influences on Turnout: Who Votes? 1984" *Journal of Politics* 54:718–40.

Leighley, Jan E., and Arnold Vedlitz. 1999. "Race, Ethnicity, and Political Participation: Competing Models and Contrasting Explanations." *Journal of Politics* 61(4): 1092–114.

Lollock, Lisa. 2001. *The Foreign Born Population in the United States: March 2000.* Current Population Survey Reports. P20-534. U.S. Census Bureau, Washington, DC. http://www.census.gov/prod/2000pubs/p20-534.pdf.

Luker, Kristin. 1984. *Abortion and the Politics of Motherhood.* Berkeley: University of California Press.

Lupia, Arthur. 1994. "Shortcuts Versus Encyclopedias: Information and Voting in California Insurance Reform Elections." *American Political Science Review* 88:63–76.

Lupia, Arthur, and Matthew D. McCubbins. 1998. *The Democratic Dilemma: Can Citizens Learn What They Need to Know?* New York: Cambridge University Press.

Malone, Nolan, Kaari F. Baluja, Joseph M. Costanzo, and Cynthia J. Davis. 2003. "The Foreign-Born Population, 2000: Census 2000 Brief." http://www.census.gov/prod/2003pubs/c2kbr-34.pdf.

McClain, Paula D., and Albert K. Karnig. 1990. "Black and Hispanic Socioeconomic and Political Competition." *American Political Science Review* 84(2): 535–45.

Meier, Kenneth, Eric Juenke, Robert Wrinkle, and Jerry Polinard. 2005. "Structural Choices and Representational Biases: The Post-Election Color of Representation." *American Journal of Political Science* 49: 758–68.

Meier, Kenneth J., and Joseph Stewart Jr. 1991. "Cooperation and Conflict in Multiracial School Districts." *Journal of Politics* 53:1123–33.

Michelson, Melissa. 2001. "Trust in Chicago Latinos." *Journal of Urban Affairs* 23:323–34.

Michelson, Melissa R. 2003. "Getting Out The Hispanic Vote: How Door-to-Door Canvassing Influences Voter Turnout in Rural Central California." *Political Behavior* 25(3): 247–63.

Miller, Warren E., and J. Merrill Shanks. 1996. *The New American Voter.* Cambridge, MA: Harvard University Press.

Mollenkopf, John H. 1994. *A Phoenix in the Ashes: The Rise and Fall of the Koch Coalition in New York City Politics.* Princeton, NJ: Princeton University Press.

Mondak, Jeffery J. 1999. "Reconsidering the Measurement of Political Knowledge." *Political Analysis* 8(1):57–82.

Moreno, Dario. 1997. "The Cuban Model: Political Empowerment in Miami." In *Pursuing Power: Latinos and the U.S. Political System*, ed. F. Chris Garcia. Notre Dame, IN: Notre Dame University Press.

Muñoz, Carlos, and Charles Henry. 1986. "Rainbow Coalitions in Four Big Cities: San Antonio, Denver, Chicago and Philadelphia." *PS: Political Science & Politics* 19(3): 598.

Newton, Lina. 2000. "Why Some Latinos Supported Proposition 187: Testing the Economic Threat and Cultural Identity Hypotheses." *Social Science Quarterly* 81(1): 180–93.

Nagourney, Adam, and Jennifer Steinhauer. 2008. "In Obama's Pursuit of Latinos, Race Plays Role." *New York Times*, January 15, 2008.

Nie, Norman H., Jane Junn, and Kenneth Stehlik-Barry. 1996. *Education and Democratic Citizenship in America*. Chicago: University of Chicago Press.

Niemi, Richard G., and Jane Junn. 1998. *Civic Education: What Makes Students Learn?* New Haven, CT: Yale University Press.

Oliver, J. Eric, and Janelle Wong. 2003. "Intergroup Prejudice in Multiethnic Settings." *American Journal of Political Science* 47(4): 567–82.

Olson, Mancur. 1971. *The Logic of Collective Action: Public Goods and the Theory of Groups*, rev. ed. Cambridge: Harvard University Press.

Orfield, Gary, and Mindy Kornhaber. 2001. *Raising Standards or Raising Barriers? Inequality and High-Stakes Testing in Public Education*. New York: Century Foundation Press.

Orfield, Gary, and Chungmei Lee. 2004. "Brown at 50: King's Dream or Plessy's Nightmare?" The Civil Rights Project, Harvard University.

Orfield, Gary, and Chungmei Lee. January 2006. "Racial Transformation and the Changing Nature of Segregation." The Civil Rights Project, Harvard University.

Overton, Spencer. 2006. *Stealing Democracy: The New Politics of Voter Suppression*. New York: W. W. Norton.

Pantoja, Adrian D., Ricardo Ramirez, and Gary M. Segura. 2001. "Citizens by Choice, Voters by Necessity: Patterns in Political Mobilization by Naturalized Hispanics." *Political Research Quarterly* 54: 729–50.

Pardo, Mary. 1997. "Mexican American Women Grassroots Community Activists: Mothers of East Los Angeles." In *Pursuing Power: Latinos and the Political System*, ed. F. Chris Garcia. Urbana: University of Illinois Press.

Park, Robert E. 1928. "Human Migration and the Marginal Man." *American Journal of Sociology* 33: 881–93.

Petrocik, John A. 1996. "Issue Ownership in Presidential Elections, with a 1980 Case Study." *American Journal of Political Science* 40:825–50.

Pew Hispanic Center. 2007. "Changing Faiths: Latinos and the Transformation of American Religion." Pew Hispanic Center and Pew Forum on Religion and Public Life.

Popkin, Samuel. 1994. *The Reasoning Voter: Communication and Persuasion in Presidential Campaigns.* Chicago: University of Chicago Press.

Portes, Alejandro, and Ruben G. Rumbaut. 1992. *Immigrant America: A Portrait.* Berkeley: University of California Press.

Posner, Daniel. 2005. *Institutions and Ethnic Politics in Africa.* Cambridge: Cambridge University Press.

Putnam, Robert D. 2000. *Bowling Alone: The Collapse and Revival of American Community.* New York: Simon and Schuster.

Pycior, Julie. 1997. *LBJ and Mexican Americans.* Austin: University of Texas Press.

Ramirez, Ricardo. 2005. "Giving Voice to Hispanic Voters: A Field Experiment on the Effectiveness of a National Nonpartisan Mobilization Effort." *Annals of the American Academy of Political and Social Science* 601(1): 66–84.

Ramos, Jorge. 2004. *The Latino Wave: How Hispanics Will Elect the Next American President.* New York: HarperCollins.

Randall, Nancy Horak, and Spencer Delbridge. 2005. "Perceptions of Social Distance in an Ethnically Fluid Community." *Sociological Spectrum* 25:103–23.

Romer, Daniel, Kate Kenski, Kenneth Winneg, Christopher Adasiewicz, and Kathleen Hall Jamieson. 2006. *Capturing Campaign Dynamics 2000 and 2004.* Philadelphia: University of Pennsylvania Press.

Rosenstone, Steven J., and Mark Hansen. 1993. *Mobilization, Participation, and Democracy in America.* New York: Macmillan.

Saito, Leland. 1993. "Asian Americans and Latinos in San Gabriel Valley, California: Ethnic Political Cooperation and Redistricting, 1990–92" *Amerasia Journal* 19(2): 55–68.

Sanchez, Gabriel. 2006. "The Role of Group Consciousness in Political Participation Among Latinos in the United States." *American Politics Research* 34(4): 427–50.

Schmal, John P. 2004. "Electing the President: The Latino Electorate (1960–2000)." www.laprensa-sandiego.org/archieve/april30-04/elect.htm.

Scott, Steve. 2000. "Competing for the New Majority Vote." *California Journal,* January.

Segal, Adam J. 2002. "The Hispanic Priority: The Spanish-Language Television Battle for the Hispanic Vote in the 2000 U.S Presidential Election." Hispanic Voter Project. Washington, DC: John Hopkins University.

Segal, Adam J. 2006. "Bikini Politics: The 2004 Presidential Campaigns' Hispanic Media Efforts Cover Only the Essential Parts of the Body Politic." Hispanic Voter Project. Washington, DC: John Hopkins University.

Segal, Adam. J. 2008. "Democratic Candidates Spent Millions of Dollars on Univision, Telemundo Stations This Year." Hispanic Voter Project. Washington, DC: John Hopkins University.

Shaw, Daron, Rodolfo O. de la Garza, and Jongho Lee. 2000. "Examining Hispanic Turnout in 1996: A Three-State, Validated Survey Approach." *American Journal of Political Science* 44:338–46.

Shea, Daniel M., and Michael J. Burton. 2006. *Campaign Craft: The Strategies, Tactics, and Art of Political Campaign Management*. Westport, CT: Praeger.

Sinclair, Betsy, Margaret McConnell, and Melissa R. Michelson. 2008. "Strangers vs. Neighbors: The Efficacy of Grassroots Voter Mobilization." Working paper, June 2.

Skerry, Peter. 1997. "E Pluribus Hispanic?" In *Pursuing Power: Latinos and the Political System*, ed. F. Chris Garcia. Urbana: University of Illinois Press.

Smith, James P. 2001. "Ethnic and Racial Differences in Welfare Receipt in the United States." In *America Becoming: Racial Trends and Their Consequences*, ed. William Julius Wilson, Neil Smesler, and Faith Mitchell. Washington, DC: National Academy Press.

Sonenshein, Raphael. 1997. "Post-Incorporation Politics in Los Angeles." In *Racial Politics in American Cities*, ed. Rufus Browning, Dale Rogers Marshall, and David H. Tabb. New York: Longman.

Sonenshein, Raphael J., and Susan H. Pinkus. 2002. "The Dynamics of Latino Incorporation: The 2001 Los Angeles Mayoral Election as Seen in Los Angeles Times Exit Polls." *PS: Political Science & Politics* 35:67–74.

Song, Min H. 2005. *Strange Future: Pessimism and the 1992 Los Angeles Riot*. Durham, NC: Duke University Press.

Stokes-Brown, Atiya Kai. 2006. "Racial Identity and Latino Vote Choice." *American Politics Research* 34:627–52.

Suro, Roberto, Richard Fry, and Jeffrey Passel. 2007. "Hispanics and the 2004 Election: Population, Electorate and Voters." Pew Hispanic Center, June 27.

Tobar, Hector. 2005. *Translation Nation: Defining a New American Identity in the Spanish-Speaking United States*. New York: Riverhead Books.

Tocqueville, Alexis de. 1904. *Democracy in America*. New York: D. Appleton.

Uhlaner, Carole J., Bruce E. Cain, and D. Roderick Kiewiet. 1989. "Political Participation of Ethnic Minorities in the 1980s." *Political Behavior* 11(3): 195–231.

U.S. Census Bureau. 2007. "The American Community- Hispanics 2004." American Community Survey Reports. http://www.census.gov/prod/2007pubs/acs-03.pdf (accessed July 2, 2008).

Vaca, Nicholas. 2004. *The Presumed Alliance: The Unspoken Conflict Between Latinos and Blacks and What It Means for America.* New York: HarperCollins.

Vaillancourt, Pauline M. 1973. "Stability of Children's Survey Responses." *Public Opinion Quarterly* 37 (Fall): 373–87.

Valentino, Nicholas A., and David O. Sears. 1998. "Event-Driven Political Communication and the Pre-adult Socialization of Partisanship." *Political Behavior* 20:127–54.

Verba, Sidney, Kay L. Schlozman, and Henry E. Brady. 1995. *Voice and Equality: Civic Voluntarism in American Politics.* Cambridge, MA: Harvard University Press.

Welch, Susan, and Lee Sigelman. 1993. "The Politics of Hispanic Americans: Insights from National Surveys." *Social Science Quarterly* 74: 76–94.

Wilcox, Clyde. 1990. "Race Differences in Abortion Attitudes: Some Additional Evidence." *Public Opinion Quarterly* 54:248–55.

Wolfinger, Raymond E., and Steven J. Rosenstone. 1978. "The Effect of Registration Laws on Voter Turnout." *American Political Science Review* 72(1): 22–45.

Wong, Janelle. 2006. *Democracy's Promise: Immigrants and American Civic Institutions.* Ann Arbor: University of Michigan Press.

Wu, Frank H. 2002. *Yellow: Race in America Beyond Black and White.* New York: Basic Books.

Zaller, John. 1992. *The Nature and Origins of Mass Opinion.* New York: Cambridge University Press.

Zhou, Min. 1999. "Segmented Assimilation: Issues, Controversies and Recent Research on the New Second Generation." In *The Handbook of International Migration: The American Experience,* ed. C. Hirschman, P. Kasinitz, and J. DeWind. New York: Russell Sage Foundation.

Index

CPSIA information can be obtained at www.ICGtesting.com
Printed in the USA
LVOW07s0856040216

473670LV00003B/18/P